To MICHAEL,
WHO HELD THE LIGHT HIGH,
AND TO GREG,
WHO SHOWED ME THE WAY

BEAN BLOSSOM DREAMS

BEAN BLOSSOM DREAMS

A CITY FAMILY'S SEARCH
FOR A SIMPLE COUNTRY LIFE

Sallyann J. Murphey

HEARST BOOKS

New York

Illustrations by Glenn Wolff

It is the policy of William Morrow and Company, Inc., and its imprints and affiliates, recognizing the importance of preserving what has been written, to print the books we publish on acid-free paper, and we exert our best efforts to that end.

Library of Congress Cataloging-in-Publication Data

Murphey, Sallyann J.
    Bean blossom dreams : a city family's search for a simple country
life / Sallyann J. Murphey.
        p.   cm.
    ISBN 0-688-12325-2
    1. Murphey family.   2. Murphey, Sallyann J.   3. Country life—
Indiana—Brown County—History.   4. Brown County (Ind.)—Biography.
I. Title.
CT274.M86M87   1994
929'.2'0973—dc20   93-33502
                                                                    CIP

Printed in the United States of America

First Edition

1   2   3   4   5   6   7   8   9   10

BOOK DESIGN BY PATRICE FODERO

$\mathscr{C}$ONTENTS

'Tis the gift to be simple, 'tis the gift to be free,
'Tis the gift to come down where we ought to be,
And when we find ourselves in the place just right
'Twill be in the valley of love and delight.
When true simplicity is gained,
To bow and to bend we will not be ashamed.
To turn, to turn will be our delight,
And by turning, turning we come 'round right.

—EIGHTEENTH-CENTURY SHAKER SONG,
   "SIMPLE GIFTS"

CHAPTER 1

HE WINGS OF CHANGE

HE FLASH OF ORANGE HOVERED FOR A SECOND, THEN settled on the cream petals of a climbing rose. New wings, damp from the chrysalis, slowly stretched out to expose black fringes and delicate white spots. The butterfly paused to balance herself, then got down to the serious business of soaking up the afternoon sun.

A groan issued from the depths of the deck behind me. My husband was sprawled, gray faced, by the garden table, nursing his long, aching limbs. Greg had just come home from a two-week photo shoot that had been the usual combination of late planes, crowded airports, unfinished projects, and clients with a "good deal" on their minds. He was exhausted. We'd barely had a chance to say hello before the baby-sitter came to whisk our two-year-old daughter away so that I could meet my deadline for the *London Daily Mail*. I shouldn't have been downstairs at all. There were fifteen hundred words to write before breakfast the next morning and I'd already been up for most of the night before.

"Why do we do this to ourselves?" Greg muttered through clenched teeth.

I pointed to the pile of bills on the table. "Got to pay the piper if you're going to play the tune."

And we had played—hard—mostly before we met, when I was a British TV producer on assignment in New York and Greg was jetting around the world, photographing palaces of American corporate chrome. We had both traveled first class, too consumed by our careers to even notice our good luck. Then, in 1985, we attended the same party and our priorities began to change. For the first time, the idea of family became as attractive as success. "*When* we get married . . . " Greg had said one day, as if it were old news. I'd gaped at him and was about to argue when I realized that I, too, had assumed it from the start. We moved back to his hometown, Chicago, where our daughter, Charlotte, appeared in 1987.

Like all babies, the little munchkin seized possession of our lives and kept us too busy trying to stay awake to notice the second seismic event of that year. In fact, we didn't connect the stock market crash with our increasing struggles until 1989, when we found ourselves mudwrestling for work that used to come with ease.

The butterfly fanned her wings and prepared for flight. "It's only going to get worse, you know." I settled into a chair next to Greg, shoving the bills and my deadline aside. "Next year we'll have to pay Charley's school fees as well. I don't know where it's going to come from; we both put in seventy hours a week as it is."

Greg stared gloomily into the garden, a little patch of color in a row of concrete yards. It was our oasis in the stresspool of the city, the place where we went to find brief peace of mind. "That," Greg said, waving at his vegetable patch, "is the only work that gives me any pleasure. I'm not even sure why we're doing this anymore."

He had a point. Since Charley's birth we had withdrawn

increasingly from urban life. The openings, the parties, the pretty things to buy, did not compete well with a pair of large blue eyes and the few precious moments we had to enjoy them. We paid premium rent, premium everything, to live in an area where she could never play alone outside, or go to a school with a cross-section of her peers.

Dry at last, the butterfly took wing. She circled the bright blue delphiniums before settling on the honeysuckle to take delicate sips from each golden cup. In her brief eight weeks, this beautiful creature would drink deeply from many flowers. Between meals she would find herself a mate and they would dance their courtship through the blossoms before she laid her eggs and faded away.

I envied her the joy and simplicity of her short time. They were qualities I'd been looking for all my thirty-six years and had only found in snatches. One day, we vowed, we would retire to a farm and spend what time we had left trying to reconnect to a more natural way of life.

"But why then—why not now?" I asked out loud. Greg's eyes opened a crack. The solution was suddenly very clear. I tugged at his sleeve to get his attention. "We could change it all. Why dream of ending up in the country when we could be living there today?"

"Oh yeah." Another of his wife's madcap schemes. "And just what would we do for money?" My husband was leaning forward, hoping to hear an answer.

"What we always do. Greg, do you realize that since we got the fax machine I never leave the office? The business of business is done down a telephone line, which could be set up anywhere. You're okay as long as you're near an airport, and in time we might be able to look to the land to provide our basic needs."

Greg's eyes followed the direction of my finger to the little sea of green in front of the garage. He had every right to be proud of his plot—the last harvest had included a whopping two hundred pounds of tomatoes from ten square feet of polluted dirt.

"And we'd be there to watch Charley grow up as part of a family—not as the only child of absentee parents." A bottle of wine was opened and we got the calculator out.

As the sun dipped in the sky, the butterfly spiraled upward. Fully refreshed, she glided out on the warm breeze, over the garden fence. For a moment she hung like polished amber in the air, pausing to take a last look at the place where it began. Then she turned southeast toward the lake—and the promise of a new and richer life.

CHAPTER 2

AND WEEDS AS TALL AS TREES

IT WAS A BOOBY TRAP. THE HORSE HAD CAREFULLY dug a hole in the barn floor, expressed his opinion into it, and then rearranged his bedding to camouflage the dip.

As the morning routine began, he assumed a gentle pose. The sun streamed in through the open Dutch door and I crossed his stall humming to myself. "Oh, what a beautiful morning. . . . Oh, what a beautiful . . . " Then the ground disappeared. As I pitched forward into his dawn offering, I saw my right knee floating in a pool of brown sludge. There was an audible snicker from his feed bin as I squelched back to the house.

Hotshot's revenge came two days after we had electrified his fence. No more great escapes, no more calls to the animal control officer, no more sprints down Schooner Road at six in the morning. Just the soothing rhythm of a pulsing red light. The horse looked appalled as we installed it all—apparently he never would have predicted that we could have been that smart.

It's been fifteen months since the Big Move, and we all have learned and changed a lot. Gone is the driven, nervous man I was once married to and the shy and whiny child who was my little girl. In their places are two people I hardly recognize.

My tall and skinny Greg has filled out: his shoulders widened from all the outside work, his tummy a tribute to an abundance of fresh food. Charley has grown, too, her legs strong from long walks in the woods, her mind frighteningly unafraid of everything around her. They both glow with good health and a general enthusiasm for life.

For my part, unlike Sisyphus, I have dropped the rock. I still have to work as hard—even harder—but every moment is a pleasure. My legendary redhead's temper has evened out into a beatific smile, and problems that have had me smoldering for years just seem to solve themselves.

The mother of all this improvement is a 42-acre farm in the beautiful hills of Brown County, Indiana. Hills and the Hoosier State may seem like a contradiction in terms, but the four glaciers that created the great plains of the Midwest stopped just south of Indianapolis, at the foot of a huge ridge known as "the Norman Upland." Eons of time and melting waters from the ice eroded this peak into rounded waves of deciduous woodland, where bear, bobcat, and wolf roamed freely into the latter part of the last century.

Settlers started coming to Brown County in the 1820's, but most of them moved on. The dense forest and steep slopes made it difficult land to build on or to farm. Even the native Delaware and Miami tribes only passed through, using the hills as holiday hunting grounds—the area's first tourists.

Those who did stay were made of stern stuff. They usually eked out an existence in log cabins on dirt roads, without power or inside plumbing well into the 1950's, when some statisticians claimed that the county was the poorest in the Union. We even have a village called Needmore, because "folks there needed more of everything."

Then, in the sixties, the community's fortunes changed. It was the dawning of the technological age, and the beauty, the isolation, the very backwardness of Brown County became the main attractions to thousands of artists, tourists, and retirees. They came, in increasing numbers, to enjoy a display of fall color that is as magnificent as any to be found in New England; to buy the crafts from the blacksmiths, the potters, and the basket weavers; and to taste a life that is simpler and slower than the world outside. Many never went back. They stayed to form the vanguard for a new group of settlers, of which we are a part.

Our piece of this paradise has it all: a lovely old greenhouse, a 3-acre lake, 22 acres of woods, 17 acres of pasture, an orchard, and a small Dutch barn.

The day that we first turned down the driveway was full of magic. Roses wound their way over the walls of a stone cottage that lay hidden from the world behind banks of tall locust trees. The outside reminded me of home, taking me back to windswept days on the Yorkshire moors or long hikes in the hills of the Derbyshire peak district.

Inside, it was the cozy farmhouse we had hoped for. The ceilings were low, meeting walls of rich red ponderosa pine. Sunlight streamed in everywhere through sugar-pane windows, dappling the floors and warming the colors of the wood. The living room, dining room, sunroom, and kitchen all flowed from one to the other, giving the family plenty of room to cook, play, read, or just doze by the old woodstove without falling over each other's feet.

The landscape beyond the backdoor was breathtaking. Parkland swept down a hill to a stand of enormous Norway spruce. Their curved, feathery branches dripped with needles, which hid a sight that stopped us all in our tracks. I rounded one huge pine, chasing after Charley, to be confronted by a sheet of silent water. A hundred trees shimmered in the surface of the lake, framed by cattails bowing and swaying to a swarm of dragonflies that dipped to display their colors like dogfighters from World War I. This was a secret spot, undisturbed by time. The only thing missing was a white arm waving a sword from the middle of the pond.

We put in our applications the next day, and in December 1990 the Murphey household moved out of Chicago without a backward glance.

We drove down in convoy that day, each vehicle full of very different thoughts. Greg led the way with Oscar, our sick British bull terrier. My husband was feeling a sense of relief as each passing mile put more distance between him and the pressure cooker of the big city. As the tension lifted and his shoulders unclenched, he began to think about the little white "Spuds" dog at his side. Oscar has no immunity to simple staph bacteria and was being eaten alive by sores all over his body. We had spent a small fortune over three years taking him from vet to vet in Chicago, but nothing they did had worked. Perhaps, thought Greg, this move will also be the answer for him.

Hope was on my mind, too, as I bounced along in my little Yugo, crowded in by Charley; Lady, our large white German shepherd; and a very disgruntled Merry, our gray cat. Living in the country and running a small farm had been a fantasy since childhood. Whenever city life in London or Paris, where I grew up, got too overwhelming, I would retreat into my pastoral daydream of a lovely old country cottage, where I'd be living with chickens in the yard and children on my knee. When I was a young woman, the vision had faded, pushed aside by my job as a BBC producer, with all its busy trappings of "success." Now, through all those strange twists and turns of life, I was on my way to what I had really wanted all along.

My thoughts were already there, unpacked and settled in. I

was harvesting our organically raised herbs and vegetables for rich city customers and fancy restaurants, while Greg was finally doing his artwork in his new studio in the barn. I saw us as pioneers in a changing work environment—jacks of all trades and masters of some, earning our way with one hand on the computer and the other on the plow. In the beginning, we would have to pay our bills with Greg's income from his commercial photography and from my writing. But I expected the farm business to take over 50 percent of our obligations within about a year—all it would need was a little hard work.

Behind me, our good friend, Steve Kowalski, followed in his VW. A city boy to his toes, he shook his head all the way to Indy, amazed that we had conned him into helping with this craziness and concerned that we would lose him and he'd have to find his way to the "middle of nowhere" all on his own.

The three cars had already outstripped the moving van, which was being driven by some rather sinister-looking gentlemen from Chicago's southeast side. Their thoughts were in their bellies and where they might stop for a meal. We wouldn't meet up again for another six hours.

By the time the movers found us, it was ten o'clock at night. They pulled in, missed the driveway, and sank up to their axles in mud. All our worldly goods were stuck three hundred yards from the house, and it began to rain. The men crowded into the kitchen, looking mutinous. We soothed them with beer, bacon and eggs, and every dollar in our pockets, and they sullenly began to unload. The job was finished by six the following morning, and I remember drifting dreamward to the sound of spinning wheels. It was a symbolic beginning.

The next few months would be a catalog of frustrations. We were about to be given a crash course in the power of nature versus the puniness of man, which would knock all the big-city arrogance and bucolic illusions out of us. We would have to learn precisely how incompetent we were before we could begin to build the skills that we needed for the future. It was going to be a humbling year.

Since we had no idea what was in store, our first few weeks were full of blissfully innocent excitement. We rushed to get organized, burning each box as soon as it was empty. This was the fifty-fourth move in our joint and separate lives, and we planned never to go anywhere else again. Our determination was reinforced with each new sight and sound.

Everything amazed us. It snowed and we spent hours at the windows, listening to the icicles tinkle like wind chimes and watching the birds puff up their feathers to keep warm. "We should put some food out for them," I said to Greg, "to let them know that we want to be friends."

We filled a plant tray in front of the kitchen and declared "Murphey's Bird Bistro" open for business. At first, no one came. Then a tiny chickadee danced in nervously and snatched at a kernel of corn. A couple of minutes later, he was back, cocking his head and checking us out from a safe distance before dive-bombing the food again. By his sixth sortie, the little fellow felt confident enough to stay awhile and inspect the menu. Within another hour, he was bathing in the seed, throwing it around lotto-winner style.

As the snow melted, other species joined him. Merry spent his mornings with his whiskers plastered to the window, aghast at the audacity of all of them, dancing under his very nose. We had to keep a bird book by the sink just to identify them. There were bright red cardinals, who sent in their buff-colored wives to scout before risking it themselves. There were juncos, titmice, nuthatches, woodpeckers, house finches, goldfinches, and a Carolina wren. Even a blue jay passed by, when he thought we weren't watching.

The drier weather drew us outside to explore the pasture

and the woods. It was beautiful—it still is; the wonder never wears off. But on those first outings, our eyes were overwhelmed. We discovered creeks in the forest, bubbling over smooth gray boulders and flanked by strange pawprints in the mud. Sugar maples, red oaks, and a hundred nameless trees soared above wild roses and blackberry bushes. The ground was dotted with fallen branches that had been decorated by delicate shells of coral-red fungus and little velvet patches of emerald moss.

In the pasture, cedar, pine, and juniper stood out greenly against a gold carpet of sleeping grass, which crunched frostily under our feet when we went for evening walks. For the first time in thirty-seven years, this city girl saw her shadow in the moonlight. We chased each other around the lake—our lungs full to bursting with cold fresh air.

The only black spot in our bright new world was Oscar. The dog was dying. Our bumptious, bossy BT, who had once earned the nickname "White Tornado," now lay on his bed all day, curled in a tight little ball. He could barely drag himself up to eat and no one, not even his beloved Lady, could persuade him to go outside. It was breaking our hearts.

"I'm going to take him to that vet in Bean Blossom," Greg announced one day. "His parking lot is always full. He must be pretty popular." My husband gently picked up his dog, cradling him carefully like a newborn baby. Oscar closed his eyes and moaned.

Two hours later, I heard a scratching at the door. I rushed to open it and there stood a familiar white wedge head with a furiously wagging tail. "Greg! What did the vet do? Did you like him? What did he say?" My husband held up his hand like a traffic cop and took each question in turn.

"He gave Oscar two shots. I don't know what they were because I couldn't understand what he said. He mumbles a lot.

He did tell me that if Oscar makes it through the next few weeks, we can probably save him. And, yes, I did like him. He's a painfully shy man but he obviously has a real touch with animals." We didn't know it then, but we had just met Brown County's very own James Herriot—Dr. James Brester.

The man is a local legend. He never gives up on hopeless cases and takes on all types of patients. Almost everyone in the county has his or her own Doc Brester story, which range from the spectacular—giving bobcats enemas or riding a runaway llama down a hill while administering its shots—to a thousand quieter tales of the doc's compassion and kindness to all living creatures. He has an astonishing 32,000 patients on his list, but lives almost as simply as he did when he was a student. The doc says that he loves his work but hates to charge for it—much to the frustration of his many, many friends.

St. Patrick's Day came and went, and Oscar was still with us. Doc Brester put him on a course of weekly injections, using a newly developed drug to boost his immunity. He refused to bill us—"Experimental treatment," he muttered, waving us away. We had to sneak money to the receptionist, hoping that it would cover at least part of the cost.

Spring arrived at the end of March, and hundreds of daffodils burst into bloom around the farm. I had never seen so many varieties. There were proud golden trumpets the size of Charley's fist next to delicate paper-whites. There were white ones with yellow centers, yellow ones with orange—even one that looked almost pink.

A thousand tiny stars soon followed, peeking out from under the grass—tuberoses—sprouting next to a million small suns—dandelions. They were our first clue that all was not quite right. The second clue came on the day we began to dig our vegetable beds. Greg stuck a garden fork into the soil and it promptly broke off at the neck. The ground was like concrete.

Even when we cracked through the surface, we were met by networks of roots that had woven themselves together like spun steel. "I don't understand it," my husband said, examining a blister on his palm. "If I didn't know better, I'd say the place had been badly neglected. But someone cared enough to landscape the gardens and plant all those bulbs."

The ongoing surge of new life confirmed Greg's fears. Every flower struggled against undergrowth and overgrowth and weeds as tall as trees. The farm had been untended for decades.

Our new neighbors, John and Terry Dungan, solved the mystery. "Thirty years ago," Terry explained, "it was the prettiest property in the county. I've seen the pictures. It was lovely. Ruth Cull was the first florist in the area and she was the one who planted everything. Her husband, Joe, did all the heavy work until he began to get sick, in the seventies, and then he died. Ruth couldn't keep up with it after that. She just didn't have the strength." We could sympathize—we were half the old lady's age and could barely summon the stamina ourselves.

Ruth became a mythical figure to us: a Miss Havisham of the land, who had worked alongside Nature to create something of great beauty only to suffer the sadness of watching it decay. She made us determined to restore the farm to all its former glory.

But enthusiasm alone wasn't going to do the job. By the summer, Greg had planted some beans, tomatoes, and a few peppers, while I had managed to start a small herb garden by the backdoor. We were growing less than we had in Chicago and the work was backbreaking. We just weren't equipped to deal with a project of this scale.

People born on a farm grow up knowing how to clear land, burn brush, uproot tree stumps, or prune the orchard. We had none of these skills. We didn't know what tools to use or which plants to pull. Is that a weed or some rare wildflower? Should we dig this up or cut it down—and why won't the tractor start? Even the simple acquisition of some ducklings set off an overwhelming chain reaction.

Our reading had suggested that ducks were a good farm animal for novices to start with. They are very hardy and almost maintenance free. An ad in the local paper encouraged us, offering pedigree babies at a dollar a bird.

We bought six of them—charming little balls of brown and yellow fluff, all beak and big webbed feet. We planned to put them on the small pond near the barn. "They're too small as yet," our neighbor Big John warned. "Snapping turtles—even a big fish—could drag 'em down. I wouldn't put them out there till they're full grown."

Problem number one: where to house them? The barn, a pretty balloon-framed structure, had not been mucked out since the last great war and was covered in cobwebs, wasp nests, and mire. More than that, it was full of holes and was an open invitation to any predator who wanted to pop in. This was going to be a major project. We would need to hire some help. In the meantime, the ducks could live in the derelict greenhouse, which was, at least, secure.

Problem number two: how to keep them cool? It was the summer of the great drought, with daily temperatures of over 90 degrees. The little birds lay panting in the heat under the glass of their new home.

"We've got to get some water to them," Greg said, dragging Charley's paddling pool over to the greenhouse door while I set up pieces of old fence to form a run.

Finally, relief lay outside, bobbing invitingly—but the ducks weren't buying it. They scattered, squawking at the whole idea, and had to be rounded up and driven like a flock of demented sheep. Charley proved to be the best at this and was appointed chief duck herder.

The ducklings always had to be chased into the pool, but they loved it once they were there. We discovered that their biggest treat was when we turned the hose on them, set at "gentle shower." They'd fight to get underneath it and would stand, preening their feathers and shaking their tails, until another sibling bumped them out of the way. For three months, local traffic would slow down to watch the daily spectacle of "those city folk" watering their ducks.

We probably would have gone on making fools of ourselves for some years had it not been for a meeting with a man we are now proud to call our friend.

Dennis Cyrus came to sandblast the barn. He is a small terrier type of person—whip thin but incredibly strong, with bright eyes that dance out at you from untidy brown bangs. He summed up the situation in a instant: city bred, born without a clue. But he didn't take advantage of it.

He and his son Joe spent three days whirring, pounding, grunting, and sweating before they called us, a little shyly, to come and see what they had done. We were amazed to find gleaming whitewashed walls without a cobweb in sight and a pile of rich black compost heaped neatly by the toolshed. They had even raked the earthen floor. The place was immaculate— far too grand for six ducks—and I knew that it would not be long before our animal husbandry became more ambitious.

Over a celebratory beer, we poured out all our problems. Dennis sat, with an amused glint in his eye, nodding sympathetically. "Sounds like you could do with some help," he said as we finished. "Me and Joe could probably spare a little time."

They did more than that. Within a week, they had cleared away the dilapidation of decades, using chain saws, picks, shovels, and a large weed wacker. Under their tutelage, we learned about each tool and which to use for what; we learned where to clear and where just to cut and how to apply our strength, without wasting it.

By the time our first Christmas rolled around, we had finally made some progress.

A quarter-acre behind the house was ready for the family vegetable garden. A chicken coop waited in the barn. A sprouting area for seeds had been set up on the right side of the summer kitchen, while we hung heat lamps over the counters on the left, ready for baby chicks. We still made lots of mistakes, of course—such as acquiring an elderly, renegade equine—but we were beginning to learn.

Dennis and our neighbor Big John conspired to give us our rural education. They taught us to be patient: take the time to do the job well—once—using the right tools. They both said that the secret to most country work is just getting started, *but* getting started on schedule. Nature is the most unforgiving boss of all, and if you miss *her* deadlines, you don't get another chance.

We had to set up a system that would allow us to do all the maintenance that the farm required, while leaving us enough time to build up the new business and earn our normal living. It was going to be quite a juggling act.

In the quiet of the winter, we got down to some serious plans.

Ms. "I Want It All *Now*" Murphey had been mollified by our first twelve months. "We're not going to be ready to sell anything for at least another couple of years," I announced to my husband, one snowy afternoon.

"Thank you," the voice grunted from the depths of the couch, where Greg and Oscar were having a Sunday snooze.

I looked down at my charts and lists and seed catalogs,

spread out on the floor in front of the fire. "But we could grow all of our own food this season."

Greg pulled a cushion over his head. "Most," he corrected me. "What's your hurry?"

"No hurry. But we have to be able to do that before we can feed anyone else. Do you know how many pole beans it takes to provide for a family of four? Or how many acres we need for two thousand pounds of potatoes? Or what kind of potatoes or pole beans to plant, for that matter?"

"No," sighed my husband, sitting up, "but I think I'm going to find out."

By the middle of January, little brown boxes of seed began to arrive in the mail. We touched each packet, turning them over in our hands to see the pictures of glorious plants on their covers. These would be purple Brussels sprouts, and those, lemon cucumbers. Here were the heritage tomatoes with historic names like Brandywine or Mortgage Lifter. We had chosen almost exclusively from old varieties that had been grown a century or more ago, because they would look and, we hoped, taste more interesting, and the books said that they were hardier against disease.

The herbs have wonderful names, too, like Lady's Mantle or Sweet Annie, and often go back in history to biblical times. Coriander, frankincense, saffron, and rue are just a few of those mentioned in both Testaments. Moses and his family ate "bitter herbs" (probably wormwood) as the Angel of Death passed over, and aloe is said to have grown in the Garden of Eden.

Greg and I make a good horticultural team. His interests center on food, food, and growing more food, while mine revolve around these modest plants, the workhorses of the botanic world. I decided to start with three kinds of herb garden: culinary—for cooking, of course; fragrance—for sachets and potpourri; and rose—for all of the above. Roses are far too versatile to be called mere flowers. I have always grown them, even if it was just in pots. They fill the house with bursts of scent and color all summer long, then repeat the exercise in the fall, when they've been transformed into Spiced Rose Potpourri. I use them in cooking and cosmetics—even to create the occasional family heirloom.

Before my daughter's sixth birthday, I plan to make her a bracelet of rose beads. These are the pulp of wild rose petals, pounded, dried, and polished many times over before they are strung into something to be worn close to the skin. Human warmth will release the original fragrance of the flower, some say, up to a century later. I will give them to Charley in the hope that one day, when her copper hair has silvered with age, she will catch a whiff of sweet scent and remember her mama, who loved her so well.

In February, all the seeds were tucked into their new trays and put under lights to sprout. We planted them on the night of the snow moon, in deference to my husband and turn-of-the-century scientist Rudolf Steiner, who believed that seeds get special energy from a full, waxing moon. I thought it sounded silly, but Greg insisted that there was a lot of evidence to support the man. Then the spring waiting game began.

Winter in southern Indiana, in comparison with Chicago, is a short affair. On Thanksgiving, we had walked dinner off in the woods without our coats on. It only starts to get really cold around the new year, and the worst is usually over by April Fool's Day. But those last four weeks make up for all the rest.

Rural spring is a terrible tease. She'll tempt you outside with the sunshine fuzz on a forsythia bush, then drive you back in with winds that slice through sweaters like a splinter. The equinox proceeds and the robins return, but she's still refusing to come out—giggling and flirting, playing hide-and-seek behind the shortening shadows.

Finally, just as the house is about to burst at the seams with stale air, she comes roaring to the rescue.

This year, she was a little later than usual. On April 7, her breezes swept under the door, shooing away the remnants of winter cooking and unwashed dogs and spilling the whole family outside. We stood still for a moment, blinking and stretching like sleepy bears, before scattering to the four corners of the farm in a frenzy of making up for lost time.

Our first job was to electrify that fence. The second was to take the only thing of use that Hotshot ever does and spread it on the new vegetable beds in preparation for the plants. We shoveled and hauled and kicked the tractor into sputtering life—nothing was going to stop us now. By the evening, we both lay groaning on the floor, delighted with the day's progress.

The next morning, we began again—eyes stiff with purpose, legs sore with age. "I suppose it's too late to raise five or six strong sons?" I said as we struggled to divide the rhubarb.

"It would be cheaper to buy a new John Deere," Greg grunted.

By lunchtime, little rows of cabbages, Brussels sprouts, and peas were set into the early crop bed. We paused for beef soup and Ben-Gay just as Dennis pulled up in his truck.

"It's looking pretty nice," he said, approvingly.

We both went pink with pride. The people of Brown County are not an effusive lot. They set more store by good deeds than warm words. Here you may not see your neighbor for six months, but if your barn burns down, he will be the first on the scene to rebuild it. Dennis's compliment was like an award. And the best of the day was still to come.

As the sun went down behind the big pines, another car drew up. Reverend Jonathan Hutchison, former rock musician and Greg's good friend, had some business on his mind.

He followed me into the barn. "I was wondering," he said,

clearing his throat, "if you had any seedlings to spare?"

I thought of the counters covered in dozens of sprouting trays. "A few." I laughed. "Would you like some?"

Hotshot whinnied and I served him up some grain.

"Well, I have not had time to start my own this year—and I'll only end up buying them from a local nursery—so I was thinking we might come to some kind of deal."

I stared into the horse's soulful eyes. "Go on . . . " I said quietly.

"If you give me a list of what you're growing," he continued, "I'll order everything from you and give you however many hours of labor in exchange."

I will never know whether this was good commerce or a gift from a kind and thoughtful man, but he had just begun our business, way ahead of schedule, and paid us in the currency that we needed most.

"Consider yourself our first customer." I smiled and turned back to the horse. Hotshot looked up from his feed and winked.

$\mathscr{S}$NAKES, TICKS, AND TORNADOES

LADY LOOKED APOLOGETIC. SHE HAD BEEN GETTING her coffee-time cuddle when my fingers brushed across a rubbery growth on her throat the size of a quarter. "Sh—t!" I pulled my hand away. "They're back!"

A furor ensued, during which tweezers, antiseptic, rubber gloves, needles, and a blow torch all appeared on the dining room table in the family's effort to arm me for the forthcoming struggle. Greg and Charley then stood around, at a safe distance, to chorus their disgust as I pulled the tick off Lady's jugular and stabbed it to death with a kitchen skewer.

"Ewwww . . . gross," they said, before going about their business—because, after all, the return of these little suckers is as much part of spring in Brown County as a redbud in bloom.

We hadn't been quite as blasé about them the year before, when the local newspaper had carried headlines about "A Summer Plague of Ticks." They were everywhere: in the carpet, on the walls, even crawling in our beds. The dogs were infested, and we'd clean them nightly before picking through each other's hair like a family of baboons. (We didn't always find them. I nearly crashed the car on one occasion, when an ominous tickling was followed by a pinching sensation behind my left ear. I removed the offender with my fingers and torched it in the ashtray until it blew up and burst like sludge-gray bubble-gum. It's a local practice that, an entomologist told me later, is "*very* dangerous, because they release bacteria-laden liquid when they pop.")

The little beasts affected everything, especially our social life. The stream of city visitors that had followed us down since our move all but dried up. Those who did come arrived vacuum-packed like bacon, armed with frightening articles about Lyme disease. We'd find guests in the bathroom, strip-searching each other for stowaways. One friend even sent a thank-you card addressed to "Tick Acres."

We were desperate—until we discovered the combined miracle of garlic and Skin So Soft. Whenever we ate one and bathed in the other, we seemed able to walk our land with impunity. Whenever we didn't, it was bare-all time again, picking off as many as sixteen passengers in one session.

This year we were ready for them and had already laid in large supplies of both commodities. I grabbed Lady by her collar. "Time for a bath, sweetheart," I said, dragging her heavy frame outside in the direction of the garden hose.

Bathing is the one thing that Lady is almost disobedient about. She's a country dog whose beauty regime includes a regular roll in "Manure No. 5." Deer scat is her favorite variety and she'll proudly parade thick green streaks of it matted in her fur. A wash is almost an insult to her doghood—one that is tolerated only because she loves us and because she thinks we saved her life.

Lady found us on a misty night in early fall, three months before we moved here. We had been spending the weekend exploring Nashville, Brown County's pretty little market town, and were now in search of a late dinner. Suddenly, a large white wolf loomed up at us out of the gloom. Before we had a chance to take defensive action, she lunged at Charley and licked her face. The dog then turned to us and greeted the whole family like old friends. There was something about her that made you trust her instantly. I'm not sure whether it was that banner of a tail that wagged her whole behind or her extraordinary eyes. They were dark brown windows on her soul, radiating warmth, intelligence, and an anxious, pleading expression. The pupils were surrounded by a ring of topaz, which, with her huge, golden head, made her look almost leonine. We petted her and moved on, assuming that she was just another of the town's strays.

Nashville has become very commercialized over the past ten years. It's full of rows and rows of little "shoppes," many selling trash from Taiwan, though the town hasn't been completely ruined yet. Local potters, carpenters, weavers, and quilters still exist alongside the kitsch, creating the elegantly simple crafts that tourists go nuts for. We had stopped to admire some particularly attractive green stoneware when I noticed a reflection in the store window. The dog was sitting close by, staring at us eagerly. "Look"—I nudged my husband—"she's following us."

We petted her again, feeling the ribs and hipbones through her thick fur. "She's very thin," Greg observed.

"And she's just had pups," I said, standing back to get a better look. Her breasts were the pendulous bags of a recent mom, but they had a shriveled look, as if no one had suckled there for a while. "Where are your babies?" I asked her, and she put her paw into my hand. "Greg . . . " I looked at my husband speculatively.

He shook his head. "No, Sal. She's a beautiful animal. I'm

sure that she belongs to someone around here—she's probably just begging for food."

We moved on again, but the dog continued to follow. She stuck like glue for over an hour, until we found a restaurant and went inside.

"That," said Greg, "will probably be the end of that."

But it wasn't. I pointed to the window. The dog was lying down outside, ignoring all other passers-by.

"Do you recognize that animal?" we asked our waitress.

"No . . . " she said, taking a good look. "She's not a local dog. She's probably been dumped. People drop their pets off in Brown County all the time—they think that country folk are more likely to take them in."

Both Greg's women rounded on him. "Why can't we give her a home?" I asked. "She can come back to Chicago with us. It'll only be for a couple of months and then she'll have all the space a dog could want."

"C'mon, Dad," my daughter chimed in. "Can we keep her? Pleeese. . . . "

"All right," he said, shaking his head. "I can't fight both of you. As long as no one has reported her missing, we can take her in." I called the sheriff's office from the restaurant and the animal shelter from the hotel the next day. No one was looking for her. Lady, as Greg christened her, was ours.

It is amazing that anyone would have let this animal go— she's Lassie, Rin Tin Tin, and Old Yeller, all rolled into one. On her first night with us, she lay down by Charley's bed and looked up at me, as if to say, "I assume this is my job?" She has watched over my daughter ever since, accompanying her everywhere—even upstairs to the bathroom in the evenings, because the child is still scared of the dark.

But Lady's behavior has certainly suggested that she was dumped—particularly on the day that we moved down from

Chicago. As the men carried our furniture out of the old house, she came crawling to me on her belly, whining and staring up with despairing eyes. No amount of reassurance would comfort her, and once on the road, she refused to leave the car—even to relieve herself—until we had arrived at the farm. As I began to unload, she finally climbed out and warily sniffed the air. Those anxious orbs widened as she began to understand, and when she followed us into the house, her face was wreathed in smiles.

"Don't shake!" Lady's bathing ordeal was over and I had just finished rinsing her off. It was like trying to hold back a sneeze: she just couldn't stop herself. The droplets from her coat shimmered in the sun before they splattered my face and arms like slivers of ice. I shivered. The spring air had a cool edge to it, which still held the threat of frost. Our seedlings in the summer kitchen were ready to go in the ground, but they'd have to wait until the really warm weather arrived.

There is always this moment of pause in the countryside, between the preparations of early spring and the main planting in the middle of May. As the lilacs blossom, there's time to step outside, wave to the neighbors, and welcome back old friends. The robins and the red-winged blackbirds are first, lining up at Murphey's Bird Bistro to snatch the sunflower seed away from the cardinals and chickadees. They are followed by the blue-birds, who bring a little magic into each day. People around the county actually phone each other when they've sighted one of these bright creatures, as if they're an omen of general good luck.

As the dogwoods bloom, the frogs cross the road near Story and peepers in all the ponds start tuning up for the summer. Driving around involves a dozen stops a day to help the painted turtles who are wandering down the lanes, still dozy from their winter's sleep. Concerned citizens pause for a moment in their busy day to deposit the creatures in the safe shadows of the hedgerows, before they are crushed by oncoming cars.

The warmer weather also brings our first visitors of the two-footed variety. Frequent guests like Steve, or my girlfriends, Janet and Carol, have learned to equip themselves against the farm's various nasties. They come with gloves, thick boots, long pants, and a dose of pioneer spirit. The rookies are sent a list of what to pack and on arrival are sat down for a safety lecture before they are allowed outside.

First, we tell them about the snakes. There are five types in the vicinity: the black racer; the cow, or hognose, snake; the sweet little garter snake; the decidedly poisonous copperhead; and the timber rattler, a smaller relative of the diamondback, which is very shy but, if frightened into striking, could do some real damage. Copperheads and cow snakes can be easily confused by the novice, so we advise all our guests to freeze if they see something slithering on the ground, then back off very slowly. "Remember Big John's rule," we tell them. "Black snakes are okay, but never trust a brown one." We neglect to finish his advice, which is to "kill 'em on sight." That is the worst thing for the inexperienced to try—it's how most people get hurt.

My first direct contact with our sinuous brethren was a heart-stopping moment last summer, when Charley found "something" by the woodpile.

"Mama, look!" she shouted excitedly, waving an iridescent streamer in her fat little fist.

"What's that, lovely?" I asked, only half paying attention.

She ran over to the herb garden, where I was pruning mint. "Look," she said again, holding her treasure up for inspection.

When I glanced down at her hand, my stomach lurched into my throat. It was a snake skin—the recently vacated hull of a three-foot-long reptile.

"May I borrow that for a while?" I asked, as coolly as I could. "I need to make some phone calls."

There were two people to talk to. Tom Tilton, a herpetologist, or snake specialist, living in Nashville, and Jim Hawkins, one of my oldest English friends. Jim had raised his first daughter in Africa around some really deadly snakes. I began with him.

"Sal, calm down. . . . " The familiar voice reached soothingly down the line from London.

"But you don't understand, the skin was damp—I think it had just been shed. The former occupant was probably right next to it."

"You have to train her," Jim said firmly. "I started working with Sarah from the moment she could walk. Get yourself a pen and some paper, and sit down." Practice, my friend said, was the key. "Every time you are outside, pretend that you've just seen a snake. How would Charley react? Keep changing the circumstances and make her rehearse it again and again until she knows instinctively to stay away from all the places they might nest; to move away slowly, not to run, when she sees one; and *never* to touch. . . . " Jim went on to explain that snakes are actually quite shortsighted—they respond to movement and vibration. "If you think you have to kill one—if you're cornered or it has got into the house—don't aim for the head. Find something heavy and hit it in the middle of the body, trying to come at it from behind. A firm blow on the back will paralyze it, and then you can get away or finish it off. Do you know what type it was?"

"A brown one," I said helplessly.

"Have the skin identified," ordered Jim. "You don't want a copperhead nesting around the house."

"It's a cow snake," pronounced Tom later that morning. I breathed a loud sigh of relief. "You shouldn't worry so much," he went on, handing back the skin. "Snakes are very shy. They'd rather run than strike. I've never had a poisonous bite." Given his history, that was a comforting thought. Tom has been a student of snakes since the first grade and over the years has collected and bred every type, from rattlesnakes to one of the world's fastest and most venomous reptiles—the green mamba. He used to have them all on public display, unmilked and fully fanged, just a window away from the eager faces watching. In their crabbier moods, his cobras would hood up and spit venom at the crowds beyond the glass. The kids loved it.

"What do you do if you do get bitten?" I asked, just in case. His light blue eyes studied me, in their serpentine way.

"Get to a hospital, as fast as you can. And I suppose you could use one of these." He rummaged in a drawer and fished out a little yellow box. "You'll find them at all the drugstores." It was a snakebite kit, complete with razor, tourniquet, and suction cup. "I wouldn't use the blade," Tom added. "It often does more harm than good."

Greg and I have carried a kit like this on our hiking belts ever since (which, knock wood, we have never needed to open), and one is always presented to our guests, with clear instructions on its use.

Our lecture then moves on to spiders. We have two to be watched for: the black widow and the brown recluse. The widow is, of course, legendary. We all know that she eats her mate and that her venom (the male doesn't bite) is highly poisonous. But most people don't realize that she also prefers to run rather than attack and will only strike if she's guarding her egg sack—so that's the thing to watch for. I've seen one around here just once—last fall—but it was unforgettable.

Lady and I had been out for an evening walk when it began to rain. On our way back, I remembered that I had left my radio in the greenhouse several days before and went to retrieve it before it got wet. We were making progress on the restoration of the old building—half the glass had been removed and the frames repainted—and I had just finished scrubbing out the sink and storage area. I flicked the light on and was walking toward the counter when something caught my eye. A spider was spinning a web in the corner, just above the radio. It was unlike any other I had ever seen. Its body was a black metallic orb and its legs were long and very angular, like broken matchsticks. The web was irregular, as the books had predicted it would be, and as she tried to shift into the shadow, I glimpsed the famous red undermark of the female black widow.

I stared at her, fascinated and feeling slightly faint. Various thoughts stumbled across my mind: *Can they jump . . . ? Forget the radio. . . . Nature certainly advertises her dangerous species. . . . She's less than half an inch long. . . . Should I keep the light on, hoping to drive her out . . . or do we want her to stay, so we know where to find her?* The idea of carrying on normally, with the knowledge that this deadly creature was just "somewhere around," was unbearable. I tiptoed away, turned the light out, and quietly closed the door.

"Never heard of seeing 'em inside like that." The man at the hardware store the next day was visibly impressed. "It must have thought that it was in an abandoned building. You know, I've lived in the county all my life and I've never come across one." He sounded almost wistful. I bought an insecticide bomb of nuclear strength and went straight back to the greenhouse to set it off. The spider was nowhere to be seen, but I did it anyway. I assumed that she was hiding in the walls.

Usually, black widows prefer sheltered spots like woodpiles that have been left undisturbed. The brown recluse, true to its name, also likes protected places, but that can mean an old shed or a toolbox that hasn't been opened for a while. They are not as venomous as the black widow, but their bite turns into a crater that won't crust over, and it takes months, or sometimes years, to heal. We always wear gloves when we're working outside and we recommend that our friends do likewise.

"How can you bear it?" Suzie's well-coiffed hair was almost standing on end. She had tried the tourniquet, but had been defeated by long red nails that were now wrapped around a stiff drink. "It seems like an awful lot of suffering just to enjoy a pretty view."

We had been uneasy about this visit. Suzie and George were old friends, but they were wealthy urbanites down to their pedicured toes. The only kind of "country" that usually concerned them was their $30,000 subscription to the club where George played golf.

It had taken over a year to persuade them to come down, and now we were making them wince with all the gory rural details. I abandoned the safety lecture, leaving out the pictures of poison ivy and suppressing all news about ticks.

"Actually, Suz, there's a lot more to it than that." I smiled. "But I'm sure you'll see that for yourself as you get to know the place."

At least they weren't like some of our other guests, who arrive with small gifts, large appetites, and tons of good intentions. "Put us to work," they say. "Make use of us . . . we need the exercise . . . we're your new farmhands." Ten minutes mucking-out is all it usually takes before they settle back in a lawn chair, ready to be waited on hand and foot—which is normally less trouble than supervising the few that carry on. The enthusiasts will inevitably end up dismantling themselves or something around the grounds. I have lost count of the number of sprained ankles and wrenched backs we've had to nurse before going out to repair the runaway tractor or beheaded garden tool, which, according to the injured, rose up and savagely attacked them. There was no such danger with Suzie and George; they were not here to play farm.

We had first become friends some seven years ago, when Suzie and I were writing for the same magazine. I reported from the Mexican earthquake or "Undercover with the Cops," while she reviewed art and the latest trends in interior design. We were opposites, attracted to each other by the qualities that we thought we lacked in ourselves. I admired her easy elegance and sense of style, while she was drawn to what she regarded as my interesting but slightly reckless life. The friendship cemented itself when we discovered that we made each other laugh—and when our husbands met and hit it off at once. Greg and George share a love of movies and a sense of the absurd, which has allowed them to tease each other about their philosophical differences without either taking offense. At times, they've even used those differences to help each other out, George forcing Greg to keep his eye on the commercial ball, Greg focusing George on something other than "success."

The motives behind our move had been a mystery to the couple, who seemed to take our rejection of the city as a personal insult. We'd had to endure months of defensive phone calls about the latest urban thrill before they realized that our change in lifestyle wasn't meant as any kind of criticism. Sheepishly, they made arrangements for "a flying visit. Just overnight—George is so busy right now—but we have to come and see the place that we've heard so much about." They had arrived prepared to make the effort, while not expecting much.

"How pretty it all looks," Suzie said as we came inside to eat. The table was bathed in the golden glow from our kerosene lamps and the air smelled faintly of sourdough bread and lilacs. "And what beautiful flowers!" she went on, admiring an enormous vase full of white and purple blossoms.

"Now there's one of the pleasures of living here—I never

have to buy flowers," I proffered. "Come to think of it, they have changed the way I visualize my calendar, since we moved down. I don't see time as a series of numbers on a graph anymore. Janet isn't visiting on May fourth, she's coming when the lily of the valley blossoms. My feature article isn't due in August, it's due when the P.G. Hydrangea blooms. Jonathan and Jodie will be staying with us at the height of the apple harvest, which is always at the beginning of October. See what I mean?"

Suzie nodded, intrigued by the idea. "But what about winter?"

"Well . . . " I thought about it for a second. "November is bunches of bright orange bittersweet drying on the mantelpiece—and the great golden hay rolls brought in from the pasture and stacked against the barn. I see December as cedar, balsam, spruce, and the pine cones that Charley and I collect through the fall, all arranged in large vases around the house.

"And I don't just measure it by the plants—the comings and goings of the wildlife mean something, too. In January, the deer start to get hungry and they creep to the edge of the woods in search of the salt licks we leave out. Some of the shyer birds risk our feeder for the same reason—the doves, the downy woodpeckers—types that you wouldn't see at any other time of year. In February, the winter aconite blossoms, even under the snow. I remember looking out of the office window on February twenty-eighth and seeing a chipmunk, wide awake, running through their butter yellow petals—it was a double sign of the coming spring. There's always something happening, something growing, something changing—yet it is on the same schedule, year after year. The daffodils will appear in April, whether we are here to enjoy them or not. There is a security in that which allows you to move to a different rhythm—more considered, less impatient, more complete. But we still get as much done—in fact, in some ways we are busier than we have ever been before."

"Don't you feel isolated sometimes?" George chimed in. "I'm not sure that I could function outside an office, without feedback, without colleagues."

"George, my boy." Greg slapped him on the back. "If I had the choice, I'd never leave the farm."

We had decided to keep dinner simple: fresh mushroom soup, laced with the garlic chives that we grow on the windowsills over the winter; a roast free-range capon, with roast potatoes and early peas; and Russian raspberry pudding, made with what was left of the ruby-red harvest we had frozen last summer.

"You certainly eat well," sighed George, sitting back, replete.

We had coffee outside, listening sleepily to the crickets and trying to identify the stars.

"That was a success," Greg remarked as we were getting ready for bed. "I think they are beginning to loosen up."

At that very moment we heard a stifled shriek from the bathroom. Suzie flung herself into the hallway, looking white. "Your cockroaches are two inches long," she said, pointing an accusing finger, "and they have wings." Greg threw back his head and roared with laughter. "Suz," he hiccuped, putting his arm around her, "that's a wood roach—only a distant relative. They usually live inside tree trunks. He was probably as scared to be here as you were to see him!"

The next morning, we took our guests for a walk around the property. These tours always begin painfully for me. I see the place through different, more derogatory eyes. The peeling paint, the decaying fences all thrust themselves forward like a personal rebuke. I only begin to relax when we get down to the lake and the forest beyond—their beauty is undeniable, even to the most determined critic.

Suzie and George inspired a special kind of agony. It seemed as if all my senses were standing on end. The sun was too hot, the birds too loud; the barn, which usually smelled earthy and sweet, now reeked of horse sweat and rancid manure. It reminded me of the old days when they came to dinner in Chicago—days when I cared too much about what other people thought, days when I put my home under the microscope and suddenly found it wanting.

My problem has always been a lack of interest in the things that seem to excite everyone else. I can appreciate the fine lines of a piece of furniture, or the beautiful cut of a designer dress, but I can't make myself desire them. It is like having a personality gap—material autism. Other sufferers of this disease flaunt it as a philosophical choice or an act of political rebellion, but I just used to feel clumsy, and had spent my life trying to camouflage my lack of "good taste."

Moving down here has changed all that. In the country you are judged by a different set of standards. How hard do you work? How good is your word? How much do you contribute to the community around you? I remember one of our earliest acquaintances telling us that there were farmers here who had more money in the bank than most city folk we knew—"They just don't drive it, or wear it on their backs." I was comfortable for the first time in adulthood—free to be myself, finally measured in ways that I understood. The only time that I felt awkward now was during these visits from city friends, when I started to reexamine us under my old urban lens.

A nervous apology began to rise in my throat but was strangled by the look in Suzie's eyes. She reached out and wound her fingers through Hotshot's mane. "Hello, handsome," she murmured softly. The horse stood still, avoiding his usual habit of shying and nipping at your hand. Then he astonished us all by lifting his head and blowing gently down his big nostrils onto Suzie's face.

"That's a horse hug," I explained. She beamed back at Hotshot with the innocent pleasure of a small child.

George, too, seemed to have regressed thirty years. "Look at this," he said, kicking at the straw. He knelt down on one knee, ignoring the dirt on his impeccable pants, and peered into the corner of a stall. "It's a nest!" he exclaimed. We all crowded around to examine our very first clutch of duck's eggs. "May I touch?" George asked shyly. Permission granted, he picked up one of the large white opalescences and held it up to the light. "What a little miracle." He turned the egg this way and that, studying it like some semiprecious jewel.

"They should taste good, too," Greg added. "You'll have to take some home."

Our next stop was the lake, which we could now row across, thanks to a flat-bottomed boat on long loan from Dennis. Greg always pauses for a few minutes in the middle so that our guests can drink in the stillness of the air and the shimmering reflections of the trees. If they can become part of the quiet for long enough, they are rewarded with renewed birdsong and the sight of snapping turtles drifting by the boat, or our red-tailed hawk doing her daily chores.

But George couldn't keep still. His knee seemed to follow some epileptic rhythm of its own and his hands were picking and fiddling, constantly on the move. "Sorry," he said, dropping a mooring rope that he'd been twisting into a loop.

We smiled at him complicitly, remembering how twitchy we both used to be. For our first few months on the farm, I didn't notice a tenth of what was out here to see. It took time to develop the inner stillness that you need to truly observe. Now I can sit motionless for an hour or more, watching the shifts in the landscape as the wild creatures forget my presence and start to go about their usual business. As Greg says, "It's a different set of senses. In the city you learn how to shut everything out. Here you have to open wide to let it all in."

We beached the boat near the forest trail and plunged into that other world, where light and sound behave more cautiously. Spring had been busy in the woods, blurring the hard edges of winter with bright green fuzz. Bunches of wild onion sprouted through last year's leaves and the trail was dotted with pink toadstool caps and the serrated shoots of baby trees.

"Is this really all yours?" Suzie gasped. "It's like living in your own national park."

We had stopped for a rest at the intersection of two creeks, where Charley could paddle and collect pebbles and gray-blue chips of clay while the adults sprawled along the banks or sat on fallen boughs of sassafras.

"What are you going to do with it?" George's eyes ranged speculatively across the landscape, building a few guest cabins here, a clubhouse over there.

"Nothing. We're not going to do anything," Greg replied firmly.

"Nature is her own best caretaker. We're just here to make sure that no one interferes—and we're going to tie the paperwork up so tightly that it will stay that way long after we're gone."

George snorted and was about to argue when Charley ran over, clutching some new treasure hidden behind her back.

"George, I've got a surprise for you," she lisped. "Close your eyes and open your hands."

He did as he was told and she deposited a small box tortoise on his upturned palms. He started and looked down just as the tortoise peeked out of his shell to check his new surroundings.

"Well, well," George chuckled, "I haven't seen one of these since I was a boy."

"Want to see where I found him?" Charley asked, throwing out her "You're just an old man, so you probably won't" challenge. It was irresistible.

"Sure," said George, "lead the way." The two figures disappeared down the creek, jumping from rock to rock like a couple of toads. A loud splash a few minutes later, followed by my daughter's naughtiest giggle, told us that millionaire commodities broker Edward George Owen had just got wet.

"There *is* a lot more to it," Suzie whispered as she hugged me good-bye. "I can't tell you how good this was for my husband. It's been a long time since I have seen him so relaxed." She looked pretty passable herself—flushed with fresh air, dandelion seed still clinging to her sweater from one of Charley's demonstrations on the art of telling time.

"Can I leave these here for our next visit?" George came out, carrying his mud-starched pants, which now had a large hole in the left knee. "But don't clean them," he instructed. "They are my passport to respectability as far as your daughter is concerned."

We waved them off, knowing that it wouldn't be another year before we saw our friends again.

Our faith wasn't even shaken by the phone call we got four hours later. There seemed to be a lot of background interference, which sounded like screaming and the slamming of doors.

"Sal, this is George. . . . " His voice was laconic, deliberately calm. "Wonderful time," he said, raising his pitch a bit to reach above the din. "Thank you. Only, we need your advice because Suz has just found something alive in her hair. We think it's a tick. . . . "

I will always be grateful that our friends hadn't chosen the following weekend to pay us a call. They would not have enjoyed spending their stay under a tornado warning.

It had been raining relentlessly all that Saturday, so I was keeping my daughter amused in the kitchen. We had just finished baking a big batch of butterscotch cookies and were about to start on Charley's famous brownies when the TV began to transmit a piercing beep. A sign flashed up on the screen: "The National Weather Service has issued a tornado warning for the following counties in central Indiana: Morgan, Marion, Johnson . . . " Then a radar screen appeared, showing the storm activity as a series of bright blotches running in a line to the west and north of us, so far, but heading in our direction.

The information was repeated and I stood blinking stupidly at it. I knew the difference between a "watch" and a "warning," and a warning meant that real tornadoes had already been seen. "This is not happening," I announced to no one in particular. Twisters belong on the great plains, hovering over trailer parks. They do not touch down in our beautiful hills.

The TV beeped again. This time the weatherman spoke, sounding more like a sportscaster: "A touchdown has just been sighted five miles west of Morgantown . . . " *Morgantown*—that's right up the road. " . . . and is heading in a southeasterly direction." I thought I heard him add "straight toward you," but I was already halfway out of the backdoor, scanning the horizon. The sky had gone a bilious green and the wind was bending the smaller trees at a 90-degree angle. The center of the storm, a black bank of cloud that flashed every couple of seconds, still hung a few miles away to the northwest.

My mind unfroze. "Charley, I've got to bring Hotshot in. You watch me from the dining room window and stay inside the house."

"But, Mom . . . " Charley was already following me down the drive.

"Don't argue!" I bellowed, screaming above the wind. She turned and ran inside. I flew over to the barn, grabbed the horse's feed bucket, filled it with grain, and ran through to the pasture—all in one fluid motion. Hotshot was, of course, in the farthest corner of the field, looking windswept and cross. I banged the bucket on the Dutch door and he eyed me suspiciously before sauntering back as slowly as he dared. I went inside, pretending not to care. As he came into his stall, I slammed the door behind him and shot the bolt. He looked at me reproachfully before settling down to his feed.

"Just didn't want you to get blown away, you mule," I muttered as I left. Sheet lightning was now streaking across the sky every other second. I hung back in the barn, timing my run, then charged from doorway to doorway, like a cowboy dodging bullets.

Charley was waiting for me, white-faced. "Mama, what's going on?"

"Sweetheart, it's a very bad storm. We may have to go down to the basement at any moment, but we need to get some things together first. Will you help me?"

She nodded, almost standing to attention. We scattered through the house and collected a first-aid kit, batteries, a flashlight, canned beans, soup, bottled water, blankets, and a radio.

As we finished stashing it all down there, the phone rang. "Sally"—it was Big John—"have you got your TV on?"

"Yes, I've seen it." It was so nice to hear another voice. Greg was in Nebraska on a business trip, and I wasn't sure that I was doing all the necessary stuff. "Should we be in the basement?"

"Not yet." John sounded cool. "Keep checking outside, and

if you see hail or the air goes very still, get down there fast. Have you put any supplies by?" I gave him the list. "You should have some basic tools, too—a screwdriver, hammer, knife. Are you sure you're okay?"

"Yes, we're fine," I said simply, not adding that I was all the better for his call—that would have embarrassed my gruff friend.

I put the tools with the rest of the stuff, gathered all the animals into the living room, and sat by the TV to await further beeps. The first black storm line had passed to the north of us, but judging by the blocks on the radar screen, there were several much bigger ones right behind it.

For Charley's sake, I stuck to the normal routine—cooking dinner, playing games, getting her ready for bed—but the situation felt unreal, like eating bonbons while you're waiting for a bomb to drop. Every half hour, more news came in: a sighting near Franklin . . . a touchdown in Nashville . . . a tornado outside Columbus—all places that were unpleasantly close. Occasionally, the lights flickered and went out for a second, making the dogs whine uneasily and crawl toward us in the dark. Thunder crashed all around, punctuated by the crack of breaking branches and the rain beating hard on the roof. By ten o'clock, the noise had exhausted us all, and I persuaded Charley to curl up on the couch. She fell asleep almost instantly and I was tempted to follow her example but for the sign still flashing on the screen. It was my responsibility—I was the only one there. I staggered into the kitchen and made a pot of coffee.

At three in the morning, I woke up at the table with my cup still clutched in my hand. I had been dreaming about a railroad train roaring by in the distance, but now the only noise was the hiss from the TV. The weathermen had removed their warning and left the radar screen for the late-night curious. It was virtually clear, just pockmarked with a few spots of rain. I carried Charley upstairs and collapsed into bed, too exhausted to worry about what might have happened while I was taking my nap.

The sun woke us all the next day, pouring into the bedroom like a bad joke. We threw our jeans on and went outside to inspect the damage. There were broken tree limbs everywhere, but nothing dramatic until we got out to the woods. In a clearing behind the lake, fifty-foot oaks had been ripped out by the roots and laid in a neat circle on their sides. They looked as if they had been put through a giant blender—which, in a sense, they had. Apparently, my train noises hadn't been a dream but a touchdown in our very own backyard. I took my daughter by the hand. "Charley-bug, we deserve a rest. How's about a long weekend up in the Big City?"

$\mathscr{B}$ROWN COUNTY BLUES

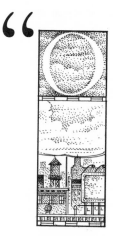

"H, POOR DADA, THE STORM HAS SQUIDGED HIS plants." We were walking back to the house by way of the orchard, which runs alongside our vegetable garden. Charley was right. Dozens of lettuces, pepper plants, herbs, corn, and tomato seedlings had been blown over the night before, or pasted to the ground by the driving rain. Green bean stakes had been torn out and hurled up to a hundred yards, while Greg's tomato netting was now lying in soggy, tangled piles.

Without being asked, Charley crouched down by the salad bed and started gently working the lettuce leaves free from the mud. I stood back for a moment and watched. The face was solemn, lips pulled together into a little pink rose of determination. Her fingers moved patiently, coaxing the tiny plants without tugging or tearing them. *Not bad for four and a half,* I thought to myself.

"It's a *big* mess," she said, standing to brush the grit from her knees. Then she put her hand to her chin, sighed, and shook her head—just like her mom, whom she studied with a wicked smile in her eyes. At exactly what point did my daughter begin to grow up? When did she learn to tease? How did she get so tall? Is this country girl really the small child who cried when we left Chicago?

"I want the Blooo Hoouse," she'd wailed, outraged that no one had consulted her. "Where's my Blooo Hoouse?" We were sitting in the parking lot in front of Franklin's Wal-Mart. Freezing December rain spattered against the steamy windows of the car as mother and daughter stared at the streetlights, both feeling bleak. I had just finished explaining to her that the farm was our new home and that we wouldn't be going back to the "Blooo Hoouse" in Chicago. She was appalled by the idea.

"Why?" She sniffled as she began to calm down.

"Because we wanted you to grow up somewhere beautiful," I explained, "where you'd have lots of space to run around, climb trees, ride your horse . . . " The word *horse* stopped her sniffing for a second. "And because Dada and I wanted to be with you, to play, to walk, to have fun all together—instead of having to work away from home." That was the clincher. The last time I'd had a job in an office, Charley hated it so much that she had hidden my car keys to stop me from leaving the house.

I was, of course, giving her the simple version of events. At the age of three, she was still too young to hear about the dark souls who stalked Chicago's streets waiting to snatch her happiness away from her. Or the hours that her parents would have had to put in just to send her to a decent school. She wouldn't have understood the seminal moments that had led to our decision, the little pushes that had made us change our life—like the man who was knocked down by a car in the alley next to our house one Sunday afternoon. His screaming had brought us rushing to the windows, just in time to see the vehicle back up and come at him again. Greg ran downstairs while I called 911. "There's a car out there trying to kill someone. . . . "

Remarkably, the victim was only a little bruised and very shaken. "I wanted to get to my garage," he explained. "They had parked in front of it and I simply asked them to move." He had never seen them before, he said, and claimed that he hadn't even been rude. The incident had haunted Greg and me for weeks afterward. It was like a thunderclap in a clear blue sky, a warning of the anger that was beginning to bubble over everywhere we looked.

There were others—little dishonesties, larger cruelties— each one more hardening, more numbing than the last. We began to witness symptoms of ethical decay in everything from our commercial dealings to the stories I was asked to write. An article about Chicago's most exclusive private schools introduced us to ten-year-olds whose hands shook under parental pressure to succeed. Another described the luxury cars lining up, just a mile or two away, to buy the bodies of fifth graders, who were learning other types of lessons. It slowly dawned on us that the rules had ceased to apply, and we weren't sure what they had been replaced with.

Our most pressing question became how to give a city child that happy, uncluttered innocence of childhood. Our answer, eventually, was that you can't—an urban kid's safety depends on his or her understanding of the streets. So we decided to raise a rural child instead. It never occurred to either of us that Charley wouldn't approve.

As it turned out, life was too busy for her to dwell on the problem for long. Every day there was some new miracle to be discovered, some new treasure to be found. Her closet began to fill with collections of abandoned birds' nests, buckeyes, and dried cicada skins, while we had to rescue frogs and baby turtles from their "new home" in the bath.

She was full of questions. In the mornings, she'd drag her small white chair to the kitchen window, where she could watch the cardinals and blue jays at the bird feeder. "Do they have homes?" she asked, and we'd put the nests on the dining room table and talk about eggs and baby birds and where she'd been before she was born. In the afternoons, we'd explore the woods, and there'd be inquiries about acorns and oak trees, and why the leaves turned red. When we came home, she'd pound apple seeds into peat pots and plant pine cones in the garden in the hope that they would sprout.

I found myself racing to keep ahead of her. Books like *The Audubon Field Guide to North American Trees* and Blakeley and Bade's *The Science of Animal Husbandry* piled up on my bedside table, as I crammed at night in anticipation of the inevitable stream of queries to come.

One of the best things about having children is the excuse it gives us to be kids again—to rediscover everything from Christmas to favorite bedtime stories, from the delights of peanut butter and jelly to games of Let's Pretend. In this case, Charley opened the door to a country childhood, and her curiosity prompted us to learn more than we ever would have done alone.

She was particularly fascinated by the advent of spring. Each new flower was carefully identified, smelled, and sometimes picked, while the arrival of the wild ducks and geese inspired our first discussions about geography.

"Why weren't they here in the winter?" she demanded, and "Now they have come, will they stay?"

We brought out maps to follow their long journeys north, and Charley discovered, coincidentally, that she was an American living in the state of Indiana near the city she called "Edanapolith."

I suppose the next question was predictable. "Where's the blue house?" she inquired.

I pointed to Chicago.

"Oh," she said, and went off to feed her rabbit.

"Thumper" had been a present from John and Terry's daughter, Rebecca, in honor of Easter Day. She was Charley's first pet—a real white bunny complete with floppy ears and big pink eyes, who did, indeed, thump her back leg whenever she was scared. Rebecca had asked me, not long after we'd arrived, whether the gift would be okay, and initially I hadn't been sure whether our little girl was old enough to take on that kind of responsibility. I was wrong. Within two or three days, she realized that this fluffy creature was totally dependent on her; by the end of that week my daughter was marching out of the house in her jammies each morning to dig up the most delicate dandelions she could find.

Charley's dedication to Thumper's well-being lasted until the rabbit decided to bust out of her cage and go walk about one night. We found what was left of her the following day, after one of our local foxes had turned her into a meal.

"What do you think, Greg—should we tell her the truth?" I asked my husband as we cleaned up the remains.

"Well . . . " He thought about it for a second. "I think she's a bit young yet. Maybe we should soften the blow." We settled on a story line, then went inside to give Charley the bad news. The Bug (as in "cute as a . . . ") was finger painting, head bent in concentration, with a blob of purple on her nose. She looked up, smiling.

"Charley . . . " I began reluctantly. "I'm afraid that Thumper has run away."

She looked blank, unmoved. "Run away . . . where?" Her question was almost casual.

"We think she went off to the woods, to find some rabbit friends."

"Oh . . . " shrugged my daughter and went back to her paint.

We put her stoicism down to a small person's rather selfish view of life and assumed that Thumper was now relegated to the place where she sent discarded toys. We couldn't have been more wrong.

A few days later, we were out on one of our walks when Charley pointed excitedly at the ground.

"Look!" she said. "Thumper has been here." She was gesturing happily toward a fresh pile of rabbit droppings. "She's all right, she's all right," my daughter crowed, dancing around. Then she stopped and looked at me solemnly. "Do you think that she'll ever come home?" Her eyes were eager, full of hope. I felt like a total heel.

"Probably not, Bug—but we can get you another rabbit." She shook her head, her expression strained.

"No," she sighed, "he'd only run away."

Children are very resilient. I realized, too late, that I would have hurt my daughter much less with the truth than I had with this lie. That restless night I swore that, no matter how hard the facts were, I would never deceive her again.

I didn't have to wait long for another sticky situation. One afternoon Charley found a cardinal lying on the drive. Her red hair brushed its wings as she brought it to me, cupped in gentle little hands. "Mama, he won't wake up," she said, expecting me to work the usual maternal magic.

"Darling, he's not asleep," I replied, and we faced death and parental fallibility together for the first time.

Most of Charley's animal encounters have been much happier. Almost every new member of the Murphey menagerie has had something important to teach her, from the turkeys— whose puffed-up belligerence used to scare the socks off her, until she learned that a bully is only as strong as his victim is scared—to our beloved Lady, who recently introduced Charley to the miracle of birth.

We bred Lady with Dennis's black Labrador, Sam, in the hope that a new litter of pups would finally extinguish that haunted look in her eye. Charley was made privy to the process from the word go, when I explained the basic biology behind it and what the final outcome would be. She was sick with excitement, particularly when she discovered that she could keep one of the babies to be her very own dog.

As the great day approached, Charley helped me clear out and disinfect my closet, which would serve as the whelping area, and came shopping with me for all the paraphernalia of delivery. As we laid out the forceps, antiseptic, flashlight, scissors, dental floss, and so on, I demonstrated what each piece was for, using a bean bag in place of a pup.

"Now, you know this is going to be messy," I warned her. "But it is all a good kind of goo. The puppies come in their own little water bags, which have kept them safe inside Lady, and which have to be broken when they're born. Lady will probably do that. In fact, she'll be in charge—we're only there in case of emergency. Each baby will then be followed by what we call the afterbirth, which looks like bits of beef liver. There should be one for each pup and your job will be to count them, just to make sure, because if any get left inside Lady, it could make her very sick."

My daughter was so impressed by the importance of her role that she went off immediately to her bedroom to practice. She was still at it when I peeked in a little later, sitting between two piles of marbles, chanting "one puppy, one goo; one puppy, one goo . . . "

One of the many contrasts between Charley and her city playmates is their respective definitions of *dirt*. The Bug is fully equipped with the four-year-old's fastidiousness about "germs," but she has learned not to be bothered by life's "precious bodily fluids." As one friend pointed out, "There's always something bleeding, defecating, or throwing up at the Murphey household," and my daughter has become quite impassive about it, announcing the latest disaster without her eyes even leaving the TV. I was sure that Lady's delivery wouldn't present any problems.

Since the puppies would destroy our social life for about two months, we decided to throw a small Sunday party in early spring, the week before they were due. We invited seven of our favorite reasons for being in Indiana: the friends we made when we first arrived. Both Greg and I used to believe that the relationships we form in youth, at college, or at school are of a depth and closeness that can't be matched by any friendship made in adulthood. Then Greg went to photograph the Eiteljorg Museum in Indianapolis for its young architect, Jonathan Hess. He called me from his hotel, raving about our new client.

"We really hit it off. He's such a neat guy—none of the ego B.S. you'd expect with his talent—and he *is* talented . . . " I was surprised—not by Greg's conclusion, which I had already come to myself during the negotiations with Jonathan prior to Greg's taking the job, but by his enthusiasm, because my husband is not normally an effusive man. As the week's work continued, Greg's excitement increased. Jonathan invited him to a party at his house. "I had a great time," he reported. "I liked everyone there—his fiancée, Jody, his circle of friends—just wonderful people. I felt more comfortable than I have in years."

Greg continued gushing when he got back to Chicago. "You wouldn't believe what a great city Indianapolis has become," he said. "Indiana No Place, we used to call it, but not anymore. It's really cosmopolitan. As Jonathan says, it's got everything Chicago has—you just have to know where to look. I'm telling you, Sal, you'd really like it." I called Jonathan.

"What have you done?" I wailed. "My husband wants to move to *Indianapolis,* for heaven's sake."

Jonathan laughed, paused, then said, "Really?"

"Yes," I replied seriously. "Got any land around there with bumps in it?"

He thought for a moment and remembered Brown County. "Lady," he said. "Boy, do I have bumps for you!"

Jonathan and Jody have since become two of the people we value most in life. In Chicago or New York, their sophistication and success would probably make them one of society's "beautiful couples"—a lifestyle that they would both hate, because it would compromise their simplicity and openhanded way of dealing with the world. Dinners and parties at the Hess home are not Social Events, but gatherings of good friends who are as straightforward and cheerful as their hosts. Their guests are usually the same group who would be visiting us this weekend: Jeff Rouse, a dentist and very talented sculptor, whose pragmatic sensitivity makes for a very balanced soul; Jonathan's colleague, Mike Brown, a big bear of a man, whose saturnine sense of humor and pseudo black moods camouflage a 24-carat heart; and one of the world's most eclectic couples, Miles and Nancy Kappes, with their beautiful children, Elizabeth, Clarey, and the "Divine Miss" Em.

Very few things have given me more pleasure than the affection that has blossomed among all our daughters. Charley, Clarey, and Elizabeth have become the best of friends, who all hero-worship Emily, the coolest twelve-year-old I know. This young lady has a unique quality of calm. Her tranquility is like a pool you can dip your hands into. It was entirely appropriate that she would be the one to call me and say, "Sal, I think you should come here—Lady's just had a puppy."

She was right. Lady had stationed herself on the landing at the top of the stairs and a small black figure was now sniffling around her legs.

"Lady," I cooed at her, "Lady, don't you want to come somewhere quiet?"

She looked at me, unimpressed.

"Look, Lady, over here," I crooned, trying to con her.

She didn't move.

I took her big head in my hands. "This is *the* most uncomfortable place you could pick . . ."

She snorted dismissively and lay down. Thirty minutes later, the second puppy came. Apparently, Lady preferred the hustle and bustle of family and friends to the sanitized sterility of the room beyond. She also relished the attention from Charley, Clarey, and Elizabeth, who came to watch in awe. The little girls, ranging in age from two to four, crept up the stairs, saucer-eyed, to sit for a few minutes at a time, until the urge to touch a pup became so unbearable that they retreated to restore their self-control.

The adults slipped smoothly into their sexual stereotypes. The men hid in the kitchen, telling loud jokes and taking bets on the total number of pups, while the women hovered like hummingbirds, eager to help a sister in need, no matter what her species. For my part, I was stationed on the top step, prepared to catch any small thing that might come tumbling my way. "Paws," the third pup to arrive, was born into my outstretched hand, where he was brought to life by Lady's licking. His first act was to give me a snuffly kiss—a gesture that promptly guaranteed him a home.

By 1:30 A.M., it was all over. Nine pups had been safely brought into the world and Lady had settled in comfortably with her brood, following a light chicken dinner. Greg and I collapsed into bed, exhausted but pleased. The house seemed to be bathed in a happy haze.

"Life," commented my husband over a late breakfast the next day. "Life is contagious."

Although she couldn't vocalize it, my daughter thought so, too. In a great display of trust, Lady had given us tacit permission to touch the pups and Charley spent the morning stroking their scrunched-up faces and examining their tiny pink paws. She was concerned to learn that they would be blind for the first fourteen days and set her feet down among them with exaggerated care. When the puppies went to nurse, Charley put herself in charge of ensuring fair shares for all, moving the big boys out of the way so that the little ones could have their turn.

Eight weeks is an eternity for a four-and-a-half-year-old. It's a sixth of the way to Christmas, and it can still be measured as a fraction of their lives. But Charley's devotion to the puppies didn't waver once in all that time. I watched with interest as the lessons that she was learning from the whole experience began to spill over into other areas. She started to do little things for us that she hadn't done before: offering us cookies, straightening her bed, and tidying away her toys. She expressed unusual concern for our well-being, asking questions like "Are you happy?" and confiscating my cigarettes because "they are *bad* for you." Then, one Sunday, while she was watching a movie, she began to cry. On screen, a baby bear had just lost his mama in a rockfall, and I turned around to find my daughter with tears streaming down her face.

"Bug, what's the matter?" I asked, thinking she was feeling ill or had hurt herself somehow.

"Poor baby bear," she sniffed, "now he won't have anyone to take care of him." She had seen the movie a dozen times before but had never reacted like this. For the first time in her life, she was empathizing with someone outside her own small world.

The birth of Lady's litter also sharpened Charley's curiosity about other forms of life. "What do plants eat?" she inquired one day while I was weeding the strawberries.

"A combination of things," I replied. "They need water, they need sunlight, and they need soil. Earth isn't just dirt, it's a living thing, full of tiny little animals—micro-organisms, we call them—that are usually too small to see with your eyes. They make the food that plants need, and the plants eat it by sucking it up through their roots. That's why Dada and I are always so careful about what we put into the ground. Plants are just like people—the better they eat, the healthier they are." Charley picked up a trowel and poked at a worm.

"Do you think that I could have a garden, of my very own?" she asked a little shyly.

"Bug, that's a wonderful idea!" I hugged her. "What would you like to grow?"

Charley considered for a second. "Carrots, bematoes, pasta, and popcorn," she decided, naming four of her favorite foods. "And some flowers," she added, "smelly ones."

"We can do all of that—except the pasta," I said, suppressing a smile. "That doesn't grow on trees."

Charley's garden kept Greg and me talking that night long after our daughter had gone to bed. We wanted to help her plan something that was simple enough for her genuinely to take care of alone, but varied enough to produce a season-long display of different colors, textures, and tastes. "Otherwise," Greg pointed out, "she'll lose interest and it'll turn into a weed patch."

"Annuals would give her a kaleidoscope of colors all summer." I thought for a moment. "But they probably aren't as 'smelly' as she'd like. She's always loved lavender and lemon balm. Perhaps she could interplant her flowers with some of those, and I'll donate a Tropicana rose. They have a beautiful scent."

"Don't make it too complicated, Miss Ambitious," warned

Greg. "You'll overwhelm her. What about the edibles?" he asked, turning to his favorite topic.

"Well, she wants tomatoes, carrots, and corn," I reminded him, "and she'd probably enjoy growing her own pumpkins for Halloween."

"That's a good idea," Greg agreed. "But we need to add some drama to all this. Kids love spectacular stuff."

"Like what?"

"Like mammoth sunflowers or a walking-stick cabbage," Greg said, sounding quite young himself, "or an Atlantic Giant pumpkin!"

"Don't talk to *me* about ambition, Ambitious." I smiled. "I think we should let her decide."

When Charley came downstairs the following morning, she found the dining table covered in seed packets and pictures cut from catalogs, of all the appropriate plants we could think of. I sorted them into piles for her.

"These are vegetables," I explained. "These flowers come in bright colors. These smell good. While these," I said, pointing to Greg's assortment of garden oddities, "these are just for fun."

Charley studied each illustration carefully, setting aside a little pile of her own, which was shuffled every now and then, when she found something better. By lunchtime, we were called in to inspect her selections, which had been laid out in the way that she wanted to plant them.

Charley's garden would be fringed by Russian sunflowers and strawberry corn, under which she planned to grow pumpkins, watermelons, and cucumbers—"The way Dada does it," she said. In front of these she had put pictures of bright cosmos, zinnias, and snapdragons, along with lavender, lemon balm, and chocolate mint, which, she reminded us, was her favorite smell of all. The tomatoes and carrots were set to one side, next to a patch of rainbow statice, to dry and keep—"Like you do, Mama"—all winter long. In conclusion, she said that she was going to edge her garden with alternate little clumps of candytuft and night-scented stock.

Greg and I were both stunned. Not only were Charley's choices much more sophisticated than we had expected, but they were made with the kind of awareness for detail that we hadn't realized she had. Each plant had been put out in order of size, as if she had a mental picture of how big that flower would grow, and their relationship to each other seemed anything but random.

I asked her why, for instance, she had put the corn and tomatoes on opposite sides of her garden.

"Because they don't like each other," she replied. "Dada said so, lasterday." (*Lasterday* is Charley's word for "a long time ago," and in this case must have meant last year, when we had been planning how to separate the two crops.)

"And why did you put the rose bush in front of the carrots?" Greg inquired, unable to think of any organic connection.

"To stop the dogs walking there, *Dad,* when the carrots are small." She gave us both an exasperated look for making her state the obvious. We stared back with a new respect.

It was little epiphanies like these that first made us consider home schooling for our child. The thought would never have occurred to us in Chicago, where we defined a "good education" by the upbringing our parents had given us: lots of travel, a second language, music lessons, museums, and the like, underpinned by high academic standards set at a competent school. Down here educating children in the home is so common that local teachers help parents to plan lessons and even allow school facilities like labs and computers to be used independently by the kids.

I was attracted to the idea because of the amount of attention it would allow us to lavish on Charley. At home we could be there for her 100 percent, in a situation where she could learn at her own pace, following all the paths that would capture her considerable imagination. While she's little and without prejudice, I wanted her to be excited by the world. If history was the latest craze, let's dig for fossils or pan for gold. Or if it was the sciences this week, why not build a "lab" in the basement where she could make a mess in peace? It didn't matter whether it was calculus or cooking, it was her job to enjoy it and ours to make it fun.

At vacation times, I pictured us taking long trips together to places like Harper's Ferry, where we'd sit and read about John Brown, or on a boat down the Mississippi, while we discussed the Old South. "You couldn't buy a better education than that," I told myself, forgetting for a while that there's a lot more to school than what we learn in books.

My daughter reminded me, at the beginning of this year, when a plea to see Elizabeth and Clarey was followed by an outburst of tears.

"She's lonely," I admitted guiltily to Greg. "We do all this stuff together, but in the final analysis, we can't *be* four years old."

"We could keep doing all that *and* send her to school," my husband pointed out. "Then she'd have the best of both worlds."

Three weeks later, Charley set off for her first day at kindergarten. As I left her at the door, she began to cry. I could still hear her in the car half a block away, as I sat by the side of the road sobbing myself—aware, like all parents, that this was the first step toward a longer, more painful parting.

It is, nevertheless, one of the wisest decisions we have ever made. My shy Charley has blossomed into a gregarious little girl with bunches of "best friends," who are all convinced that my daughter lives in Disneyland. They are eager to come down and spend many happy hours boating on the lake with Greg or riding Hotshot around the backyard. Charley indulges them, but in her heart she doesn't rate Hotshot as a real mount. That honor is reserved for the horses she rides at our local stable. She's been learning now for nearly a year and has graduated from being led around the arena on a lunge line to starting, walking, and stopping "all by myself." The sight of my small child perched precariously on top of a barrel-chested pony, with her big black riding hat slipping down over her eyes, has been known to give me palpitations, but I put up with them because the experience has been so good for her posture, co-ordination, and, especially, her self-esteem.

Recently, Charley entered her first show, competing in the beginner's horsemanship class. The ponies were put back on lunge lines and each child was led at a walk by its nervous parent. A disembodied voice on the loudspeaker then instructed us to "trot." I broke into a little jog, which made Charley roar with laughter as she bounced along behind. The voice broke in again, telling us to bring our mounts to the center of the arena and stand still for the judges. Charley sat erect and very proud. When a judge came over and told her to "back the horse up," she looked at first confused and turned to me for clarification. As I sent semaphore with my eyebrows and not-so-subtle wavings of the hand, her face cleared and she clicked her teeth, pulling back so hard on the reins that I thought she was going to tumble off. Her pony, experienced in the schooling of small children, backed up three paces and came to a digni-fied halt. The crowd was very quiet as the judges consulted each other.

Finally, a cough and some thunderous tapping exploded across the speaker before they announced the winners, in their usual reverse order. Charley, who hasn't developed a compet-itive bone in her body yet, was so busy waving at her dad that she missed the announcement: "And the first prize, the blue ribbon in horsemanship, goes to Miss Charlotte Murphey on Ginger."

My daughter may have been unimpressed, but her parents certainly weren't. We bore her trophy home in triumph, tied it to the dining room window, and threw her a celebratory meal. As we chowed down on Charley's favorite, "Cheezy Scalloped Potatoes," I took it into my head to ask her a question I had been wondering about for months. "So, Bug, now are you pleased that we moved?"

"Of course," she said, looking shocked at her mother's stupidity. "But," she added, after a pause, "I still want the blue house."

I almost didn't dare go on. "Sweetie, don't you like the farm?"

She was emphatic. "Oh, I do! But I want the farmhouse to be blue."

$\mathscr{T}$OOLS OF THE TRADE

THE CRASHING IN THE UNDERGROWTH WAS SO LOUD that it propelled Oscar off the couch. Doc Brester continued to keep him alive, but the little dog's paws were still very sore and he usually got up only to eat or pay a brief visit to the pooch room.

The sight of him standing foursquare next to Lady, barking his head off, was almost as startling as the noise outside, which was getting closer to the house. I called the sheriff's office.

"I'm sorry, Mrs. Murphey, but we've only got one deputy on tonight, and he's down in the south of the county dealing with a traffic accident. . . . Mrs. Murphey, are you still there?" The kind lady at the office could tell I was perturbed. "Could the sound have been made by a deer? One was run down on the road just outside your place last week." I felt like a fool. Of course it was a deer—mass murderers don't make a point of announcing themselves.

"I'll be Joke of the Week," I grumbled to Greg in bed that night. "Calling the sheriff in to arrest an innocent doe. Where do people get the idea that country nights are quiet, anyway? I mean, listen to that!" I flung open the window to enhance my point and a cacophony of chirrups, beeps, barks, and yowls flooded into the bedroom. "I'm surprised we can sleep. I'd feel a lot happier if we knew what each sound meant."

My husband was in no mood to sympathize. "You'd better put it on our list of 'Things We Must Learn,' " he said bitterly, "right under 'Fixing the Tractor Each Time You Cut the Grass.' " Greg had spent his day on the garden tractor until a faint whiff of ozone and a nasty bang had brought the machine to a grinding halt. "You would think," he went on, "that having mowed the equivalent of our way to Colorado and back, we would have found every hidden root, rock, and tree stump on this property. But oh, no! This'll be the third new blade I've had to buy this spring."

"Perhaps you'd like to start working with a bush hog again," I reminded him sweetly. "That'd be good for your blood pressure."

Greg winced, remembering last year's disasters on the old tractor, with its big bouncing steel plate (known as a bush hog) dragging along behind.

Handling farm machinery is not as easy as it looks. Even driving a pickup truck takes practice, and controlling our elderly Ford tractor, with its complex gearing and three-point hitch, was a job strictly for the skilled.

Greg had been the first to try, climbing aboard on a sunny spring day, ready to cut the new grass of the season. Charley and I had watched from the house: Farmer Dad, with his faithful dog Lady running along behind. He seemed to be enjoying himself, so I left him to it and went upstairs to bathe the Bug. The thrumming of the motor through the open window was a pleasantly soporific sign that all was well, and I didn't look out again until my daughter was drying off. Greg had made progress. In fact, I could tell exactly where he'd been from the bald brown strip he was gouging in his wake.

"Stay here," I ordered Charley. "I've got to stop your dad." Outside, the sound of the engine was growing fainter as my husband made his happy way down to the shores of the lake. A picture of those lush banks stripped of all their green flashed into my mind, and I broke into a run. "Greg . . . Greg . . . stop!" I shrieked as I scrambled over his path of destruction. But he couldn't hear me. By the time I had flung myself in front of the tractor, the bush hog had ripped the grass out by its roots all along the dam. "How could you?" I wailed, almost in tears.

"How could I what?" He barked back defensively, shocked at his wife's hysteria.

I gasped, trying to catch my breath. "Just look behind you," I finally managed to spit out before marching back to the house. They were the last words we spoke to each other for quite a while.

The next time we got the tractor out, it was my turn to drive. We had consulted with Big John and Kenny Burker, owner of our General Store, and the consensus was that the bush hog had been set too low. I carefully set the beast on "high" and practiced in the driveway for a few minutes before tackling the grass.

My session began as pleasantly as Greg's had done. It takes about eight hours to cut the grass on our acreage and, accidents aside, it is the most relaxing job around the farm. It's like a sauna for the mind, which is released by the monotony of the task to float off wherever it feels like wandering. After a day like this, we always sleep our deepest sleeps, blood fully oxygenated, brain powered down.

I was just getting into this semi-Zen state when the bush hog lurched and started dragging along the ground. I applied the brakes gingerly and reset the height control. Ten yards farther on, it happened again. This time my temper got the better of me and I slammed my foot on the front brake, almost flipping the tractor on its nose. Big John's cautionary words echoed back. "Always use the front and back brakes together," he'd said. "Tractor accidents are one of the biggest killers on a farm."

No daydreaming today, I thought grimly to myself. I am going to beat this machine. The real problem was that we had bought two lemons in a package deal: the old Ford needed new gears, new brakes, new everything, while the bush hog it was pulling was at least one size too big. It was an impossible battle, but I persevered until I discovered on our way down a hill, that the brakes had failed. My mind began racing as the tractor gathered speed. Should I hurl myself off or try and steer it to a stop? Do I aim it at the bushes or drive into the lake? Is Greg watching this? I was half hoping not.

The runaway machine was now out of control. All I could do was cling on for dear life as it careened across a hollow and started up the next slope. Gravity did what it could to help and a crabapple tree finally brought us to a halt. I climbed down shakily and threw up in relief.

"You don't really need a big tractor like that," Big John said later, when he'd finished laughing his head off. "Not unless you're going to plow up your back field." He sighed and wiped his eyes. "A twenty-horsepower garden tractor like mine could do just about everything you want, and it'd be much easier to handle." It was typical of the man that he went on to lend me his machine so I could finish the job I had started.

We had hoped that moving to the country would slow, if not end, our need to consume. From clothes to cars, we'd thought, serviceable would replace smart and the urban pressure to constantly polish up one's image would simply fade away. But we were disappointed to find that there was now a whole new list of things to buy: a tractor, a tiller, a chain saw, and a truck just for starters. Self-respecting members of the diesel set also owned wood chippers, log splitters, hay bailers, post diggers, and toolsheds that put our local Sears to shame. And the equipment alone isn't enough. You need to know how to use it, too. Despite thirty-eight years of schooling between us, Greg and I have had to start again from scratch, learning to be carpenter, electrician, plumber, veterinarian, orchardist, blacksmith, mechanic, forester, poulterer, and general ranch hand. I don't know what we would have done without friends like John and Terry, who've seen us patiently through the process, step by faltering step. This couple have stood over us like guardian angels for the past eighteen months, reluctant to intervene but always materializing when we're about to make a serious mistake. John was first on the scene, for instance, when he heard that we'd bought a chain saw, quietly inquiring if he could be of any help.

"Brace your arms, *brace your arms!*" John drilled me a little later, "unless you want it kicking back into you." I poured mental concrete into my elbows and reapplied the saw. The chain whirred and screamed as it tore through the wood, splattering sawdust against my protective goggles. We had been at it for most of the morning and those wicked teeth were getting blunt. "We'll walk across to my place in a moment and I'll show you how to sharpen them," John said. "But first, let's go back over what you've learned."

I took off my gloves and sat down on a log, trying to focus past the ringing in my ears.

"Okay. Types of wood to use," I began. "Softwoods like sassafras or apple are best to start the blaze, followed by hardwoods like oak or black locust for a strong, slow burn. Avoid evergreens like pine, because the resin in the wood will clog up the chimney and could start a fire. Right so far?"

John nodded. "What about chain saw safety?" he asked.

"Always wear goggles and gloves; brace your arms and legs;

examine the wood for knotholes and nails first, and never try to cut it on the ground."

"Good," John said simply, "and what else?" My mind went blank, so he answered his own question. "Make sure that you keep the blades sharp."

Maintaining your equipment is the first rule on a well-run farm, for three very good reasons: safety, independence, and thrift. Any tool is an accident waiting to happen; using a defective one is like playing Russian roulette. And you can almost guarantee that the tool that isn't cleaned, oiled, and put back in place is the one you're going to need in a crisis. I'm still looking for the pipe wrench, for instance, that could have spared my blushes a few Sundays ago, after I heard water pouring into the basement.

It was an ominous sound, which I had heard once before when our entire septic system backed up, last year. It had been an eight-hundred-dollar mess—one I wasn't anxious to repeat. "Please don't let it be that," I prayed as I clattered downstairs. But, of course, it was. The tank outside was obviously full, and water was flowing back down our main drainage pipe, which had sprung a leak under the pressure.

At least this time, I thought, I know what to do. Just tighten the pipe joints until we can get the tank pumped out. I had bought the wrench for that very purpose, but when I looked for it, it was nowhere to be found. The cap on the pipe was loosening more, and brown sludge was beginning to fountain onto the floor. I headed for the phone.

My first two calls to plumbers met with maddeningly upbeat message machines asking me to call back on Monday. My third option was the disagreeable prospect of disturbing Big John on his only day off. Since the basement was filling up like a bathtub, I didn't have much choice. "I'll be right over," he said, his kindness making me feel worse.

The water had slowed down by the time John arrived, but he rejected my plan just to tighten the pipe. "There may be a blockage in there, as well as a backup. We should take the cap off first and check it out."

My mind thought "no," but my mouth said "yes," and Big John began to loosen the bolt. There was a bubble and a pop as the piece came off and two turds, followed by a wad of "female cotton," shot over my friend's right shoulder. We tried very hard not to look at each other.

"Well, no blockage there," said John, studying the inside of the pipe for an unduly long time. "I guess I'll just tighten it up until they can pump it out tomorrow."

Our eyes still hadn't met by the time we said good-bye.

A new wrench now hangs from its hook on the basement wall, serving to remind us that organization and self-reliance are two responsibilities of rural life. Husbanding resources is another. On a well-run property, nothing goes to waste.

When I think of what the city Murpheys used to throw away, I feel thoroughly ashamed. We must have junked mountains of good food, fixable commodities, and perfectly usable clothes, all in the name of clearing up clutter or keeping up-to-date. Down here there are coils of wire that have been hanging on nails in the barn for the past forty years, and Dennis built our entire chicken coop out of what I called the "rubbish" in the loft.

"Poor man," he says, "has poor man's ways." The first time I heard him use the expression, he had just borrowed a screwdriver to turn the ignition on his truck, having busted the lock on one of his hair-raising rides around the hills. I looked at his broad grin set in its sunburnt face and thought that Dennis is probably one of the most prosperous men we know. The knowledge that you can find food and water and build shelter for your family under almost any circumstances brings with it a peace of mind that money can't buy.

I think this is one of the things we were looking for, sub-consciously, when we moved—the safety of knowing that the land will provide. In the city, our most basic needs depend on a grid that is beyond our control. We are driven by a deep-seated fear that financial disaster or the loss of a job could mean hunger and homelessness in a quite literal sense. In the country, those catastrophes feel much further away.

The point was proven last March when we woke one morning to a freezing-cold house. A quick check revealed that our propane gas had run out, which was a real problem because the tank costs five hundred dollars to refill. Greg's photography business is a seasonal one, and unless he is commissioned to shoot an annual report, winter is usually belt-tightening time, with March being the leanest month. This particular year was worse than normal, thanks to the re-cession, so there was no question of ordering the fuel re-quired. In the city, we would have had to buckle down to a miserably cold home for a few weeks, but down here we had other options—such as the cord of firewood stacked behind the house and the mass of logs just waiting to be lifted off our forest floor. We had all the fuel we needed, and the Franklin stove blazed away happily night and day, keeping us toasty warm until spring.

In time we plan to be as self-sufficient as possible by using all the wonderful things that the latest modern technology has to offer. Solar power, for instance, is getting so efficient that you don't actually need much direct sun anymore to make electricity, nor do you have to set half a field aside to house the plant. There are units on the market now that would fit neatly behind the house and generate enough energy to cover all our needs, plus an excess to sell back to our local electric company. We plan to install one as soon as they get within our financial range, which shouldn't be too long, because prices are dropping every year.

We also want to reconvert to our own spring water. When Ruth Cull originally bought the property, forty years ago, she built a sophisticated setup of water tanks and cisterns to fully exploit the farm's vast network of underground springs. After she sold the house, the new owners capped the pipes and hooked into the county water line, which draws off local reservoirs that are full of lime. In the summer, the water pressure can reduce to a dribble, and what you do get is so full of deposits that it is disgusting to drink. We'd like to go back to Ruth's system, boosted by modern pumps and a backup flow of water from the springs that feed our lake.

In a sense, we have to. Our dreams for the greenhouse would be too expensive to run without our own sources of water and heat. One day, we want to grow food in there hydroponically, which means that the plants' roots will be suspended in water rather than in soil, while they grow under metal halide lights. The advantages of the technology are enormous: crops grow at an incredible rate and are almost pest- and disease-free because their environment is clean. Hydroponics would allow us to grow our own fresh food all winter long and also enable us to produce reliable harvests of herbs and salad-greens for local restaurants or stores. It could be quite a profitable sideline, and one that would take only a few hours' work each week. But the system is so energy-intensive that there is no point even in starting until we can run it off our own power.

In the meantime, we'll use the greenhouse the old-fashioned way and concentrate our main energies on the gardens outside. Greg and I have cleared some considerable growing space since that first frustrating spring, and my husband has just finished four backbreaking weeks building our first raised beds.

Raised beds are the foundation of an organic garden. They are made by "double-digging" the soil to a depth of about three feet, then sifting the earth for weed roots and seeds. Next, wood frames are built around the beds, and the cleaned soil, mixed with natural fertilizers like compost and guano, is heaped back in. Over the years, the earth becomes virtually weed-free and, with regular seasonal amendments, develops into a richly nutritious medium for even the most demanding crop. If the beds are built up properly, you can also grow more prolific harvests, because the sifted soil and minimized pest problem makes for strong plants that will flourish in a much smaller space.

The advantages to this method are so well documented that you would think all gardeners would be eager to use it, but the problems for the commercial grower are that getting started is very labor-intensive, and achieving the best results takes time. Greg says that it will be ten years before our soil reaches its peak: a decade of forking, feeding, turning, and weeding until we can look forward to a blister-free spring. I can understand the temptation to use chemicals—no bugs, no weeds, no backache—but they are also a form of asset stripping.

Chemicals just take from the soil, they don't put anything back. If a gardener is only looking for short-term ways to maximize his bottom line, I suppose they might make sense. But a garden is a long-term endeavor, the success of which depends on our willingness to reinvest. The more patience, labor, and capital you put into it, the more profit it will yield over many years to come.

I suppose all this self-sufficiency stuff makes us sound suspiciously "fringe," but Greg and I enjoy our comforts and conveniences too much to be survivalists. Before we moved, I might have entertained romantic notions about us eventually providing everything by hand, but those were smartly laid to rest our first autumn here, when I met a woman named Cecille.

We came across each other when I was looking for stories
to tell in the "Murphey's Lore" column that I write for our local
paper, *The Brown County Democrat*. Mary, at the county library, said, "You should interview Cecille Marasco. She survives on a couple of acres without using money or modern
technology of any kind." Mary volunteered to drop her a note
about me because, of course, Cecille has no phone.

The following Saturday, I drove deep into the hills to find
her. As I pulled up, a hen was scratching in the flowers outside
the tiny wood cabin, stolidly followed by four baby quail. Dozens of baskets hung above the front porch, and I could see more
in the main room beyond the window. The door was open, so
I knocked on the screen.

A figure raised her head from the shadows on the floor.
"Come in," she said, "this is my sabbath, so I'm resting." Cecille
lay on a roll-away mattress in the place where, she told me
later, she had had the last three of her four children. Her first
was a babe in arms when she and her husband had come to
this place from Detroit, twenty-two years before, to create their
dream homestead out of a tumbledown shack.

Two luminous brown eyes regarded me from a taut face that
could have been anything from forty to sixty years old. Strands
of gray hair escaped from under a dainty white cap, which
looked incongruous above the woman's thick working clothes.

"Do you search for the truth through God?" Cecille asked,
finally, before going on to explain that she bases her lifestyle
on the Book of Revelations. "It states clearly," she went on,
"that all technology is the work of Mammon."

Her self-denial, she said, begins with coal and oil. "What
can you do with coal ash?" she asked, almost affronted. "Nothing useful. Now wood ash will fertilize your garden . . . you can
make lye from wood ash, which is good for dozens of different
things . . . wood ash is an insecticide. . . . You see, you pick

the firewood up off the ground—then, eventually, you put it back. It's all one big circle."

While Cecille got herself up, I waited in the living room under bunches of herbs and garlic that hung drying from the rafters. The weather was warm, but a fire had been lit so that she could boil water in the iron kettle that was suspended over the hearth. Baskets of peaches and apples were piled on the simple wood furnishings. The only decorations in the room were a few afghans, made from wool, which, Cecille said, she gathers, spins, and dyes herself. A large Bible lay propped open on the table, with a couple of half-burned candles by its side.

"My entertainment," Cecille observed briefly, as she conducted me through to the back, where she grows all her supplies.

It was like stepping into another age. A huge stone well, the type you see in biblical pictures, flanked gardens bursting with green abundance. Lettuce, peas, beans, tomatoes, corn (which she also grinds for flour), cabbages, grapes, peaches, plums, pears, apples, and every herb I could name grew in raised beds divided by thin rock paths. There were flashes of color here and there, where Cecille had planted bright patches of marigolds, pansies, and roses, which wound their way over rough trellises made from tree branches, tied together with twine. The same manufacturing technique had apparently been applied to the small stable on the other side of the yard, home to the goat and the sheep that supplied Cecille's yarn.

"I want for very little." She smiled. "Just some animal feed, and iron products: tools, pots and pans. I barter my baskets for those."

As we sat by the well to enjoy a cool drink of water, Cecille went over her schedule for the fall. There were the forest hickory nuts and walnuts to gather and her own harvest to put up, which would be stored in the root cellar that had been built into the side of a small hill. "Then"—a shadow crossed her face—"I have to worry about wood. I need it for everything, but I can never get enough. My whole winter is just a struggle to keep my fire going."

Her strong, callused hand rubbed the problem away from her eyes and I realized that what looked so picturesque in the gold September sun was actually a very hard life. Survival takes 100 percent of Cecille's time. She is now a widow, with children grown and gone, so she only has herself to rely on. If she falters, she has nothing to fall back on. The stark reality of her circumstances was brought home by the story of Cecille's broken ankle. With no way of calling for help or getting to a hospital, she sat down on the floor and set the bone herself.

Greg and I are willing to devote about 40 percent of our time to the farm at the moment. If the farm business takes off in future years, that could go up to 60 or 70 percent, but no more. Our new country life was always intended to complement, rather than replace, the other things we love, and neither of us could imagine a life without writing or photography, even if we were doing them just for our own pleasure.

Nor was our goal to substitute one overwhelmed schedule with another. We want to achieve a balance among all the different elements: family, work, creativity, growth, peace of mind, and play. The only way that's going to happen is if we simplify our demands enough to enable the farm to support a moderate list of requirements. In fact, it already does by giving us food for the table, fuel for the stove, and an interesting list of "Things We Must Learn" that gets longer every day.

"Where are you going?" The spicy aroma of taco meat wafted from the stove to blend with the sharp smell of cilantro that Greg was cutting by the sink.

"You weren't listening, as usual," I commented as I stole a scallion from under his knife. "Chirrup, chirrup, bark, bark," I went on, trying to give him a hint. Greg looked at me as if I had finally gone mad.

Reluctantly, I put his mind at rest. "The state park," I reminded him, "to meet Skitz Everard."

"Skitz Everard." Greg labored over the name. "Who's that?"

"You really didn't hear a word. Skitz Everard is queen of the night hike."

" 'Who-cooks-for-you, who-cooks-for-you-all'—that's a barred owl." Skitz switched off the tape in her pickup truck as she pulled into a clearing in Brown County State Park. A woman in her mid-twenties, Skitz is the archetypal product of a life spent outside. She glows with good health, her skin that soft gold of an incidental tan, her dark hair cut short and shiny for manageability under the most primitive conditions. Her heavy denim clothes, her fresh-scrubbed face point to someone who lives entirely for her work, with no time for the world's more superficial habits. Skitz describes herself as a "transient naturalist," which means that she spends her life traveling the country, spreading joy and edification about wild things to anyone who's half willing to listen. Fortunately, some summers bring her to our neck of the woods, where she teaches the ignorant like me about the creatures of the dark.

"Hear that? Sounds like a broken banjo string. That's a green frog." Skitz was marching me off to her favorite forest hideout, a peak deep in the woods that towers above a huge natural amphitheater.

As we stood there listening, June's strawberry moon rose above the trees and cloaked the hills in a soft pink shimmer. The local symphony struck up in unison.

First, the broken banjo strings, hundreds of them, followed by the aria of a mournful whippoorwill, who probably sounds sadder these days because the birds' habitat is being devastated by the park's overpopulation of deer. The tenors—gray tree frogs, I was informed—sounded like rusty bedsprings, while the bass came courtesy of the bullfrogs, who say, Skitz believes, "Jug-o'-rum, jug-o'-rum." The crickets provided a descant in the background. Insect sounds, she says, come in three types. The flute players (cockroaches and the like), who blow their tunes; the fiddlers (crickets and katydids), who move their wings, sometimes up to forty times a second, to sing their songs; and the percussion players (the cicadas), who contract their muscles over a large open area in their abdomens, which resounds like a drum. The frogs apparently sing for four reasons: to mark their territory, to attract a mate, to warn other amphibians of impending danger, or to signal a fellow frog that he has made a terrible error of judgment. Skitz has named this last sound the "I've Got a Headache" call, and it evolved from the males' somewhat dubious practice of climbing aboard any sedentary frog who happens to be around. Occasionally the intended turns out to be another male, or a female who is otherwise engaged, so the creatures have developed a polite way of saying no.

I could have been standing in my own backyard, but a few elements were still missing: the yipping and barking that wasn't a dog; a faint cooing, that sounded like doves; and a pseudo-electric clicking, which Skitz thought must be bats. "We'll go down to Strahl," she suggested. "There's a bat roost there."

On the way over, the road was lined with deer who barely reacted to the truck. "They're too tame," said Skitz sadly. "All the tourists have trained the wildness out of them and they have overbred so much that they're stripping the forest floor of its vegetation. If something isn't done soon, they'll drive all the ground-living wildlife out of the park and the deer themselves will starve. They can't live on the Twinkies that sightseers insist on feeding them."

Skitz broke off as a pair of glittering eyes, set in a familiar bandit mask, was suddenly caught by the headlights. She pulled the truck off the road and a raccoon family of two parents and four babies sat back on their haunches and studied us curiously. "I might be able to get them to come closer," said Skitz, rolling down her window. She emitted a series of yips and barks that were supposed to be a greeting.

Unfortunately, the animals misunderstood and took it as a battle cry. Mama Raccoon's face widened in horror and she chased her babies up the nearest tree, as Dad prattled angrily and prepared himself to fight.

"Oops," said Skitz. "Came on a little too strong there."

She tried again, and the male cocked his head, looking puzzled. Eventually, he decided that caution was indeed the better part of valor and followed his family into the brush.

"I'm sorry about that," my guide said ruefully.

"Don't worry," I replied, "you've just identified another of our mysterious sounds."

We left the truck a few yards from Strahl Lake and crept through the darkness to a small wooden shelter. Skitz shone a flashlight up into its beams, revealing half a colony of dozing brown bats. "Most of them will be hunting right now," she said. "We'll go out and listen to them in a moment."

We left the shelter to take up position on top of the lake's big dam. Skitz had brought a detector that would amplify the bats' sonic language. She pointed it toward one of the few outside lamps. The light had attracted hundreds of moths and bugs, which were being hunted by members of the bat colony.

She switched the machine on and we could hear a thunderous clicking, which got faster and faster as a bat swooped in for the kill. The noise would then tail off to a languid rhythmic beat until another bat began his fly-by. This slow pulse was the "electric" noise we heard over the house each night.

Standing on the dam, the wall of sound around us began to

separate and make sense. It was like that moment of revelation when you begin to hear each word distinctly in a foreign language. The bats, the cricket frogs, the leopard frogs, the bugs, and the toads all have unique voices that, once learned, can't be forgotten. For the first time since we moved, the cacophony of the night sounded almost soothing.

Skitz will be visiting us soon, and I'm looking forward to showing her that my "doves" were in fact a hoot owl who's taken up residence in the barn. I'll be cooking her dinner as a thank-you for solving all our nighttime mysteries. All, that is, but one. This creature slips soundlessly to the side of our lake, where, judging by the lay of the grass, it stands on two feet overlooking the water for long periods of time. I look forward to observing it more closely soon, perhaps when we invite the sheriff over for a bit of late-night fishing. . . .

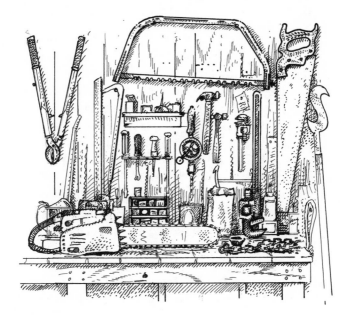

CHAPTER 6

OUR FURRED AND
FEATHERED FRIENDS

HE SMALL PILE OF FEATHERS BY THE POND WERE part of the story. The tracks in the mud told us the rest. Ralph had laid down his life for his flock.

Dennis interpreted the signs. "See, this is where he drew the fox away from the rest of them. . . . Here he was dragged under the gate. . . . He got away for a moment here . . . and this is where the fox finished him."

The drake had fought hard to the end. It had been a heroic struggle, befitting his station as top duck on the pond. There'll never be another Ralph. He was one of our first birds—a fluffy duckling with a cocky attitude who eventually became our friend.

As to the fox, I suppose he couldn't be blamed. Food is hard to come by, and judging by the number of hides Dennis found, this had been his home for a long time. If he struck again, we'd have to find some way of moving him on. For now, we decided, we'll fix the fences and try to live together in peace. The small brown feathers have gone into a box—to be scattered under a weeping cherry by the pond next spring.

Learning to be unemotional about our stock has been one

of the farm's sternest lessons. We are still trying to master it.

In the past eighteen months, seventy-one creatures of various types have taken up residence here. They have arrived in dribs and drabs. The halt, the lame, the unloved, the hungry—all have been drawn to us like muggers to an out-of-town tourist.

First, there was Calico, our tortoiseshell cat, who we met as an abandoned kitten the day after she had been dumped on a friend's doorstep. She attached herself instantly to Charley and wouldn't let go until she was brought home. We hadn't wanted another cat, but who could resist those enormous green eyes blinking up at you with such trust? Calico firmly established herself in the family hierarchy that first night by facing up to Oscar in a fight that was worthy of David against Goliath. The bullterrier was just curious, in his usual clumsy way, and approached to have a sniff. Calico stood her tiny patch of ground on the dining room floor, an outraged sphere of fur. She drove the dog off, lacerating his nose, then calmly washed her paws. Ever since, he has treated her with a respect entirely out of proportion to her size.

The next to come was the horse—our walking cautionary tale against city-style sentimentality—who should have been converted into cans of dog food long ago.

We met last October, after I'd put the word out that I was looking for a mount. It had to be big enough for me, but small enough for Charley to handle. I didn't care about looks, sex, or breed, but it had to be well trained and not more than $300. That probably sounds like a tall order to anyone living in town, but this is horse country, where the whole world owns some kind of mount. Our first call was about Hotshot. A dealer had bought him as part of a lot and had originally intended to send him to the sale barn, where renderers and soap companies come looking for raw material, before she had thought of us.

The animal had heaves, a form of incurable equine asthma, and wasn't good for much more than glue. She wanted $150 for him, which is what he'd fetch in meat.

We went to see him. He was a mess. His mane stood up like a bristle brush, shorn back to the neck, Trojan style, and his hooves were horribly cracked and split. His breathing was positively bronchial, his teeth told us that he was at least twenty (as opposed to the dealer's estimate of fifteen)—but he had a very sweet face. Charley climbed aboard and he moved off gently around the paddock. When she lost her balance and began to slip slightly to one side, the animal stopped, turning his head to point to the problem. All common sense flew away on wings. If we didn't take him, he was condemned to an undignified death. A week later, Hotshot was delivered to our barn, with newly trimmed feet.

At first, he was very well behaved, accepting pets and allowing me to brush his strawberry roan coat up to a shining chestnut gleam. But then he figured out that we'd never owned a horse before. He tested the water one day by kicking me in the knee while I was cleaning out his hooves. When I didn't haul off and cuff him on the nose, he felt free to push a little further. The next day, he jumped his fence and went to visit the horses next door. Our neighbor called. Would we care to come and get him, she asked sweetly, before he caused a multicar pileup along the main road?

He came quietly, the first time, lured by carrots and the promise of a walk in the woods. As the weeks went by, he was progressively harder to convince.

No amount of fence fixing seemed to keep him in. He wandered the property at will, rearing and kicking at anyone who tried to corral him. Any pretense at good behavior was abandoned in favor of a coldly cocky attitude designed to drive us mad. Then, one freezing night in January, he went too far.

Unbeknownst to us, Hotshot had developed a fondness for our neighbor's filly, Precious, and had taken it into his head to move to her place. I had been at a business meeting most of the day and spotted him from the car as I turned into our drive. He pretended not to see me. Cursing, I climbed into my boots, grabbed some fruit, and went to get him.

For two hours, he took my apples and treated my soft, wheedling words with total disdain. When I lost my temper and threw his halter at him, he stared in disbelief and chased me around the barn. It must have been quite a sight: me in my city suit and garden boots, running for my life from a peevish pony with love on his mind.

I escaped and called the sheriff's office to report a mad horse on the loose. They had the kindness not to laugh and sent Leroy Collins, the animal control officer, to meet me at my neighbor's. With the help of the filly fatale, he got Hotshot back into his stall. It took about ten minutes. The horse, recognizing real authority, had followed Precious like a lamb. I was ready to send him to the sale barn myself, but my daughter intervened.

"Hotshot," she announced, "needs a friend. He's lonely, that's all." The pleading look in her big blue eyes was impossible to ignore. We hot-wired his fence and started looking for a mare.

Since then, our relationship has eased. We haven't found his ladylove yet, but the acquisition of thirty-eight chickens, nine ducks, four guinea fowl, and eleven geese seems to have provided him with the company he craved. And the arrival of April, the goat, a couple of weeks ago, has made his world complete.

April is the founder of our milk flock. In my city days of pastoral dreams, I always imagined that our farm would have a cow. I saw her chewing daisies in the pasture or standing quietly in the barn at sunrise, while I drew off the family's milk supply. I didn't realize, at the time, that it takes about 35 pounds of feed to produce a single gallon of cow's milk. Nor did I know that a cow in full flow is not like a spigot to be turned on and off, but will yield more milk a day than we could drink in a month. Five minutes with a dairy farmer at last year's state fair set me straight and turned my attention toward goats as an alternative. A good nanny will produce just enough for a family of three and will forage most of her feed for herself around the farm. Goats are great weeders. They'll munch through whole thickets in a matter of hours. Two nannies will keep our hedgerows clear and allow me to experiment with yet another craft: cheesemaking. Goat's milk tastes very similar to cow's and can be turned into much more than the usual Feta. Some goat keepers claim that it will make everything from Swiss to the finest Stilton. That remains to be seen. First, we have to have kids to get the supply going.

April will go into heat soon and be whisked away to the local billy goat, where she will stay until she is bred. In the meantime, you will find her standing companionably in the barn with her new friend, Hotshot, a chicken or two roosting on the horse's back, as they both share their grain with the geese.

We never planned to have so much poultry. Five or six geese, maybe, about a dozen chickens, and a flock of ducks was all we'd had in mind. The problem began when we bought the two turkeys.

Cornbread and Cranberry are American Bronze—a relative of the type that Ben Franklin wanted to adopt as the national bird. They are deeply stupid beasts, with just enough brain to keep breathing, but magnificent to look at. When they fan their tails and puff up their mass of chocolate and cream feathers in a misguided display of machismo, they can stop traffic. One day, they literally did. A truck pulled into the drive, disgorging a white-haired man with a suntanned face wreathed in smiles. "I was wondering if you'd be willin' to sell one of your turkeys . . . " he began.

I wish, I thought grimly, but Greg would never allow it. He had become very fond of their bossy ways and blue heads with eyes that blink at you like some disinterred dead thing before they bite you on the ankle.

"I'm sorry," I regretted out loud, "but they have become family pets." His cheerful eyes drooped in disappointment.

"Would you like to meet them?" I asked, thinking that a brief introduction would improve his state of mind.

"Oh, yes!" The smile came back and he fell into a jaunty step beside me.

Herschiel Boller is a truck driver with a yen to live in the country. He had been brought up on a small farm as a boy, but had moved to the city for his work, which is where he would have to stay for the time being. Meanwhile, he told me, he had been living his dream vicariously through his brother-in-law, who had recently moved to Brown County.

"I've bought him all manner of birds," Herschiel explained, "guineas, geese, chickens . . . but I wanted to get him some turkeys, too." The blue heads gobbled at him ingratiatingly. I offered him the name and number of our supplier. As he took the note, Herschiel cast around for an exchange of information. "You know, I just got some chicks from a hatchery that said they would lay colored eggs—I'd like to bring you a couple." I was duly grateful for the offer, never expecting to see him again, but true to his word, he came back at the weekend with two beautiful baby birds.

The writer E. B. White once warned the passionate poultry keeper against trying to share his enthusiasm. He did not take his own advice and nor can we, now that we've met the Auracana chicken. They are also known as the "Easter Egg Chick" and do, indeed, lay colored eggs—blue, olive or pink—and have the most spectacular plumage this side of a peacock.

Herschiel had brought us a cock and a hen—Chanticleer and Henny Penny. Chanticleer has since grown into a magnificent rooster with brown and bronze body feathers flecked with gold, red and blue and a tail of deep sea green. As a baby, he lived under the heat lamps in the summer kitchen with his sister, where he began to practice his crow. I heard him one morning as we were eating breakfast—this small strangled sound, a bit like a two-toned cough. Each day he got a little louder and added a new note to his scale. By the end of the week, he could sing the full five-note phrase, with just a touch of laryngitis.

The birds were also much smarter than we had imagined, even to the point of being friendly. Henny Penny would come to the bars of the cage for Charley to tickle her chest, and when they were big enough to be sent out to the barn, they did not forget us and would be waiting to greet us when we came to serve their breakfast.

This was the breed for us. It was time to find some companions for the founders of our flock.

There are many ways to buy chickens, but one of the most common is to order hatchlings through that hub of farm life, your local feed store. There is always one somewhere in a farming community, selling everything from boots to barbed wire.

Need straw, a saddle, fence posts, or a fly trap? The feed store is where you'll find it. They will sell you the seed to grow your crops and, when the harvest is in, will buy your corn or oats right back from you. Our local store looks like something out of a Steinbeck novel. I don't suppose it has changed much in the last seventy years. Huge silos stand guard around a square silver tower, which proudly proclaims the legend "WAYNE FEEDS." In the shadow of these giants lies a long gray bungalow fronted by a rough wooden deck. This is where daily business is done, and there are always a few trucks pulled up with their hatches down, ready to drop off or pick up.

Inside, the air is sweet with the smell of fresh grain, molasses, and good conversation. Lesa and Judy, the ebullient blonds who run the store, always make the time for a word or two—and even the taciturn Rick, a big bearded bear of a man who does much of the heavy labor, will pause to offer the occasional gem of advice. Between them, these warm people have taught me everything from how to tie a slipknot to when to worm the horse. They are my first port of call if I have any question of an agricultural kind.

Lesa dealt with our inquiry about the chicks. Yes, she said, she could get the Auracana, but only in batches of twenty-five.

Greg's eyes rolled heavenward as he waited for my reply.

"Well," I sighed, "we can always give some away, or stock the freezer for the winter."

Killing, in the country, is as important as giving life. It is the inevitable conclusion for those who wish to raise their own meat and is as much part of rural living as knowing how to start seed. Most born-and-bred Brown Countians have tagged along with their hunting, fishing, or trapping fathers since they were babies and don't give the matter a second thought. Many city settlers give it a third or fourth consideration before deciding it's not for them. Greg announced from the very start that this was a skill he was not keen to acquire, so I was appointed family butcher.

Last winter, I researched the matter thoroughly. The books describe several popular methods of execution: beheading; strangulation; or the "Farmer's Wife" technique, where you pick the bird up by the neck and whirl it around in the air on the way to the kitchen.

Big John favors a .22 rifle, which he uses with murderous

accuracy following his tour as a 17th Cavalry (Air Cavalry) scout in Vietnam.

This is not a man one would wish to annoy, as Terry discovered on the day she forgot to do the grocery shopping. John went outside, shot all the chickens, and hung them on the fence as a reminder to his wife to fill the freezer from time to time. All but one, that is, who to this very day gives him a wide berth and one of the dirtiest looks you've ever seen on the face of a fowl.

My favorite book recommended a spike through the beak into the brain, because it makes the bird's feathers drop out spontaneously. It takes a little practice, they say, but it does cut cleaning time in half.

"Dressing" a chicken is actually a contradiction in terms. I have only done it once, during a vacation with a French friend on her parents' farm, but I can report that "stripping" a chicken would be more apt.

I was all of ten years old at the time, feeling very shy and far from home. I had never been parted from my parents or big-city life before, and the experience was a little overwhelming.

The family did their best to make me feel welcome and went out of their way to keep me from getting bored. Within the first few days, I was taught how to deliver piglets, feed minks (the farm's main source of income), and fend off a rat, which had attacked me in the barn.

I was grateful when Sunday morning arrived and they all went off to Mass, leaving me alone to read in the garden.

It was midsummer and the sunlight made my hair feel hot. Even the droning of the bees sounded drowsy, and I began to doze over my page. An indignant squawking woke me with a start, just in time to see the flash of an axe, followed by a fountain of scarlet. The grandmother was preparing dinner. Without a word, she pegged the bird's feet to a clothesline and shuffled back into the house, her old carpet slippers slapping up the stone steps. I sat there stunned, watching the headless body dance and jerk as its blood drained out over the marigolds.

Grandma and I hadn't had much to say to each other since my arrival. She spoke no French—only Breton, the ancient Celtic tongue—and was a frightening figure in black, with a few yellow stumps where there should have been teeth. She did, however, have a kind smile, which she used to good effect an hour later, when she motioned me into the house. The chicken was lying on a thick wood slab near the stove, where a huge cauldron of water was bubbling away. Judging by her pantomime, I was to help her clean the bird—as a special treat.

Being a well brought up and curious child, I followed directions with a will—plunging the body into the boiling pot and watching as the lice and mites in the feathers jumped for their lives. The bird was then dried and left to cool for a minute or two before the plucking began.

Grandma held the body up by its feet and motioned me to start at the tail, pulling the feathers out along their grain. They came easily, some with the soft sound of tearing silk. They were still wet, of course, and stuck to everything they touched. My hands, arms, and chest were soon covered in white and the floor was speckled with the few I managed to brush off. As the feathers dried in the sun, they became airborne, filling the kitchen like drifting snowflakes. It was a mess—a big mess— but the old lady didn't seem to mind. The mess was obviously part of the fun.

When the chicken was bare, she laid it on the wood block and, in the blink of an eye, removed its feet and split its bottom up to the breastbone. She reached inside and, with all the experience of more than seventy years, eviscerated the bird with one sharp twist of the wrist. The guts came spilling out in a neat, shining heap of purple and dark pink. The old lady then poked at the entrails like some ancient priest before seizing the lungs, liver, and heart, and throwing them into a pot.

At this point, I bowed out politely, vowing never to eat meat again. But my promise melted away when I saw the succulent roast on the table that night. It was the best chicken I had ever eaten, and my part in its demise didn't bother me one bit.

It was hard to imagine doing any of the above to the twenty-five chicks who arrived in late May.

We were astonished to discover that they had been sent by mail in a small cardboard box. Apparently, it takes a hen a day or three to hatch all her brood, so the chicks are born with an inbuilt food supply, in the form of undigested yolk, to keep them quiet until Mom has time to teach them how to eat. The hatchery takes full advantage of their "packed lunches" by parceling them up on their birthdays, for immediate delivery.

Our crowd did not seem particularly perturbed by their ordeal and soon settled down to an early supper under the warm lights. There is no prettier sight than a newly born chick. As we gathered around to watch Charley hold each little powder puff in turn, I knew that these birds would probably die of nothing worse than old age.

If we weren't going to kill our chickens, we could still dream of our very own fresh foie gras. Goslings were next on our shopping list, and we were determined not to get too attached to them.

My parents, who now live in the Périgord, were the first to introduce us to France's most celebrated pâté. Foie gras is a goose's liver that has been fattened on a diet of pure corn. French farmers force-feed the birds, pouring the grain straight down their throats through a large funnel. The name means, literally, "fat liver," and the organ from one of these overfed fowl can weigh up to four and a half pounds. The end result is a pink-tinged potted pâté that is the most subtle and delicious spread you have ever had on a piece of toast.

The means of getting there bothered us both, however, until we discovered that the Romans, who invented the delicacy, had an alternative method of production. They considered their geese too sacred to mistreat, so they fed the birds normally and waited until butchering time, when they took the still warm liver and soaked it in milk and honey for several hours. This seemed much more to our taste. The only remaining question was: what variety of gosling to buy?

As I fussed over the virtues of the Toulouse versus the Chinese, Herschiel pulled into the drive again. He did not look happy.

"I've come to see whether you'd like some more birds." He went on to explain that his brother-in-law had been taken ill and was undergoing major surgery. There would not be anyone to take care of the creatures for a long time to come. "I was going to sell them," he said, "but I'd prefer them to go to a good home, and I like the way you look after your animals." After a compliment like that, how could anyone turn him down? Greg was away, so I saw no reason to be circumspect. "I'll take whatever you've got," I replied expansively, "except for the turkeys—my neighbors might help you there." In the absence of my husband's wiser head, I had neglected to ask Herschiel how many orphans we were talking about, or even what breed or sex they might be. The questions entered my mind only as his taillights disappeared from sight.

When the early evening sunshine began to brush the face of the barn, he came back. His truck was exploding with beaks and beady eyes, all squawking and jostling for a better view.

The back of his van looked like some feathered Medusa, alive with sinuous necks straining to catch a glimpse of their new home. My jaw dropped.

It took Herschiel, Janet (who was visiting from Chicago), and me twenty minutes to carry them all to the pasture, two at a time. The scene by the pond was chaos. Hotshot had stepped on a greylag's foot, who was now hobbling around in circles, honking pathetically. The turkeys had one of the new ducks pinned down in the mud and were attempting to mount her. Old chickens squared off to new, while the guinea fowl, with their black combs and Phantom of the Opera masks, were trying to break out under the fence.

There were thirty-one new birds in all, bringing our poultry population up to a staggering sixty-two. Gradually, order was restored. The greylag was caught and hospitalized for the night, her huge orange web just a bit bruised. The turkeys were pulled off the duck, who was removed to the safety of the summer kitchen to recover from her assault. She nibbled my fingers in thanks and settled down so sweetly in her cage that she was christened Dolce on the spot. The rest were fed and left alone to establish their new pecking orders. By 7:30 P.M., all was still.

Big John and Terry came over to sneak a peek at the new flock. They joined Janet and me on the front porch, where we sat in the gathering gloom, watching the fireflies and listening to the frogs.

The conversation was the easy staccato of good friends, teasing each other about the best way to hatch an egg and the laying qualities of each type of hen. Janet, my intellectual sparring partner from city days, was just sitting with a broad smile on her face, unusually quiet.

Her thoughts translated themselves into a letter the next day, after her return to the Big City:

Dear Sal,

After being chased home by a wild stampede of lawless truckers barreling their way up to Chicago and points north, I finally fell asleep with visions of chickens—and ducks, geese, and one very threatening turkey—prancing and dancing in my head. A natural herder I am, I am. What a hoot.

I love how the birds group themselves. They move and merge together like waddling water—so fluid and graceful, around and around the field they go. It's a wonderful image to drift dreamward with. Then add a picture of you, talking turkey to the turkey: "Well, mister, if you think you're going to challenge *me,* you'd better think twice! You're in over your head!" (from the "shout loudly and carry a big stick" school of agrarian psychology). . . .

Yes, Sal—you have changed. . . .

I don't think that moving to the country has made us less aware. We still read *Time* and *Newsweek* and watch *Nightline* every night, and can argue art or politics with all our city friends. But the farm has given us new intellectual priorities. We now have an ever-shifting landscape to watch over, which suffers for any lapse in our concentration. An apple tree collapses because we missed the webworm in its crown; some tomato plants are suffocated by slowly leaking septic waste; a lavender bush dies, left unmulched out in a frost. They are all our responsibility, as stewards of the land, punishments from Nature for not paying attention.

It's the same with our animals. Signs of sickness or small injury often begin slowly, little hints of trouble ahead. Someone's slightly off their feed or lying down more than they should; there's a dullness to the coat, a loss of sparkle in the eye. They are all little inconsistencies that you wouldn't even notice unless you know each creature well. A phlegmatic fowl, for instance, may not be any cause for alarm—but if she was top gossip on the compost pile, take note. You had better isolate her before she gives the barn blackhead, or bluecomb, or one of the dozen other disgusting diseases that can decimate a flock. It only takes twenty minutes a day to monitor them all— a short interval of peace and quiet that is the main pleasure of my morning.

Our birds seem to live happily together and almost never fight. Poultry will naturally peck at one another—ours did— until the barnyard social stratum is established. Once everyone knows who is who, the feathers should stop flying. But it does not always work like that. Chickens can be vicious when confined. If living quarters are cramped, they will often lash out, maiming or even killing a fellow fowl. In the worst conditions, they sometimes turn cannibal and feed on each other in an effort to gain a few extra inches of space. The books' solution to this problem is to de-beak the birds so that they cannot do each other any harm; we prefer to rely on decent housing, good food, and the freedom to explore in the fresh air. Like most living things, they do best that way.

The closeness of all this human-bird contact can be a problem sometimes, too. The geese began by looking all the same, but their personalities were so different that they soon separated into individual birds.

We ended up with three different breeds: the Emden, the Toulouse, and the long-necked white Chinese. The Chinese geese are led by Yang, a huge, gregarious gander who is always first to tell you the news. He will insist on pets for his neck and soft chest before yielding to number one wife, Yin. She is quieter than her husband but every bit as affectionate, jealously nipping at the other girls until she has had her full share of loving. The only goose who does not compete for attention is little Water Lily, who has spent the past few weeks lying patiently on a nest, waiting for her probably infertile eggs to hatch.

It is impossible to look at their eager faces and think "pâté de foie gras." Like the turkeys, they are becoming beloved pets who should be with us, barring disasters, for the next fifteen to twenty years.

We could, I suppose, learn not to name our animals, in an effort to put food on the table without the whole family going into mourning. Or maybe we just have to admit that this is the one area where we will always be soft city folk who cannot bring themselves to eat any meat that isn't plastic-wrapped.

"You're not going to eat them?" Dennis was incredulous, one evening over a drink. There it was again, that cardinal sin: waste. "But . . . then . . . what are you keeping them all for?" I didn't have an acceptable answer for him—until the day the ducks died.

"Look over here!" I ran toward a white pile of feathers lying hidden in the long grass. Not content with Ralph, the fox had returned to the pond for dessert. A second bird had been pulled to the middle of the big field, where her attacker had apparently been scared off by the dogs. She had been abandoned with a broken back and was struggling weakly to get up. It was Dolce. The duck laid her head across my arm.

"I'm sorry, sweetheart, but I'm not sure I can help." Her eyes were full of understanding as she let me stroke her, speaking softly while I screwed myself up to do the only thing I could. Finally, urging me on, she moved her head aside to rest her neck along the ground. She looked away toward the lake.

It took just a second, a small heartbeat of time. Her neck snapped with one sharp twist of the wrist.

Later, after I had buried her little body under the pines, I

wandered over to see our living birds. The inside of the barn
was cool and very quiet. Strips of dusty sunlight cut through
the shade, spotlighting three chickens roosting in the rafters.
A fourth was trying a nesting box out for size in preparation
for her egg-laying days to come. She clucked contentedly to
herself, well pleased with the accommodations, and settled in
for a midday snooze.

The bird barely twitched when sounds of battle broke out
in the pasture, just outside. One of the turkeys had been making advances on a hen, who was outraged by the whole idea.
The rooster rushed to her defense, flinging himself in fury at
her assailant's head. Cornbread took off across the field as fast
as his lopsided gait would let him, while Chanticleer stood on
top of the well cap, crowing his contempt.

"Eggs and smiles . . . " I muttered to myself.

"What did you say?" Greg came up behind me and put his
arms around my waist.

"Eggs and smiles—that's what we keep the birds for."

"Yes," he said approvingly, "*and* those bright blue heads."

CHAPTER 7

THE GLITTERING PRIZES

AN I DO SOME?" AN ENORMOUS WICKER BASKET PRE-
ceded my daughter through the bean plants and
she arrived panting at my side.

"Only take the bigger ones, here at the bottom," I showed her. "I'll get the ones at the top."

Charley's rapt concentration as she carefully
measured each pod was an echo from many
years ago, when my beloved Nana Moyce had
instructed a muddy-kneed, much smaller me in
the art of picking beans.

I can still see the kitchen garden on the
chalk cliffs, hovering above the gray mudflats of
the Thames estuary. As we left our harvest by the sink to be
washed, the sea breeze from a mile or two away would rush in
through the scullery window and blend with the fumes of
bleach from the old laundry tub. The rest of the house would
still be asleep when we tiptoed out to my grandmother's silver-
blue Austin and drove to our secret spot by the railway tracks.
There we would wait for a whisper of sound in the distance,
which would mount to a deafening roar as the steam train
rushed by on its way to London. Occasionally, the driver would
spot two figures at the top of the embankment waving like

windmills and he would wave back, pulling on his whistle in a personal salute. That made our day.

My Nan died when I was ten, leaving me with the cozy memories of early childhood securely wrapped in the smell of her glorious steak and kidney pud. I never knew her as the tiny battle-ax who became one of Britain's first female dentists. To me she was just the warm hand in a white suede glove, who took me on adventures that taught me to love the simple stuff of life.

"Put them on the back porch, by the little table." Charley's basket was full to the brim with beans, enough for a dozen dinners to come. June's rains had finally been chased away by July's radiant skies and the gardens were beginning to explode with color. Lemon cucumbers peeked out from the ground cover, next to the cream skins of baby melons, while our tomatoes hung above them like various stages of the sunset: pale orange-yellow ripening to the deepest dark pink. In the herb garden, the cornflowers and nasturtiums glistened like jewels in a green crown of parsley, basil, and apple mint.

"See if you can find ten beans that look the same."

Charley looked suspicious. "Why?"

"Because Dada might want to enter them in the fair."

My daughter's face lit up. "The fair . . . " she whispered reverently. "Is that coming soon?"

To Charley the state and country fairs rank right up there alongside Christmas. We were called upon to visit the county fair twice last year, so the Bug could examine all the animals at her leisure and try out every one of the rides. Mom and Dad were dragged from tent to tent as she took in the arts and crafts, the tap dancers and the swing bands, the antique engines, and the occasional tractor pull. She is not alone in her enthusiasm.

Across the road, the Dungans have already been hard at work, getting ready for the twenty categories that Rebecca will enter this year. We first met this energetic sixteen-year-old on the day that we decided to take the farm. Her parents were having a barbecue and, with their usual kindness, invited us to join in. It was quite an initiation into Brown County society. Big John was roasting a whole pig over a pit in their backyard, while Terry was bustling about, setting baked beans and salad out on trestle tables in the barn. A big log fire was burning by their pond and some teenagers were doing the limbo dance under a clothesline.

The lithest and most athletic of them all was a tall, slim girl with curly blond shoulder-length hair, who broke away from the crowd and ran up to talk to us. Rebecca was fourteen, she informed us, and had just won her first steer in a roping competition at the local fair. "Come and see him," she insisted. Without waiting for a reply, the girl marched these two rather startled city folk over to a large pen and introduced the animal proudly: "This is Wild Thing."

The beast was enormous—a black bull the size of a truck. He stuck his nose through the fence and licked his young mistress's hand. "What exactly did you have to do?" I inquired, eyeing his large frame with respect.

"I had to wrassle him to the ground and tie him up," she replied, as if this were a normal activity for all young teenage girls.

Her father confirmed the story. "Yep," said Big John, with his lazy smile, "and she beat out all the boys to do it. One was even carried off with a couple of broken ribs." He was clearly delighted.

We went away shell-shocked that day, wondering whether Charley would, in her turn, be able to throw bulls to the floor with such abandon and whether that was exactly what we wanted for our daughter. It was a few months before we discovered that this apparent madness had some method to it, too.

The steer was the basis of Rebecca's college fund. He would be shown the next year, then sold at the end-of-fair auction. The girl would use part of her money to buy another animal and bank the balance in her savings account. By the time she went to school, she would be several thousand dollars better off.

I became very fond of Wild Thing, who saved a few kisses for me whenever I stopped in to do the feeding during a Dungan family vacation. I was sad to see him go, but pleased when he was replaced with another softhearted steer, called Sir Loin. For the past twelve months, we have seen this big-eyed Brown Swiss grow from a 460-pound weakling to the lumbering 1,160 pounds he is today. He will be Rebecca's headline act among the ten animals she will show this year.

From our bedroom window, I've watched the pair of them working together every morning, Beauty and her faithful Beast, marching round and round the upper paddock. Oh, the callousness of youth! Rebecca hardly seems to notice the loving look in the big steer's eyes. She doesn't see him sucking in his chest and sticking out his chin, doing his bovine best to "set up and square off," as she tells him, sergeant-major style. She won't become aware of the depths of his affections until competition day, when triumph and sadness will combine to teach her that he was more than just a mobile piece of meat.

Our animals will all be staying at home. At county level, these shows are usually reserved for the kids, or more specifically, the members of 4H. Charley can't join the Head, Heart, Hands, and Health brigade until she is eight, so she will have to content herself with contributing to her parents' efforts to fly the Murphey family flag.

There are tons of categories to choose from, but we will limit our entry to the three where we might not embarrass ourselves: herbs (two sprigs of any variety); vegetables (one plate of three, ten pods, or one head), and the pie-making contest. As Charley counted out the beans, I turned toward the kitchen garden to begin the final selection.

The combination of July's semitropical heat and humidity had encouraged the herb bed to shoot for the stars. The fennel was already five feet tall, closely followed by the lemon balm and the chocolate mint. It looked as if I would be spoiled for choice—until I got down on my knees.

A praying position is often the best way to contemplate a garden. There's another world going on under that canopy of leaves. This morning's study revealed a new crop of twitch grass twined around the parsley plants; a dead mole, deposited there by one of the cats; and a dozen Japanese beetles clinging to the large-leaf basil.

George, the small toad who had taken up residence in the garden when I planted it last year, came out for his customary greeting. "You haven't been doing your job, have you?" I chided him. He was normally a wonderful assistant gardener who kept my little patch bug-free. Apparently he drew the line at this lot—which was easy to understand. As babies, they are burrowed in under the plants—fat, grayish white maggots that squirm wetly on the end of a garden fork. The survivors of spring digging turn into little copper-coated helmets, who march into battle with voracious appetites for plants and procreation. If left unchecked, they will turn an entire bush into a stencil of its former self. I had been waging war on them for the past four weeks: hanging traps, spraying them with soapy water, and handpicking them off the roses—their favorite food—morning, noon, and night. I had not realized that they had changed their plan of attack.

The basil was too badly nibbled for entry in the fair, so I settled on some tarragon, the chocolate mint, and two sprigs of fennel. They were not showroom beautiful, having been hacked at so much for the kitchen, but they were bushy and totally bug-free. I staked up the tarragon so that it, too, would "set up and square off" by Judgment Day.

The vegetables also left a lot to be desired. Our refusal to use any form of chemical control was certainly better for the plants, but it did not do much for their physical appearance. We did not have a leaf unscarred by something or other, and nothing was quite uniform in size.

Charley was going purple with frustration. All the beans had been turned out of the basket and were scattered all around her, in little piles on the ground. She was a dejected figure. "Mama, none of these are the same," she said sadly, as if she were letting the side down. "I'm not very good at stuff."

I gathered my little girl in my arms and together we found three pods that matched out of several dozen. "See, it was not you," I said. "They just grew that way. We'll pick some later for the fair."

Although she refuses to believe me, Charley is getting so good at "stuff" that she has become an invaluable helper all around the farm.

Every day now, she pitches in with the feeding, the watering, the weeding, and our bug patrols. Her sharp eyes always spot the hornworms or the aphids before mine do, giving her an unfair advantage in our favorite game, the daily egg hunt. We are looking for ducks' eggs, which get deposited all over the field. Those shameless ladies will drop their hoard wherever they happen to be, from the top of the compost pile to the shores of the pond, where the eggs get trodden into the mud by the other local traffic. The eggs are worth rescuing because they cook wonderfully well and are a great substitute for chickens' eggs while we wait for our hens to start laying. That will be any day now, and Charley and I have been sneaking into the barn behind each other's backs, competing for the honor of finding the first one. We are best companions, she and I, particularly in the long weeks when Greg is away.

Summer isn't just a busy season on the farm; it's also when Greg's photography work is at its height, taking him on the road for 70 percent of the time. "Us girls" stage pajama parties and late-night picnics to fend off any fear of the dark, and I often wake to find a small head on the pillow beside me, filling the void that her father left behind. The depth of the darkness in the country still makes me nervous when Greg's not around—and I am not helped by phone calls like the one I got the other night.

"Sally, did you know that there's a wild dog living on your property?" It is unusual for Big John to dispense with the formalities; he was obviously concerned.

"It looks like a Doberman," he went on. "I've seen it every morning for the past few days. I think it's after the livestock."

Now he had me worried, too. Brown County is the drop-off capital of the world, and we all have found dumped pets and taken them to the animal shelter. But a wild dog, living somewhere in our woods, was a different matter. I thought of Charley being watched from the bushes as she played outside and a shudder went up my spine. "What should we do?"

"Just keep an eye out for him, and if you see him, call me. I'll deal with it." John sounded grim.

I stood guard the following morning and at nine o'clock spotted a shadowy figure slinking around the corner of the barn. The dog was painfully thin and seemed terrified, tail tucked between his legs, ears flattened against his skull. By the time I called John, the animal had disappeared, slipping away like a dark gray ghost.

I was surprised that our dogs hadn't raised the alarm. Lady is usually a vigorous watchdog and her son Paws seems all set to carry on the tradition. The pup that I had held in my hand just seven months ago now weighs in at over 100 pounds and stands a head taller than his mom. He is a giant of a dog, whose sweet nature makes up for a startling lack of brain. Paws tends to walk through things rather than around them; and when he chews, as all puppies do, he picks on more than just a pair of shoes. We've had to stop leaving him alone in the house, following one occasion recently, when we had gone out to do some shopping. Paws had obviously worked himself into some kind of frenzy and, by the time we came home, had uprooted two potted palms, eaten holes in our best rug, and ripped the sides off an armchair. The only thing that saved him from instant banishment to the barn was the dumb look of love on his vacant face—and the fact that he's an alert guard who usually uses his booming bark to deafening effect. This morning, though, both dogs were still sleeping peacefully on the kitchen floor. It was quite puzzling.

I saw the Doberman again several times in the following days. He would appear for a few seconds, in the same place, then vanish as quietly as he'd come. The livestock at each farm remained untouched, and I began to feel very sorry for our spectral friend. Maybe John could be persuaded that there was a way of saving this sad creature and finding him a home. I wish we had made the time to discuss it; we all would have been spared a lot of heartache in the end.

But fair fever was upon us, and the Dungan family were busy loading half their farm into the back of two small trucks. Their competitions began a week ahead of ours, at the Johnson County Fair.

It is only an accident of geography that Brown and Johnson counties lie together. If you judged them by appearances, they would be in separate states. Johnson County is flat, Midwest plain, full of small white houses set in large fields of corn. This is serious, full-time farming country, where people spend months preparing for their big event. It's a matter of family honor. Grandma develops a knockout blackberry jam; Mom nurtures an orchid in the cellar for nine months; Dad hovers anxiously as little Johnny works with the prize bull, blacking its hooves and shining its coat until it gleams like a new car.

At contest time, the Johnson County fairgrounds are full of severe, sunburned men in big boots and gimme caps, closely following their nervous offspring's every move. This is real business. A win here, even at this young level, can mean an increase in the value of their stock or an entry worthy of that Olympics for farm animals—the State Fair. The dads stand around the stock barns, studying the competition through narrowed, deep-set eyes.

There is only one full-time farmer in Brown County, so our fair is less competitive and much more fun.

This year, the floriculture and gardening exhibits were due in by midday on August 3. I resisted the temptation to get it all ready too soon and left what picking there was until the morning of the show. The tarragon was most cooperative, standing to attention right on cue. The beans were less so, and ten pods of "the same size, shape, and color" still proved impossible to find. We couldn't remember how strict the standards were in Brown County, so we decided to save the vegetables for next year, to give us the opportunity for some more serious research. By 11:45 A.M., the herbs were stashed on the dashboard and we were rocketing across the hills to get there on time.

It was a dazzling day. Little white clouds raced across a clear blue sky, covering the fields with dancing light. Cattle rested quietly in the shade under trees that were syrupy with sun. It would have been a spectacular drive had we not been in such a hurry.

We made it with a minute to spare.

Our entries were tagged and set on the shelves, next to a sensational sprig of borage, covered in light blue flowers, and two heads of picture-perfect dill. There are the winners, I thought to myself. But it didn't matter. It was exciting just to play a part in a real county fair. The entrants and judges chatted quietly to each other, crowded around steaming coffee urns and large plates of cookies. Women who work hard every day of the year taking unusual time out to catch up with old friends. Their warm faces smiled at each other's skill, only too aware of the effort that had gone into each display.

The exhibits were being housed in a huge steel barn, which contained an astonishing array of human ingenuity and art. There were hand-sewn quilts held together with ten thousand tiny stitches and cakes cloaked in icing that could have been white lace. There was handmade jewelry and homemade jam, and watercolors of favorite local scenes. Some of the designs were a little alarming, but a lot of the work would have fetched ridiculous prices in a chic big-city boutique.

We had been wise not to enter our undisciplined beans. The ones on show were as straight as dark green soldiers and matched each other perfectly in size. There were some green peppers that Greg could have competed against with pride, but it hadn't occurred to either of us to enter ours.

The fighting Irish in my husband flashed into his hazel eyes. "Next year," he muttered, "I'll take this a little more seriously."

As we wandered around the show, I, too, was inspired. There was a class for every simple craft that plays a part in our lives, from gift-wrapping to bread-baking to Christmas ornament design. At the fair, nothing is "ordinary," and there is at least one opportunity for everybody to shine.

Judging takes place a couple of days before the fair really begins, so we didn't see our herbs again until the Ferris wheel was up and running. Charley was in such a frenzy of fairitis that we almost walked right past the barn—which would have been a shame, because a blue ribbon was waiting there with our name on it. In the best Brown County tradition, no one in the herb section had taken less than second place, and blue and red ribbons fluttered like flags from the base of every plant. Only the borage and the dill had been set aside, proudly wearing purple championship rosettes.

We would have been quite happy to share the spoils with the whole county, if need be. The Murphey family wafted out of the barn, feeling over ten feet tall: we had become members of the community and winners, all in one evening. Outside, the night air smelled of cinnamon and fried onions as we headed for the midway and a celebratory meal.

No one, not even my husband, would normally choose to eat fair food. It usually comes floating in its own pool of oil and encourages the kinds of combinations that, in any other context, would be utterly obscene. Greg's plat du jour contained pizza, a corn dog, ribs, an egg roll, and an Italian sausage, slathered in peppers and onion—and he was being relatively restrained. All around us, bellies as big as beach balls were tucking into enormous piles of grease. Their owners weren't fat so much as sturdy and strong, their bulk some solid symbol of security or wealth.

"You know, tomorrow's going to be a different class of competition. I think we could live without it."

My husband looked at me, amazed. "What, no pie contest? Aw, come on, Sal, it'll be fun."

"Look around you, Greg. These are people who like to eat. We are going to get trounced."

My love waved his hand in dismissive benediction. "You'll do just fine."

I wasn't convinced. There is not much of a culinary tradition in these parts, but when it comes to baking pies, nobody does it better than the Brown County ladies. I was sure that this occasion would bring out their most aggressive best. It was almost audacity for an amateur like me to enter whatever misshapen contribution I could muster. But the look of disappointment on my family's face decided the matter, and I found myself sweating over apples and flour the following day.

Taking the ladies on with an American apple pie would have been madness, so we settled on a more exotic European recipe—the French almond apple tart. It's a pretty dish, covered in wheels of fruit, which are glazed in apricot jam. If I was going down in flames, at least I was going down in style.

The contest began at six thirty and, for the second time that week, we found ourselves hurtling down dangerous roads in an effort to be prompt. The atmosphere on my side of the car sang like a high-tension wire. "We're not going to make it . . . we shouldn't even have tried . . . can't you go any faster . . . mind that cat . . . perhaps I should drive. . . . " Greg's side of the car was a perfect pool of calm. We arrived five minutes late and I was dropped at the community room before he went to park.

I flung myself through the door to find that the judging was already in progress. About forty faces turned to stare and a gentle laugh began at the back of the crowd. I'm not that funny, I thought, blushing, until I looked down to find that I still had my oven mitts on.

A cheerful lady from the Brown County Home Economics Club motioned me over. "It's not too late," she whispered. "What have you brought? Oh, how pretty. Just fill this out and put your tart over there." She pointed to a long table down the other side of the room, where the pies in each group were being displayed.

I had been right. The Brown County Ladies had knocked their stockings off. There were pies of every kind: peach pies,

cherry, apricot, pecan, raspberry, and, of course, apple pies by
the mile. Each one was the finest example of the baking arts,
with puffy golden crusts, cooked to perfection. The room
smelled of spice and honey, like an orchard in the fall. My class,
"Cobblers, Crisps, Bettys, or Tarts," was headed by the most
beautiful fruit flan, which must have been devised with the
Fourth of July in mind. The crust was blue with a creamy white
filling, topped by strawberries and blueberries in intricate designs. My apple tart looked clumsy in comparison.

Greg was gazing admiringly at the panoply of food. "Told
you so," I hissed.

He pushed me over to a seat, saying, "Just wait and see."

The judging was being taken very seriously. Each pie was
held up for the crowd's inspection as its contents and creator
were announced. Small slices were then cut for the panel, who
tasted each one thoughtfully before noting their scores. There
were four judges. The two "toughies" were the chef from the
Story Inn, the county's swishest restaurant, and the manager
from Nashville's most expensive hotel. Their impassive faces
were the hardest to impress.

It takes a strong stomach, and about an hour and a half, to
taste and judge some twenty-odd pies. By the time they got to
the tart section, my palms were sweating and my mouth was
very dry. You can take the girl out of the city, but you can't
take the city-style competition out of the girl. I despised myself
for caring, but I couldn't help it. Winning was not at issue: I
just didn't want to lose.

The first up was the Fourth of July flan, which drew "oohs"
of admiration from the crowd. The lady from the Story Inn
smiled when she tasted it and whispered something to her fellow judge. I closed my eyes and prayed: "Please don't let me
be last—not last, please." Mine was next. The crowd reaction
was nice, but my eyes were frozen on the lady chef. She took

a bite, looked pensive, then noted something down.

"She doesn't like it," I whispered, preparing for the worst.

All the entries were tasted and returned to the table, while the members of the Home Economics Club figured up the scores. The little cards were double-checked, then suddenly it was all over. The nice lady who had let me in picked up a blue ribbon and moved toward the tarts. Her hand hovered above the obvious winner, then plunged over to a different plate. My mouth fell open as she attached the first place honors to the bottom of my dish.

During the applause that followed, I was handed a small white envelope, which I forgot to open until we got outside. In it was a crisp five-dollar bill, my winnings for the night. "Look," I said to Charley, "we've been given a prize."

Many years ago, I was awarded the equivalent of a thousand-dollar bonus and a letter of commendation for being one of the producers to start breakfast programming on British TV. I was very proud of that, but not as pleased as I felt now. "What shall we do with it?" I asked my daughter.

"Frame it," growled my husband, who had dinner on his mind.

"I think," I said, ignoring him, "that Charley should spend it . . . at the State Fair."

In the center of Indianapolis, just north of downtown, is a secret world tucked away behind high wire fences. It covers 236 acres of the city and is barely big enough to house the ten and a half thousand contestants who enter Indiana's State Fair. Every August, they come from hundreds of miles around and often stay for the entire two weeks, in trailers or on sun loungers in their animals' stalls. They compete in categories that range from pig racing to piano playing, cock crowing to shearing sheep; and they show all types of stock, from the humble rabbit to the hottest new thing in farm herds—llamas.

Left to her own devices, my daughter would also be willing to camp out, but she would pitch her small tent on the midway. The acres and acres of rides here are Charley's idea of bliss—complete with bright lights, tawdry toys, and every type of candy a young mind could imagine. In past years, our day trips to the state fair have been ten hours of parental hell, as we battled to focus her on anything else. We were hoping that this year's visit would be a different story.

"Charley, what are you going to spend your five dollars on?" The family was eating barbecue by the Indiana Pork tent—the first of the day's many culinary joys.

My daughter swallowed slowly, wiped her lips, and took a sip of lemonade. "Rides," she began, "cotton candy . . . elephant ears . . . more rides . . . and a toy." That decided, she returned to her lunch.

"Okay," I said. "Will you come and see some of the animals first?"

Greg and I held our breaths. The Bug nodded vigorously, through a faceful of bun.

We began at the sheep pavilion, where a flock of Hampshire were waiting for their turn in the arena. Each animal was wearing a leather mask and long raw-cotton cloak, in an effort to protect her perfectly brushed and powdered white coat from the least speck of dirt. They looked like a lineup of medieval executioners. All around the barn contestants were patiently submitting to the ministrations of their owners, allowing themselves to be washed, teased, and blow-dried into paragons of ovine perfection.

I secretly hoped that in a few years we might buy a very small flock of more unusual breeds—not to raise lambs (that way ruin lies), but to sell wool. The fleeces from a small flock of Shetland or Marino would cover the cost of all our farm animals' feed and leave us with a small profit. The sheep would also keep our acres of grass well cropped and would be worth having just for the hours they would save us in mowing time.

Charley had collected a small pile of fleece at a sheep-shearing demonstration. "Rub it in your hands," I suggested.

"Eew, it feels greasy," she said.

"That's not grease, it's lanolin, and it's really good for your skin."

Charley agreed to visit the Pioneer Farm, post rides, so she could watch her "fur" being turned into cloth. Then we moved on to the Swine House, which has become a family favorite.

Pigs have been given a bad rap. In reality, they are amazingly clean and intelligent animals who talk to people on equal terms. Greg had a long conversation with one pink swine, who was clearly complaining about the noise and the crowds, while inquiring as to the whereabouts of his owner. Charley dragged her dad away so that she could join the large group of children gathered around a bank of bright orange lights.

Under them, ten enormous sows lay protectively around litters that had been born since the beginning of the fair. The tiny piglets snuffled and squealed as they tripped over their siblings in their search for milk. The satiated ones lay in little pink rows, eyes scrunched shut, oblivious to the crowd. Charley wanted to pet each one, so we left her to it and went to investigate an intriguing banner that promised "The World's Largest Boar." We weren't disappointed. Spots Stallone, as he was called, and, Bo, "The World's Second Largest Boar," weighed in at 1,400 and 1,240 pounds, respectively. They looked like small, hairy hippopotamae, with melonlike appendages that gave the word *virility* a new dimension.

For months we had been under increasing pressure from Dennis to buy "a few hogs." His dad, a butcher, had always kept them, and Dennis was an expert in the field. "Just get a couple of sows," he pleaded. "You can make friends with them. I'll deal with the babies, before you get too attached." I had fended him off with excuses about the expense of building a sty and the unsavory smells that emanate from them. But my real reason was kneeling on the barn floor with a lap full of piglets. Charley would want to keep them all.

After prying our child away from her new pets, it was on to the Exhibitors Hall, which houses a vast array of goods to waste—I mean spend—your money on. We wandered among the water purifiers and portable barns, watching the hawkers selling everything from kitchen knives to computerized pianos. One silver-haired gentleman seemed particularly taken with a Super "Chami" mop, which was being presented by a young Dutchman. His product was, of course, "miraculous," which he proceeded to prove by throwing liberal amounts of ketchup onto a white floor.

"Looks like my house," grunted a blond mom, who "ooed" her approval as the mess disappeared.

The store price for this wonder would be $29.95, we were informed, but—"just for today"—its magnanimous makers had agreed to slash that figure to $14.95. The crowd moved off, disgruntled at the price, leaving the silver-haired gentleman still enthralled at this marvel of modern invention.

Charley's patience had finally run out.

The bottom lip quivered and her eyes filled with tears. "What about the rides?" she asked sadly, breaking both her parents' hearts. Greg swung her up onto his shoulders and we marched off for two hours of stomach-churning fun.

A day, even a long one, barely scratches the surface at the State Fair. Evening was drawing in and we hadn't seen the half of it. The harness racing, the horseshoe pitching, and the "Hands-On Bricklaying" demonstration would have to wait till next year—along with the donkeys, the dairy cows, and the dozens of cooking, craft, and gardening displays.

We had one last stop to make before we dragged our aching feet home. Every year, we finish our trip at one of the fair's best exhibits: the Pioneer Farm Show. As we really begin to learn about the business of our new farm, we realize that we have much more in common with the family farmsteads of long ago than with most of today's more mechanized setups. Very few modern machines are of much use to us. They are usually too big or too expensive, and they cater to the chemical crowd, who work enormous tracts of land. The old tools were designed to work much smaller plots by hand, which often makes them perfect for our purposes. The Pioneer Farm Show is a place to get ideas.

It doesn't change much, year to year. Reconstructions of rooms from an old farm ring the edge of the arena, where practical demonstrations of ancient skills go on all day long. At the entrance, some "pioneer" ladies in long frocks hold a very public quilting bee, while others comb, card, spin, dye, and weave wool. Charley learned about the life cycle of her fleece, while I discovered that six different "weeds" from our pasture are actually great dyer's plants. I can't wait to boil up that rich yellow from our giant crop of goldenrod.

Behind the ladies, a wood-carver was hollowing out a set of bowls, next to ironwork from a local blacksmith and a table festooned with old-fashioned candles. This is what I had come for. Greg and Charley went in search of chocolate milk, while I tried to find out more about the beekeeper's craft.

I would love to keep a couple of hives in our orchard. Bees play an integral part in the life cycle of a garden. They also would give us two new crops—honey and wax. Unfortunately, Greg was stung really badly as a boy and is almost phobically afraid of them, so we have to rely on passing visitors to pollinate our plants. Quite a few of those come from a neighbor who raises honey as a cash crop. He also sells beeswax in large butter yellow tablets that smell as sweet as their sister product. I'd always been tempted to buy some, but I wasn't sure what they were for.

"Lots of things," the beekeeper on parade settled back to give me a list. "Lubricating zippers, sticky windows, drawers—that kind of stuff. It strengthens thread, sharpens needles, waterproofs shoes, helps you sink wood screws, dresses bowstrings, makes candles, and, mind you, I don't know much . . . "

I bought two tablets from him for his trouble. "Do you get stung by your bees?" I asked him as he counted out my change.

"Well"—he scratched his head—"I used to. But I don't feel it much no more. When I open up the hive, I guess I get hit ten or twenty times."

You can't have everything—not even on our farm.

"So, did you have fun, Bug?"

We were in the car, reviewing the highlights of the day.

"Oh yes! Can we go again soon?"

"No, sweetie, not till next summer."

My daughter fell silent as she contemplated the year's remaining delights. A minute later, a chorus of "Jingle Bells" drifted forward from the depths of the backseat.

Greg was up early the following day, preparing to leave on a two-week-long shooting trip. Charley and I stood by to see him off. It was always a sad moment, and would continue to be so until we could limit his need to travel by earning some real income off the farm.

"What are we going to do today, Bug?"

The little girl looked despondent. "I dunno. . . . "

"Would you like to help me make the big herb garden for next year? So we can earn tons of money and keep Dada at home more?"

The gloom lifted. "Yes, yes, yes. Let's go."

We spent the day happily clearing and digging and playing hide-and-seek. The dogs lay close by in the shade, moving only to receive their share of our picnic lunch. Finally, Charley flung down her trowel. "I'm tired, Mama. Let's go inside and rest."

"All right, but first we have to feed the animals."

"And have an egg hunt?" My daughter was doing deals.

"Okay! and have an egg hunt."

The barn was very quiet as I slid open the big door. There wasn't a chicken to be seen.

"Mama, where are they all?"

"I don't know, Charley. Maybe they went outside." I peeked over the wooden wall of the stall. "Oh no! Oh, Charley, don't look. Please don't look."

But it was too late. Charley had a close-up view of the carnage in the coop. Blood was sprayed all over the walls. Bodies lay piled by the door. In their panic, the birds had trapped themselves in a corner. It looked as if they were all dead. I couldn't handle this alone. I took Charley by the hand and ran over to Big John's.

$\mathcal{L}$ADY AND THE TRAMP

HE MAN'S GREAT HAND GENTLY CRADLED A LITTLE broken body. John looked terribly upset. "It must have been a possum or a fox," he concluded. "My God, what a mess." For all his tough talk, my friend can be a softy at times.

The week before, John had told me the story of Sir Loin's demise. Rebecca and her steer had done really well at the Johnson County Fair, picking up six ribbons of various stripes, and had become very close—even curling up together in his stall at the fairgrounds. When auction time arrived, Sir Loin was sold easily and moved to a different pen. Apparently, the steer understood that the separation was a permanent one, and he started to cry.

"There they were," said an incredulous John, "two fat tears running down his cheeks. . . . I would never have believed it. We were pretty broken up." I turned to look at him. Judging by the wetness around the big man's eyes, he still was.

"Wait a minute, there's one here that's still alive." The bird lay panting in my hands. A huge puncture wound in her neck was beginning to congeal, while another in her wing had stopped bleeding altogether. "Do you think it's worth trying to save her, or would it be kinder to end it here?" I didn't want to seem irresponsible or oversentimental.

John looked a little surprised. "It's always worth trying, if there's a chance. Just make sure she gets plenty of water." The hen was the only survivor out of fourteen chickens. The rest of the flock had escaped and were probably scattered all over the county. "They will come back," John consoled me. "Or some will, anyway."

We cleaned up the barn and I carried the hurt bird back to the house. Charley found a cardboard box, which we lined with straw and put by the sink. As I washed and disinfected the hen's wounds, I began to take a closer look. These were not the bite marks of a fox. The teeth that did this were much too big. Nor were they the ratlike fangs of a possum—the punctures weren't deep enough. There was one person who would know. I called Dennis.

"Don't sound like a fox," he said, when he'd heard the whole story, "and it's sure not a possum. We'll be right over."

"It was a dog—look at that track." Dennis was crouched down on the coop floor next to an enormous pawprint that had been hidden by the straw. "And look over here." He went over to the wall. "See that scratch? That's where he came in." A long welt scored the white paint, where the animal had steadied himself on the way down. "It's a big dog," Dennis went on, "a good eighty pounds, I'd say."

"The size of a Doberman, perhaps?" I didn't need to hear his reply. Our dogs had been with us quietly all day. Any other canine intruder would have whipped them into a frenzy, but we already knew that they didn't react to the Doberman.

"Could be," said Dennis.

I told him about our lodger and his face got very dark. Silently, he walked to his truck and pulled out a rifle. "Once a killer, always a killer. Which direction did he come from?"

Dennis's wife, Debbie, and I waited in the gloom while her husband stalked our woods. Across the way, John kept watch with his shotgun, just in case the dog made a break across his farm.

Man's veneer of civilization is really very thin. We stomp around the planet behaving like masters of all we survey, only to be bowled over by the first strong wind that blows in our direction. The child throws a tantrum; the snake strikes; the other nation tells us that we're sitting on their land—and our initial reaction is "Slap it; kill it; let's go to war." The more vulnerable we feel, the more violent we become. Now, here we were again: Homo sapiens out hunting the latest "threat" while I sat on the front porch, feeling as if I had fallen off the evolutionary ladder.

"Well, I've found his hideout, but there'll be no catching him tonight." Dennis strode up to the table, his gun cocked over his arm. "I'll come back with Joe in the morning."

His concern for us was touching, but I had to ask the question: "Do we really have to kill him?"

Dennis didn't pause. "Now he has tasted blood, he'll be back—maybe even tonight. And once he's finished with your ducks and geese, he'll start on someone else's stock. We don't have any choice."

It was late. I put a very sleepy Charley to bed and went back downstairs to read. The quiet was soothing after the day's drama, and my nerves began to settle down. At midnight, they stood on end again when two shots crashed through the silence. A moment later, the phone rang. "I got him." John was out of breath. "He crawled off, but I hit him and he went down hard. If he's not dead now, he will be soon." There was no sense of triumph in his voice—he was simply stating the facts. I put the phone down, feeling very sad.

The next morning, Dennis and Joe came anyway—"In case

we need to put him out of his pain." We began looking in the dense thicket where Dennis had found the dog's lair the night before. The dog had built himself quite a setup in the brambles. His "bedroom" overlooked our field, so he would always be aware of our comings and goings—and in a position to flee if we got too close. A series of tunnels through the bush led off this area, which enabled the dog to go almost anywhere on the farm without being seen. He was evidently quite a strategist. Dennis estimated that he had been living here for more than a year.

The trail was cold. No fresh tracks, no bloodstains or fur— nothing to indicate that he had been back here at all.

The forest, the lake, and the big pasture were also empty of signs. "Perhaps he went north," Dennis speculated. "Who lives on the property next to you?"

"An absentee owner," I replied. "He only comes here once a year, during deer season. Do you want to take a look?"

There was nothing to see. The search party returned to base. We'd been out for over four hours, on a burning hot day, and we were all feeling dehydrated and a bit depressed. I went to fetch large glasses of ice water, while father and son flung themselves down in the shade of the pines. "I can't bear the idea of an animal suffering," said Dennis, "but I'm not sure what else we can do." We lapsed silently into our own thoughts.

I had been so busy with the fairs and the beginning of the harvest that for several weeks I had neglected just to sit and look at our land. I had missed out. The big pasture—still un-cut—had produced hundreds of wildflowers, which were now in full bloom. Orange daylilies, fuchsia fireweed, and butter yellow black-eyed Susans glittered like broken bits of stained glass in the brilliant August sun. Ruby-throated hummingbirds danced from one clump to another, taking their midday meal, while enormous bumblebees diligently gathered the day's collection of nectar from each open blossom.

"Maybe we don't have to worry about this anymore." Joe was pointing toward the sky, over to the northwest. Four buzzards were wheeling above the forest, playing their lazy waiting game with death. They were several miles from our land, but were in the direction that John said the dog had taken. We didn't have to see it to know that it was done.

"C'mon," said Dennis, scrambling to his feet.

"Where are we going?" I inquired, following his example.

"Target practice," he said firmly, turning toward the forest. He was right, of course. We could not keep relying on his protection, or John's, every time we had a crisis. We had to be able to defend ourselves if we needed to. It was time to buy a gun, whether we chose to use it or not.

At the edge of the trees, Dennis found a large chip of wood, which he set on a fallen log about fifty yards down the path. He loaded his rifle and handed it to me. Both men smiled indulgently, clearly expecting me to botch it. Not only was I a woman, a species who wouldn't normally bear arms in Brown County, but I was city bred into the bargain. They stood back to await the maiming of a few innocent trees.

I raised the weapon and fitted it snugly to my shoulder. As I looked down the barrel, the outside world melted away to leave just the target, the trigger, and me. I breathed out slowly and fired. A loud bang echoed somewhere in the distance and the chip of wood flew off its log and down the path.

I handed the weapon back to Dennis, who looked utterly amazed. "My father taught me to shoot when I was a child." I shrugged. "He thought it was something that I should know how to do."

I didn't get to the gun shop for the next few days. Charley and I were too busy in the garden. There were cabbages, peas, spinach, carrots, and kale to be planted for the fall, and the summer harvest was in full swing. The cucumbers, corn, chilies, radishes, scallions, and beans were screaming to be picked, while the tomatoes all had ripened at once and were yielding between five and ten pounds of fruit a day.

Last year, we had stored what tomatoes we couldn't eat immediately in boxes, where they had rotted within a week, leaking juice and mold all over the floor. This year, we were ready for them, and each evening was a new experiment in how to save their sunshine for the gloomy winter months. We skinned them and chopped them, stewed them and froze them, boiled them and reduced them into thick tomato paste. We made tomato soup and tomato sauce, ketchup and cacciatore (that combination of tomatoes, garlic, onion, and mushrooms that tastes so good with steak or chicken breasts), gazpacho and salsa, and stored all of it in our giant freezer, where it would keep until next spring. We also demolished as many fresh ones as we could: stewing them for breakfast, in tomato sandwiches for lunch, or making marinara sauce to sling over spaghetti at night. The best were saved for Greg, to go into the family's favorite salad at his welcome-back meal.

My husband was coming home. His women were excited. We scrubbed the house from top to toe and filled half a dozen vases with roses, Queen Anne's lace, and wild pink geraniums. We washed and hung cotton shirts in the sun to dry, so that they would smell of fresh air and warm grass when we wore them. On the afternoon of his return, "us girls" repaired to the bathroom, where we fussed and primped until we both felt pretty enough to meet him. In the kitchen, Greg's famous "belt buster" cut of sirloin steak lay marinating in ginger and soy sauce, next to a glistening *Insalata Tricolore:* rows of tomatoes, fresh buffalo mozzarella, and large-leaf basil, arranged as are the colors of the Italian flag.

The first floor was fragrant with mustard vinaigrette and

freshly baked bread, which I had pounded into submission that morning. We were as ready as we could be, so we went outside to play on Charley's swings.

At six o'clock, the old VW wagon pulled up to the gate and Greg's tired face emerged, wreathed in smiles. Charley ran toward him, arms opened wide. Her father scooped her up and put his other hand around my shoulders. "Hello," he said, and we all cuddled for a long time.

Later, when dinner was done and the plates were cleared away, Charley and I went to fetch the evening's entertainment: our new "house chicken." The injured hen—Honey, as she was now called, in deference to her nature and the colors on her wing—had fully recovered and become so tame that she would sit for hours on my shoulder, quietly grooming through my hair. She endeared herself to Greg straightaway by hopping onto his arm and inspecting him with that sidelong stare that makes chickens look even sillier than they are.

"I wish I had been here," he mused, stroking the soft ruff of feathers around her neck. "I think everyone overreacted."

"You wouldn't say that, if you had seen it," I bristled.

"I'm sure it was terrible," Greg went on, "but I don't think the dog deserved to die. He was just hungry and went a little wild . . . "

"Both Dennis and John were sure that he was dangerous," I countered, "and they know much more than we do."

"Maybe." My husband was unconvinced. "I just wish I had been here to keep you all calm."

It takes Greg several days to reorient himself after a working trip. He potters in the gardens, sits and reads out in the sun, and goes for long walks with the dogs. We also spend many hours just catching up with each other's thoughts—sharing every conversation and idea until we feel that we're in synch again. This time, our minds had apparently been wrestling with the same problem: which aspects of the country business to kick-start into making some kind of money?

"I'm going to begin shooting landscapes around here next week," Greg announced over a pitcher of lemonade. "Once I've got four or five good images, we'll put them into Nashville stores as mounted prints. If only a few of our four million tourists like them, they might make a nice little income."

I had been thinking along similar geographical lines. "Nashville has just started a farmer's market. We may not have enough for a full-scale business yet, but we could fill a stall with a whole variety of stuff once a week. Not only fresh veggies and herbs, but baskets filled with eggs, bread, preserves, and all the herbal stuff I normally make. I've talked to a couple of stall-holders who go to Bloomington on a regular basis and they've been earning up to three hundred dollars on a decent weekend."

Greg looked pensive. "It sounds like an awful lot of labor for little return," he began, trying to shelve the subject.

I was ready for him. I had sensed for a while that our views about the farm had begun to diverge. We both agreed that the greenhouse business was a practical possibility, but my dream of making real money from the garden was getting less and less support. It was time to have it out.

"I just don't think you're realistic, Sal," Greg admitted. "The food baskets would be a great idea if we were free and in our prime. But we're not. I'm forty next year and you'll be thirty-nine. We're already too old to do it, Sal," he argued. "Any business we start here has to be built on the basis that we'll be in our fifties before it's up to speed. It has to be low on physical labor and high on financial yield. In other words, the complete opposite of any kind of farming."

"I disagree," I said, trying to keep calm. "You have to think smaller. Most people around here do more than one thing to make ends meet. Jo Park—you know, the owner of the feed store—also teaches agriculture at the high school and farms one hundred and fifty acres of corn, soybeans, and wheat. Dennis has his carpentry business, as well as his sandblasting and painting. Even Doc Brester raises cattle in the few hours when he's not being a vet. Any one activity may not seem to pay too well, but when you add it all up, you're looking at some cash. If we only did half the other stallholders' business, we'd make six hundred dollars a month, which is six hundred we don't have now. We have to learn to diversify, or living here will be no more than a heck of a long commute."

"I'm not suggesting," Greg countered testily, "that we give up trying to make money from the farm. All I'm saying is that we should be practical about how. The hydroponics makes sense, both now and long-term. Baskets and farmers' markets aren't the best choices for two middle-aged artists." My husband had made a serious strategic mistake and he knew it.

"That's right, middle-aged," I spat out. "It could take us ten years to finish the greenhouse, and I don't intend to spend the next decade packing and unpacking your suitcases—that is, of course, while you can still get the work. I plan to use what little strength I have left to fulfill our original vision. If you don't want to help, I'll do it on my own."

"My tempestuous redhead." Greg gave me a hug. "What a character you are. All right, we'll try it your way. What do you want *us* to do?" He smiled wryly and we talked on, taking notes on what would have to be fixed around the farm. With just a little work, we could manage with things much as they were. The existing greenhouse glass would be recaulked over the winter and the interior cleaned out to handle all the plant starts. Greg's raised beds could handle the more delicate produce, while the ordinary open beds had already been cleared and just needed to be turned over to the eighteen-inch depth that would guarantee the roots of all our crops some reasonable room in which to grow. The only major investment would be to rewire the outbuildings and run a good water supply to the greenhouse from the pond.

We decided to ask Dennis to quote on the jobs first, or at least recommend someone we could trust.

I was quietly weeding the roses when Dennis and Joe came by the next day, pulling up in their pickup just as Greg arrived back, panting, from the lake. "I've seen him," he gasped. "He ran right in front of me, over the dam."

"Who? Who have you seen?" we chorused.

"The Doberman," Greg replied. "He's not dead—John missed him!"

"Well, here we go again." Dennis reached into the back of his truck, pulling out a rifle each for himself and his son. Before anyone had time to think about it, the three men were off in the direction of the woods, escorted by an enthusiastic Lady.

This is evolving into some awful kind of game, I thought to myself, deciding not to follow. I turned back to the hybrid teas, hoping not to hear any rifle fire.

It was a more subdued group that returned, twenty minutes later, with a strange story to tell.

They had caught up with the dog very quickly and flushed him out of the forest. In his panic, the animal had broken across the back of the pasture, giving them the first clear shot they'd had since this fiasco began. But they were prevented from taking advantage of it by Lady, who had put herself squarely between them and their target. She then proceeded to greet the Doberman like the old friend he obviously was, and ran with him back into the trees until he was safely out of sight.

"That explains why our dogs never reacted to him," it dawned on me. "They know each other well."

Greg nodded and raised his eyebrows in that look that means, "We'll talk later."

"I don't think this animal should be shot," he said firmly when everyone had gone.

In my heart, I agreed with him, but there were two practical considerations that concerned me. "What about the birds?" I asked.

"He has only attacked them once," Greg pointed out, "and when he's being fed, I'm sure it won't be a problem."

"If he'll take the food," I said doubtfully. "When I first saw him, he was obviously terrified of people. I wouldn't think our hunting him has done much to improve our image. The dog is wild. Trying to approach him could be risky."

My husband looked confident. "If he were really dangerous, Lady would have driven him off our land long ago."

Winning a feral animal's trust is a painstaking process, demanding tons of patience with no guaranteed return. I had never tried to do it before, but I had heard many stories about its hardships and heartbreaks from one of my dearest friends in the county, Pat Richardson.

Pat runs a state and federally certified wild animal shelter ten minutes away from where we live. In her time, she's taken care of them all: from cougar to coyote, raccoon to the occasional skunk. The animals usually have been orphaned, injured, or maltreated in some way. Pat raises them until they are well enough or big enough to be released into the wild again. My visits to Pickle Meadows are one of life's great treats, which always begin with an introduction to her new guests.

"This little guy was brought in with a broken leg," Pat explained to me the next morning, motioning toward a young fawn who was studying us with large liquid eyes. "He's almost ready to go."

"Where will you take him?" I asked.

"He'll probably leave of his own accord. The deer usually do."

Pat's an attractive woman with short silver hair and an intelligent face filled with the stoic calm that comes from successfully conquering real problems in life. She and her husband, Jim, moved here from the city twenty-two years ago, after doctors had given her twelve months to live. She had incurable breast cancer, they said.

"If I was going to die," she told me, "I wanted to do what I wanted to do." Pat's father had been born in Brown County, and she had fond childhood memories of the peace and quiet, and of canning with her grandmother.

The couple resolved not to talk about her illness and to avoid doctors until she absolutely needed them. Instead, they threw themselves into living their new life to the full.

Pat remembers that nature seemed more intense that year. The flowers bloomed brighter; a row of crabapple trees blossomed in their pink best, filling the air with honey. When winter came, the snow was picture perfect, glittering on the trees. She felt wonderful.

She played in the drifts and went ice skating on a pond, forgetting for increasing lengths of time that she was supposed to be so sick.

By the end of their third year here, Pat and Jim decided that it was time to discuss her cancer again. A visit to the doctor was arranged. He ran a series of tests before pronouncing that she was in full remission. "I don't know how," he had said, "but just keep on doing whatever it is you're doing."

Pat has since raised two sons to strapping manhood, lost a six-week-old baby in a car crash, watched her house burn down and be rebuilt, and lived to see her gorgeous grandchildren arrive. The shelter is a kind of ongoing thank-you for a rich and varied life. "I had to do something," she says matter-of-factly, "and I prefer animals to most people."

Her advice about our problem was quite simple: At the same time of day, every day, put the food out where the dog will feel safe to approach it; talk to him in a calm, low voice whenever you see him; gradually move the food closer to the house; and be prepared for the fact that he may never let us near him.

We began the process that very night, putting a bowl out in front of the barn, where it would be lit by the hayloft lamp.

At about ten o'clock, the dog slunk into the light, snatching at some meat, almost on the run. A minute later, he was back again to make his second pass at the bowl before disappearing into the shadows.

On his third attempt, he stuck his nose out and pushed the bowl out of the light, where he stayed to finish its contents in a matter of seconds.

The next night we set his food down in a darker spot and waited on the front porch to see what would happen. Right on cue, at ten o'clock, our guest reappeared. This time he approved of the location and began eating straight away. Our presence outside didn't seem to bother him—there were still a hundred yards between us—but his ears twitched constantly as they scanned for strange sounds. A domestic dispute between two blue jays in the trees finally ended his dinner, making him bolt toward the lake—although we saw him later on, sneaking back to check his bowl.

The following morning, I let Paws and Lady out and stood by the back door to monitor them. As they played by the vegetable garden, twenty feet in front of me, another dog appeared and joined in without introduction. It was my first close look at our Doberman friend.

He was a handsome dog with the slim elegance of a young deer. His ears and tail had never been cut, so he looked more like his weimaraner ancestor than the breed we know today. His head was gray-blue, darkening into a black body, with the classic rust patches on his paws, cheeks, and chest. A white flash ran from the base of his throat to the top of his thighs.

I knew a bit about the breed, because I'd had one in New York. That lonely and threatening city had driven me to the dog pound one day to find myself a dependable companion. I had been looking for a terrier, or something small, to fit into an apartment the size of an outhouse. But the first dog I saw was a magnificent King Doberman, looking miserable as a poodle peed on him from the cage above. "Could we let him out for a minute?" I asked the lady keeper. She unlatched his door and Luca came straight to me and laid his big head in my lap.

We walked across Central Park that day, because he was too big to get in a taxi. By the time we reached the West Side, we had become the firmest of friends.

Like most people, my image of Dobermans up to that point had been of canine concentration camp guards who, like their handlers, had dripping fangs and brains too small for their badly designed skulls. I was surprised to find that they are actually highly intelligent and very affectionate dogs with an instinct to protect rather than attack.

Luca and I spent some happy months together before he went off to his new country home, and I had looked forward to getting another "Dobie" when I had the space to let him run.

My reading about Dobermans had taught me that white patches were considered a flaw—a half-inch square on the chest was the only kind allowed by the American Kennel Club. Our wild one's markings had made him worthless from the moment he was born. The breeder probably dumped him before going to the expense of having his ears cropped, which is usually done when the dogs are three months old.

Judging by the way he was playing with Paws, he wasn't

much more than a pup now—a year to fifteen months at most. They were wrestling like littermates who had spent their lives together.

This was my chance to talk to him. I began in a low, quiet voice, introducing myself and hoping that he could learn to like us, too. He froze as I spoke, head cocked slightly to one side as he listened intently. His body was wound tight, ready to spring away if I made the slightest move, but I just kept talking, as calmly as possible. My voice seemed to spin an invisible thread between us, keeping the dog still and fixing his attention on my face. He looked almost mesmerized. The spell was broken only when sounds intruded from inside the house, which made him start and take off for the nearest bank of trees. He was still very scared, but now he was curious, too, and he gave me three more chances to talk to him as the day progressed.

That evening we brought his food in a bit closer—about twenty yards from the house. When he turned up, he went straight over to his meal. The distance didn't seem to bother him, and after he had finished eating, he lay down by his bowl, listening with half-closed eyes to us chatting together on the front porch. He seemed pleased to be included, even on the periphery, and dozed fitfully—nodding off for a few minutes, then shaking himself awake.

"He probably hasn't had a full night's sleep since he started living wild," Greg said sadly.

By the fifth day, Tramp was following us all over the farm. We can't remember who came up with it, but the name suited him perfectly. He continued to keep his distance, no closer than ten feet, but you could tell that he wanted to trust us. Dinner was now put out by the blue spruce in front of the porch, and he would eat greedily before settling in to observe us for the evening. Lady and Paws took to lying with him, as if they were encouraging the dog to relax.

Things were going better than we ever could have hoped for. We decided to celebrate our first week's wooing with a large steak on the grill.

There wasn't a whisper of breeze as Greg began his barbecue ritual. Streaks of blue smoke hung above us like cobwebs in the air and the smell of frying beef started to make our stomachs growl. I opened a bottle of Burgundy and sat back to watch my personal master chef perform his magic in the flames. He was accumulating quite an audience. Lady and Paws positioned themselves close by, and a black silhouette emerged from the lilac bushes to take up his usual spot under the spruce.

When the meat was ready, the family fell on it like wolves, filling ourselves to bursting before another word was said. Lady watched us anxiously, with that "leave some for me" look in her eyes. Finally, we sat back, gorged and greasy-chinned, happily contemplating the banana splits to come.

The dogs followed me inside as I went to make coffee, bumping each other out of the way to be first for any scraps. I loaded up their bowls and was on my way back for the rest of the dishes when I spotted Greg through the dining room window. He was not alone.

Standing next to him, tentatively taking strips of steak out of his hand, was Tramp.

The dog was looking up at Greg demurely, his ears lying flat along his head. There was a pleading look in his eye, as if he were saying, "Please don't hurt me."

My daughter and I crept outside. Tramp backed off, but only by a few feet. We sat down and I held out more steak. The dog inched toward me and took the meat gently from my hand. He came back twice for more, then, wonder of wonders, he let me touch his head. He stood looking into my eyes for a second, as if he were searching for my soul, then pulled back to the darkness at the edge of the porch.

That night we put a blanket down for him just outside the front door and were delighted to find him on it when we came down the following morning.

It took a rainstorm, three days later, to actually get him inside the house. We didn't push it, but had left the door open, just in case. Five minutes after the first thunderclap, we saw a nose coming shyly around the living room wall. Tramp tiptoed across the room and laid his big head in my lap.

"Three *large* dogs!" said Greg bitterly, two weeks later. His breakfast was splattered on the kitchen floor, the victim of a two-pronged raid by Paws and his new partner in crime. The young dogs had become inseparable friends, scrapping, eating, playing, and sleeping together. "It's like living in a kennel," my husband grumbled.

No one could care about our canine crew more than Greg did, but we were both rather alarmed at our sudden lack of space. You couldn't move in the house anymore without falling over a large body of fur, and we were wondering what was going to happen when the weather got cold and they all wanted to stay inside.

That wasn't too far away. It was mid-September, and we were busy planning the prewinter work around the farm. "We've got to seal the barn," Greg muttered, checking down his list, "fix the fences, clean the inlet to the lake, start cutting firewood. . . . By the way, the hot wire's not working."

"I know," I groaned from the kitchen, where I was clearing up the mess. "It's gotten overgrown. Something's touching and shorting out the circuit. I'm going to walk the perimeter tomorrow and clear it all back. Then I'm going to run a new strand to the gate, because the dogs have been getting out into the road. It's dangerous, so I thought I'd wire along the front, about eighteen inches off the ground."

"Good idea. And there's the rest of the pepper harvest to

put up, the melons to bring in, the last big grass cut to do. Maybe I'll tackle that tomorrow. It's going to take most of the day. What time are you getting up?"

"About six-thirty," I called back. "The blacksmith is coming at eight to trim Hotshot's hooves."

"You'd better give yourself an hour at least to catch the horse," Greg laughed.

"Tell me about it," I said, only slightly amused. "Pick some carrots later, would you? There's nothing like a little bribery."

The following morning, I emerged from the backdoor with an armful of payola. It was a beautiful day in early fall, when the sun colors everything a soft peach and the breeze smells fresh.

I let the dogs out and sauntered over to the pasture to deal with Hotshot. He was reasonably cooperative for once, allowing me grab him by the ear to put his halter on, and we were outside by seven-thirty, enjoying an apple together.

At eight o'clock precisely, Randy drove up the drive. His usually cheerful face was somber. "Got a tarp?" he drawled.

"What do you want a tarp for?" My heart was beginning to rise into my throat.

"Your dog's out in the road." He looked unspeakably sad.

"Oh my God, oh my God . . . " was all I heard myself say, over and over again, as I brushed past him—like a prayer to hold the truth at bay.

It was Paws. He lay in the gravel, his head nestling in a pool of blood. He had been hit once, hard. Death had been instant. I stared at him uncomprehendingly. He looked every inch the puppy that he was—suddenly small, terribly vulnerable. All his clumsiness and gangly size had disappeared, leaving a soft baby, seemingly asleep. I half expected him to wake and scramble to his feet, bruised and dizzy, in search of comfort. But he just lay there, beyond my grasp for the first time in his life, a traveler on a journey that must be made alone.

Randy was getting concerned. A car was coming. "You'd better move, else you'll get hit, too."

I turned back to the house in stunned silence. A band had wound its way around my chest and it was difficult to breathe. I couldn't even call Greg. I just grabbed the old dog blanket and took it back to the road. We lifted him onto it gently, then carried him to the side of the barn. The birds had gone quiet. Lady came over, nuzzled her son, and lay down beside him. She, too, made no sound, her eyes wide with loss. She understood, but looked at me pleadingly as if I could somehow ease the pain. The band around my chest burst and I began to cry.

We all shed tears that day. The death of someone we love breeds such a terrible conflict of emotions: guilt that we didn't watch him more closely, that his size would make us forget what a baby he was; regret for the times we could have cuddled or played and didn't (did he know how much we loved him? Probably not; the pain we felt at his death surprised even us); and overwhelming sadness—for the dog he would have been and for the dog he was.

Nature abhors imbalance as much as the renowned vacuum. She solved our canine overpopulation problem in her usual way: by taking the weakest animal, the one least able to survive. The thought didn't make us feel any better.

It was Lady who led the way to our recovery. She played with Tramp, made a fuss of Charley, and took us on long walks around the lake. The only signs that she remembered anything at all were her insistence on sleeping in her son's old spot and a faraway look in her eyes when she thought that we weren't watching.

She made her attitude plain on the night I went to visit Paws's grave, under the pines. I almost couldn't bear to go, but I wanted to put some rosemary (for remembrance) under his stone marker. Lady sniffed around the site, then came quietly to my side. She knew exactly where she was. She leaned into me as we both said our good-byes. Then she turned firmly and made her way back to the house. Halfway across the grass, she checked over her shoulder to confirm that I was following. The look on her face said plainly: "That's enough now. It's time for us to get on."

Tramp also mourned. He lay around the house listlessly for a couple of days before it occurred to him that he was now the lead male of the pack—sworn to defend us all, whether we wanted it or not. His rules were laid down from the start: trips outside only to be taken under escort; all visitors to pass his personal inspection; property to be thoroughly patrolled, three times a day. Every night his sleek form glides through the shadows, checking the perimeter one more time before retiring. I pity the intruder, if he ever comes across one.

The only danger we face from him in the home is being beaten to death by his tail. Tramp is the most extraordinary dog that Greg or I have ever met. He prefers love over food and will leave his dinner if there's a chance of a cuddle. He tries to climb into our laps and wants to be held like a chihuahua. Everyone is worthy of his notice, from Charley, who gets chased in a gentle game of tag, to Oscar, who has his wounds washed, doggie-doctor style. He pays special attention to Lady, whom he treats with the greatest respect. In the mornings he grooms her coat for her and cleans up her eyes before attending her on her early morning run. He's a much faster dog than she is, but he will always pause and wait if he has outstripped her by mistake.

The rhythms and routines of the house seem to give him the most pleasure. He knows the time for breakfast and the time for Charley's bath, and is always there, waiting to participate in whatever way he can. His two favorite points of the day seem to be the Bug's bedtime story—he hasn't missed one yet—and feeding time at the barn.

The first time I took him over there, he lay down outside and looked utterly ashamed. "I know what happened," I assured him, "but I trust you not to do it—ever again."

He understood the conditions of his reprieve and has since become a dedicated guardian of the flock. When the chickens leap the fence or have to be herded into the coop, he runs point for me, nipping at their fat behinds—without touching so much as a feather.

$\mathcal{J}$UST ANOTHER DAY

October 1992

Dear Michael,

It was lovely to get your letter. London sounds exciting, as always—and no, I don't miss city life in the least. I was amused by the implication behind your question: "What exactly do you do with your time down there?" It conjured up visions of us sunbathing by the lake, reading P. G. Wodehouse and peeling grapes. Life is a little busier than that. I thought the best way to answer you would be to catalog a 24-hour period. Since there's no such thing as an average day, I picked last Tuesday at random.

4:00 A.M.: Am woken by a disgusting slobbering sound. Oscar, our British bull terrier, has discovered the cat litter in an empty bedroom closet, and is savoring the delicacy in stereo. Throw the alarm clock at him, followed by my sneakers and the Sunday edition of the *Indianapolis Star*.

6:15 A.M.: Charley crawls into the "big bed" for comfort, following a dreaded "monstur" dream. Proceeds to kick me in the knees until I surrender my side and stagger downstairs to make coffee. The sun is barely up. Two woodpeckers are fighting over breakfast at their suet feeder, and a bluebird has just emerged from the brushpile where its nest is hidden. It's going to be a good day—it always is when a bluebird starts it off.

6:45 A.M.: Coffee down at the boat dock, where a beaver and a black heron carry on their dawn chores, blissfully unaware of my presence.

The beaver appeared here sometime over the summer. I first noticed it on a morning much like this, as it was taking a leisurely swim. Initially, I thought it was a giant muskrat until it took a dive and flapped that famous paddle tail. It won't stay, I thought sadly. A lot of wild creatures drop by our lake. I've seen families of mallard and Canada geese—even an eagle fishing, on one occasion. They always disappear, scared off by the dogs. But this animal is a tougher customer. A week or two later, we noticed an igloo-shaped structure a few feet from the shore, a perfect piece of natural architecture. The lodge is made from mud, tree bark, stones, and branches, and is a little like a delicately proportioned iceberg—only revealing a small part of itself above the waterline. Somewhere deep in the murk, there are two or three entrance tunnels, built safely beyond the grasp of any predators. The occupant climbs up these to the enclosed, dry comfort in the chamber above.

This morning the beaver was busily dragging brush across the lake, apparently gathering stores for his underwater larder. Time is running out. Within the next six weeks, the surface will begin to freeze and won't fully melt until the first few weeks of spring. Before winter arrives, this provident chap will have buried a season's supply of branches in the bottom of the pond so that he can eat without having to break through any ice.

His appearance here has presented me with one problem. Our dam is infested with muskrats, who are threatening to breach it with their maze of burrows. We certainly don't have the $25,000 it would cost to rebuild, so we have to get rid of them before they destroy the lake and the other wildlife in it. Originally, I had planned to trap them, but now that the beaver is here, I'm reluctant to try it. The alternative is to pick them off, one by one, but I'm going to wait until our other guest is fully settled in.

Shooting is a skill I never expected or desired to perfect, but since I got my new 20-bore shotgun, I felt that I should know how to use it well. I've been practicing on Coke cans, scaring the fur off the dogs. The gun has rifle sights on it and I had been setting my mark on the fence, where I could take my time and fire. Then my friend Big John told me that the real trick was being able to "point and shoot"—hitting your target without really taking aim. So now I go out into the forest and throw the can into the creek. As it bobs along, I try to ambush the "baddy" cowboy style, sneaking up on it from behind the tree trunks. The dogs have decided to take cover in the house.

The hardest part of maintaining a man-made lake is balancing between the needs of the structure and the creatures that live in it. Ours was neglected for years and nature has gotten the upper hand. Sumac and sassafras have sprouted on the dam, forming a cool green tunnel on hot summer walks; reeds dance along the shore and little areas of wetland have sprung up, full of thistle, teasel, and bright orange butterfly weed. Our wildlife love it. The deer eat the sumac berries on their way down for a drink; the reeds house a multitude of singing toads and frogs; while the wetlands provide birds and butterflies with all their favorite foods.

The experts, on the other hand, think it is a disaster

area. They have told us to hack it all down before the roots break through the dam or the weeds overtake the water. They may be right, but we are trying some simple containment first—just keeping the inlets and outlets clear and not allowing the growth to spread. I spent a couple of days in September cutting cattails before they went to seed. They are now in dried-flower arrangements all around the house.

The most delightful part of good lake management is that it has to be fished. We are stocked with bass and bluegill, which will thrive only if the bigger ones are removed on a regular basis. It's wonderful to be able to tell people, without a trace of guilt, that we've "gone fishin'," and they have become an important part of our food supply.

The first time we tasted bass from our lake, they came courtesy of our neighbor Steve. He has fished here since he was a boy and continues to do so with our blessing. It had been a particularly good day's catch and he brought a large bowl of it back the following morning, cleaned and ready for the stove. At dinnertime Greg dipped the pieces in a light batter, then pan-fried them in peanut oil and butter. We ate them al fresco, drenched in lemon juice, with baby potatoes dug that day and a large salad. "Delicious" doesn't cover it.

I realize now what a good angler Steve must be. Most of the lake's fish are easy pickings, even for novices like us. Choose the right time of day and some nice juicy bait, and the bluegill, crappie, or catfish practically jump into the boat. Bass are a different story.

They are the foxes of the fish world. A visit to a tackle store will tell you all you need to know. Just walk along the shelves of lures. You'll find one or two for each of the other species and a whole section devoted to these guys alone. There are livid yellow worms to catch them in the sun and dusky scarabs to attract them in the shade; the fluorescent green frogs are supposed to fool them in the reeds; while the turquoise minnow works on every second Tuesday, when there's an *r* in the month.

I haven't caught one yet. Our friend Dennis has suggested that half a stick of dynamite would be more productive than a hook.

7:10 A.M.: A loud slapping sound bounces off the trees. The beaver has been startled by a slamming door up at the house and is whacking his tail on the water as a warning to his fellow wildlife. The dogs have been let out, which has set the geese off, beginning the morning's cacophony of honking, crowing, cackling, and quacking. I leave the dock reluctantly to go and feed the birds.

Last time I wrote to you, the hens hadn't started laying. Well, they are making up for it now. I suppose that it would be obvious to most people that if you have a lot of chickens, you're going to get a lot of eggs. Frankly, I didn't think about it.

We collect about two dozen a day. Now just stop a minute and imagine how quickly that mounts up. Twenty-four turns into 168 by the end of the week, which means that we are producing 672 eggs a month.

At first, the enormity of it all escaped me. I baked some cakes, made some quiche, and gave a few away. Then I opened the fridge one day and found it overflowing with these "little miracles of life." Our preservation efforts were stepped up a notch, as we pickled them and froze them, broken into ice trays. At the end of our first session we were stocked with more eggs than we would eat in the next six months.

Clearly, an alternative arrangement had to be found. We

did not want to sell them from the house and the farmer's market is closed until next May, so we are giving our surplus to a homeless shelter in the city. It was Greg's good idea—one that will continue for as long as we have hens.

7:35 A.M.: The kitchen is declared officially open. The cats and the dogs stand in line, followed by Charley, who orders "shaushage, pancakes, and *lots* of syrup." My husband demands a full ration of bacon and eggs to kick start his day every day. He is reed thin and has the cholesterol level of a teenager, which drives both his doctor and his wife up the wall. Greg is planning to write a best-seller called *Eat and Sit: The Way to Better Health.*

8:15 A.M.: Somebody has to take Charley to school. No big deal, you say, but it is a fifty-mile round-trip that has to be driven twice a day, so strict rules of sharing apply. It's her father's turn this morning and they leave the house, hand in hand, singing the song from a Kit Kat commercial.

8:30 A.M.: The business day begins. The computer is booted up, calls are returned, proposals and invoices are faxed, and outstanding checks are wheedled out of accounts departments. I wear about four hats in my working world: business administrator to Greg's photography company; columnist and writer; television correspondent; trainee farmer. What goes on in the office is predicated by which deadline is the most pressing.

Today I have to make travel arrangements for a shoot in California; collect money from a particularly recalcitrant client; and write the outline for an article about companion planting—you know, if you plant the corn next to the cucumber, will the cauliflower mind? Most scientists deny that plants and pests have specific friends and foes, but our experience tells us that onions do deter rabbits, roses like rue (which their enemy, the Japanese beetle, hates), and a basil plant next to a tomato will make it thrive as never before.

Organic gardening is not popular in America, which came as quite a shock to me. After all, in Britain that's how we have been doing it for hundreds of years. How could anyone improve on Nature and what she provides for free? I didn't realize that there was even a debate about it until Greg and I rented our first garden plot in Chicago. I turned up with trays of seedlings and some tools, while he brought along a bright blue powder called Miracle-Gro.

"What's that for?" I asked him as he watered it onto our plants. "And why is it that color?"

"It's fertilizer. What do you normally use?"

When I told him about compost and manure, his fastidious lip began to curl. "No, no," I assured him, "they're not dirty, not in the least." We bought a couple of bags to prove my point. When my husband ran his fingers through the soft black loam and sampled its earthy-sweet smell, it was his turn to be surprised.

One of the many things I love about Greg is that he reads everything about a subject, once his curiosity has been aroused. For the next few months our dinnertime chat revolved around the history of chemical agriculture—which sounds very dry, but is actually a catalog of skulduggery, fraud, and criminal greed.

Since you are such a smarty-pants, Michael, you probably already know that the father of all our modern pesticides and fertilizers was a German by the name of Justus von Liebig. In the mid-nineteenth century he claimed to have isolated the three chemicals that nourish plants— nitrogen, phosphorus, and potash—and went on to develop what we all know as the "superphosphate." He utterly pooh-

poohed the idea that plants got any nourishment from the soil around them and wrote so strongly on the subject that by the time he changed his mind ten years later, no one was willing to listen. The modern chemical industry had been born and men were already getting rich on synthetic drugs, dyes, and explosives. Arming two world wars merely added to their coffers, and the chemicals that they sold to agriculture kept them going in between. Innocent farmers bought pesticide made from the same poison gas that had floated over Ypres. They didn't stop to ask what it might be doing to their land—after all, this was the "farming of the future," which, they were assured, would minimize their labor and multiply their yield.

In the short term, it did—particularly after World War II, when the agricultural "wonder drug" DDT came on to the general market. It was capable of killing an enormous range of bugs. The American countryside was soon drenched in it, before anyone understood the damage it could do—both to crops and to the creatures who consumed them.

The situation escalated over the fifties, as farmers discovered that the more they used these expensive herbicides, insecticides, and fertilizers, the more they needed to apply. The moment they stopped, their plants became choked with weeds and infested with pests. It was a vicious circle that would eventually bury the family farm under a mountain of debt.

A few voices were raised in protest, but big business ensured that they were dismissed as kooks or pinkos of the Left (a dangerous thing to be in the American 1950's). They tried the same tactic on Rachel Carson when she published her book *Silent Spring* in 1962, documenting the poisoning of nature and our food supply. In her case, the smear campaign didn't work. The book shot to the top of the best-seller lists and Carson became the mother of the modern environmental movement. Today DDT is off the market and our ecology was recently an election issue in a country where the public have really started to care. Unfortunately, the agricultural establishment hasn't followed suit. It is still too closely linked to the chemical companies, who give millions of dollars in research and grants to guarantee its compliance with their worldview.

In a farming area like ours, there is no compromise. You either use chemicals or you are part of the lunatic fringe who, at best, knows nothing about modern agribusiness or, at worst, is vaguely un-American.

I am not exaggerating. I experienced it for myself, this summer, when I was looking for someone to cut our hay. One of our local farmers came by to see if it was worth his while, and we got to talking about our future plans for the place. He told me that he had some interest in organics, so I gave him the full tour.

We began in the greenhouse. "One day, this will all be hydroponic," I explained, "giving us a new crop of herbs and greens every thirty days."

"How does that work?" he asked skeptically.

"Basically," I went on, "hydroponically raised plants have more energy than field-raised plants. They get all the food, light, warmth, and CO_2 they need without having to waste their strength fighting off any bugs or disease."

"Oh yeah," he said, looking unconvinced. "A bit experimental, isn't it?"

"Well," I sighed, "not really. We have a friend who's making two thousand dollars a month raising herbs hydroponically, and some supermarkets on the West Coast are

selling produce straight out of hydroponic displays. I think
that the technology is here to stay."

He sucked his teeth silently and I led the way outside.
My ears were beginning to burn.

The man did know something about raised beds, he said.
He had dug one for his wife's flowers. He agreed that the
plants had flourished in this supernurtured soil, but when
I told him that we will eventually grow all our crops this
way, he almost laughed. "I bet you read *Organic Gardening*
and *Mother Earth News*," he sneered.

"Of course," I said sweetly. "Don't you subscribe?"

We never heard from him again.

Get a load of me, Michael—I'm a radical! The irony is
that the man was scared by technology that has been
around, in the case of hydroponics, for over a hundred
years. Raised beds go back to some famous gardens in Bab-
ylon.

11:00 A.M.: Time for some real work. Early frosts have
been predicted, so we're frantically harvesting the fruits of
the summer. Today there are 100 pounds of apples to be
peeled, cored, and washed before they can be turned into
applesauce, apple butter, apple pies, dried apple rings, and
apple chutney.

It's a curious exercise, because we never used to eat any
of the above. Our diet has definitely changed since we left
the city. Gone are the days when we could rush out to the
supermarket at eight o'clock at night or pick up a phone and
order dinner in because we were "too tired" to cook. A trip
to the grocery store here is a twelve-mile expedition, and if
you want a Chinese meal, you'd better buy yourself a wok.
Now we have to rely on what we have in stock—which is no
hardship. We eat better than we ever did in town.

At the moment, there are huge piles of food stacked all over the house. Onions, garlic, spinach, beans, cucumbers, carrots, peppers, collard greens, marrows, melons, plums, cauliflower, red cabbages, potatoes, and twenty-six types of herb are waiting to be put away for the winter. You can't move in the dining room and every closet is full of drying plants.

Fall is a bit like childbirth: We forget the pain until it happens again. For the rest of the year, I will remember the autumn harvest as a few gentle hours in the kitchen spent making jam. I'll be suffering from selective amnesia. The reality is more like a battlefield of scalded fingers, bruised feet, bad tempers, and aching backs. There are nights when Greg and I collapse, speechless, on the couch, too tired even to moan out loud.

It is unrelenting work on a large scale, which has to be fitted around life's normal daily demands. It will take about four days to clean, chop, and blanch a winter's worth of spinach, beans, greens, and cauliflower, in preparation for the freezer. Some of the cauliflower will be kept back for the sixteen pints of mustard piccalilli that I'll make next with the marrows, cucumber, and pearl onions. Now this might seem rather excessive, but you can't train vegetables to stop growing once you've got enough for the four jars you'll actually eat. Last season we could have survived the winter on our mashed potatoes and marinara sauce—in the old days we would have *had* to, because we had precious little of anything else.

Everybody around here ends up in the same boat. I have one friend who just canned five years' worth of blackberry juice. You just have to store, sell, or swap the surplus and grow something new next season.

While it is all cooking, we leave the house to avoid choking on the smell of pickling spice. We decamp to the summer kitchen, where the carrots and potatoes are waiting to be packed in boxes filled with earth. The summer kitchen is actually the old well house, which has been joined to the main building. In the days before air conditioning, the women would move out here in July and August to cook, because it was the coolest part of the home. It was then shut off in the winter, to avoid draining heat. It serves us as a decent makeshift root cellar until we have waterproofed the greenhouse basement, within the next couple of years. "Root cellaring," as it's called, is a whole art in its own right: balancing air flow, temperature, and humidity until all your roots are happy. Our friend Cecille, the lady I told you about who uses no technology, stores a lot of her crops this way and has been teaching me some of her secrets.

Once the air in the main kitchen has cleared, I'll return to deal with our fifty pounds of red cabbage. Ultimately, this will metamorphose into a mere twenty jars of sweet and sour pickle. But first it has to be shredded and stewed with ten pounds of peeled apples, five of chopped onions, brown sugar, and spiced cider vinegar. The twenty jars will then be sterilized before their union with the cabbage—which will be consummated in a boiling-water bath for twenty minutes.

Greg is king of the peppers. We grow six kinds, which produce at a civilized pace for most of the summer before a final profligate spurt at the start of fall. We have four large boxes full.

The chilies, cayenne, Tabasco, and paprika are already drying in baskets on our bookshelves. Once they are nicely desiccated, Greg will grate them and pack them in spice jars for cooking and for Christmas presents. Some of our green and purple sweet peppers will also be given as gifts— suspended in olive oil that has been infused with garlic and herbs. As you may remember, my husband is a classics nut who happens to know this ancient Roman technique for preserving a lot of their food. It works just as well today, and when the peppers are all gone, you can use the liquid as a delicious salad dressing.

I don't envy our ancestors in the fall. We had a taste of their past agonies in our first year here, when an ancient pressure cooker was the only "modern convenience" we owned. We prepared everything by hand and what wouldn't fit into our tiny freezer had to be canned. I could never get the hang of the thing. It would explode on a regular basis, covering both ceiling and cook in applesauce or dripping bits of stewed tomato. This would lead to mutual recriminations and marital strife about who had peeled what and how much time they had wasted. Our harvest lasted past Thanksgiving and the food began to rot. Most of it ended up on the compost pile—one of the biggest in the county by the following spring.

Since then, kind ladies from around the county have taught us all sorts of ways to preserve, can, and dry. The art lies in choosing the right method, keeping everything scrupulously clean (don't process the bacteria along with the pickles), and not using old procedures just for the sake of it. We are now the proud possessors of a chest freezer, a state-of-the-art food processor, a juicer, and a peeling/coring machine. Twentieth-century technology is a wonderful thing—particularly when it comes to saving your time, money, or marriage.

The ordeal should be all over by the end of October. Our freezer will be full of vegetables, fruit, fish, and the freshly butchered pig that we just bought from a local hog farmer (organically raised, for 40 cents a pound!). And the pantry will be overflowing with gleaming jars of every size and description.

Will it be worth all the work? Well, we will have enough food to see us through to March—which is about three months short of our original target, but a great deal better than we have ever done before. Next season we'll have a more accurate idea of what each crop will actually produce on our land and how much we'll need to plant of it. That is invaluable information that only comes with time and experience, and which is essential for our budding farm business.

If we had to put a real price on the whole process today—including our hours, charged at their usual professional rate—we'd probably be looking at a two-hundred-dollar tomato. But it has a deeper worth than that.

Producing food for your family, raised by your own hand, empowers the spirit. It speaks to our history and our hopes, reminding us that there was and will be no greater prosperity than the warm and well-fed child. Our optimism for the future is directly linked to our ability to provide—the urge is fundamental in us all. Like the beaver, we are driven by instinct to stock our larders before the hard winter sets in.

2:30 P.M.: With fingers suffering from rigor mortis of the apple peeler, it's time to run the day's errands in town. For once the list is a short one: we need some office supplies, a birthday card, and a new jackshaft for the tractor. It should only take about three hours.

People in Brown County spend more time behind the wheel than they do in bed. It is made tolerable only by some of the most beautiful scenery on God's green earth. Unfortunately, lots of tourists think so, too, and today's trip is extended by 45 minutes as I wend my way to Bloomington behind an Iowa family doing 20 miles per hour. I wish that people would have the courtesy to pull over and let us locals past. We don't want to spoil their vacations, but we don't want to be part of them, either.

The only advantage to my slow journey is that I get to study the landscape in detail. The trees are wearing their autumn best, splashed with flaming orange, scarlet, and bright yellow. Little columns of smoke rise into the air from piles of burning leaves, while a farmer cuts the last of his feed corn, followed by a noisy escort of crows. They are too busy to notice the red-tailed hawk, riding the airflow high above, until he plunges past them to snatch his supper from the stubble.

Did I say I wasn't homesick? That isn't entirely true. Once in a while, a color or some faint image will take me by surprise and I'll ache a little. National identity is greatly to do with atmosphere, and Brown County in the fall is a very British place.

The mornings are misty and the grass, seen through a veil of raindrops, goes bright green. Herefords and Black Angus graze by the roadside and the air is full of the peppery smell of sunshine on wet earth. It's the kind of weather when steak-and-kidney pie or bread-and-butter pudding come into their own. I find myself sneaking into Blooming-ton to buy the London Sunday *Times,* and taking tea most afternoons at four.

My family is used to it. Every year they expect to spend a few weeks on a diet of roast beef and *Masterpiece Theatre.* They know that when the snows arrive we'll be eating meat loaf once again.

Greg delights in our differences, which, he says, he's still discovering. Over the years, he has learned that I mean an eraser when I ask for a rubber, and that a nappy is a diaper and a van is a truck. But it goes deeper that the divisions in our "common language."

"You're so serious," he teased the other day. "All these 'matters of principle' and 'It's only fair play.' Take it easy, Toots—you're in America now." At the time, he had been soothing my outrage at a male friend who had told me to "shut up."

"What are you going to do?" Greg asked. "Call him out on the field of honor? He was probably only joking." He probably was. Sometimes I find American codes of conduct very confusing.

In Britain the rules are so clear-cut. We have spent hundreds of years perfecting them, so that we could all live on our tiny island without having the world's highest murder rate. The British survive on a curious mix of etiquette and tolerance for extremes. A Brit could declare a Communist revolution, but he'd better do it politely or people will get upset.

At first glance, Americans appear to be much more relaxed. It took me a while to learn that in some ways they are every bit as formal as we are, with standards of courtesy that seem to vary from state to state.

In New York, for instance, "Good morning" has been dispensed with and "Hey, you gimme . . . " usually replaces "please." It is understood that survival time is too precious to waste on words and the polite just turn the other cheek. It took months for me to make friends in Manhattan—but once I had gotten beneath that tough New Yorker hide, I found a witty and passionate people with an insatiable energy for life. They tolerate every type of ambition, dream, or eccentric opinion, provided that you can shout loudly enough to make yourself heard.

This is not the case in Chicago. Algren's "city on the make" has a smile on its face—which sometimes doesn't reach its eyes. Initially, the pleases and thank-yous made such a pleasant change, until I realized that they were often just tools—wheel greasers—that help the machine work. And work in Chicago is what counts most. Having said that, some of my best friends come from there. They are a practical, no-nonsense people who will bluntly tell you what they think, in the name of honest friendship. My good buddy Janet listed every objection she had to our move— before pitching in to help with the sorting, wrapping, and packing up.

"Pitching in" is expected behavior in the Hoosier state. I have never lived anywhere before where people give so freely of themselves. Initially, the big-city cynic in me was suspicious—"Where's the angle? What's the gag?"—but then I realized there wasn't one. In Indiana, what you see is what you get.

My first lesson in Hoosier hospitality came not long after we had arrived. My car broke down (it often does), and I found myself stranded between towns on Route 135. Within minutes, two drivers had pulled over and were discussing what to do. They insisted that one would call the wrecker and direct him to my car, while the other drove me the fifteen miles back home. My protests were firmly brushed aside. "No point in you hanging around in all this freezing rain," they said. They were just doing the decent thing and barely wanted thanks.

This "old-fashioned" attitude also translates itself into

business. We have had to adjust to clients who honor their word, pay their bills, and give credit where credit is due. Greg still can't get over it.

Hoosiers aren't perfect, of course—they can be very conservative and suspicious of change—but usually they will tolerate a difference of opinion. Pat Richardson's husband, Jim, for instance, can't agree with Greg about the time of day. The two men will sit and argue for hours—but they remain the best of friends.

As Charley grows up, I hope that she combines a little of all these traits. If she can mix Hoosier sweetness, Chicago pragmatism, and New York spunk with good British manners, she'll have a happy mom.

6:15 P.M.: Home in time for the domestic rush hour. The evening will, as always, disappear in a blur of daily caretaking. There's wood to be gathered, fires to be made, mouths to be fed, and games to be played. Oscar will require his four outings of the night and everyone will take their turn at disseminating the day's news. The air will ring with conversations, disputations, and my daughter's gurgling laugh. It's my favorite part of the day, when the candle burns brightest before it starts to fade.

Greg and I love it here so much that, if it weren't for Charley, we would probably never go out. But that wouldn't be fair to her. When we moved here, we promised ourselves that we would expose her to all the wonderful city experiences, as well as the country ones. We thought we'd probably have to travel to do that, but that hasn't been the case. Between Bloomington and Indianapolis, there is every kind of theater, museum, restaurant, and club that a metropolitan heart could wish for. Charley has seen the Great Impressionists, been to the ballet, heard musicians like

Rostropovich and Robert Levin, and eaten every type of food from Greek to some of the best Thai that we've had in this country.

Eventually we will travel, too, but it won't be for lack of things to do back home.

Charley doesn't approve of the idea. "I don't want to go anywhere," she announced firmly the other night. "I want to stay here with you guys, for ever and ever." We had just finished one of our international evenings—eating chapatis and chicken curry and watching *Gandhi* on tape.

"One day," Greg told her, "we'll take you to India and show you the tigers, the elephants, and the tea plantations in the jungle."

Her response made us smile—it was the highest compliment that she could pay her parents, and entirely appropriate for her age. If we do our job well, she'll pay us another one in fourteen years' time, when she bounces off to college and away to explore the world.

11:15 P.M.: The house is finally still. Upstairs, Charley sleeps the sleep of the innocent while Greg dozes off despite his sins. Downstairs, I sit for a minute and drink in the peace. The living room smells of woodsmoke and applesauce, and the dogs are dreaming of rabbits.

My last task, before bundling off to bed myself, is a letter to an old friend who seems to be concerned about the level of challenge in my life. He will discover that this career woman turned country wife didn't know what fulfillment was until she made her home in the beautiful hills of Brown County.

Yours, not quite as ever,

CHAPTER 10

FOOTPRINTS IN THE SNOW

"DID YOU SPIT?" MY HUSBAND WAS OUTSIDE THE FRONT door, in the cold. He had just quoted the unmentionable—Shakespeare's Scottish play—and was going through the required rites to counteract bad luck. "Turn around three times, spit, and knock on the door," I yelled from the warmth of the dining room.

Greg came back in, looking bemused. "I can't believe I just did that," he said. Greater love hath no man than that he lay down his pride for his wife.

The Murpheys can be a superstitious household, particularly around Halloween. As the days draw in and the ground cools off, mists rise in the hollows along Bean Blossom Creek and glide across the road like lost ghosts. Almost everyone decorates their home in some way, from the modest jack-o'-lanterns flickering on front porches to the giant rolls of hay spray-painted with monstrous faces and stationed in driveways to leer at passing cars.

People in the county take these festivities quite seriously—urged on, perhaps, by their Celtic ancestors, who celebrated the last day of their calendar on the night of witches and warlocks, several thousand years ago. The same blood runs in my veins, compelling me to chuck around chunks of salt for every grain spilled or, to my husband's astonishment, turn all the silver in my purse in the light of a new moon.

Greg is superstitious in less specific ways. His good fortune relies on "gut feelings," which may seem to be totally unfounded but which I've learned not to ignore.

"I think we're going to have a rough winter," he said, warming his toes in front of the fire.

"The weathermen always predict that," I replied through a mouthful of pins, "so that no one can blame them later." Half a black umbrella lay spread out on the floor, waiting to be turned into bat wings for Charley's Halloween costume.

"That's not what I meant," Greg sighed. "I meant that it's going to be rough on us." I put down the ears I had been piecing together and studied my husband's face. He looked very tired. "Haven't you noticed how quiet it has been?" he asked. "The phone has virtually stopped ringing."

I had been so busy with the harvest that Greg had been carrying this burden all alone. I suddenly realized that he hadn't shot a job for nearly a month.

"Don't worry so much," I said, assuming the reassuring-wife role. "We've got enough in the bank to see us through the next few weeks, and something is bound to come in by then. Anyway, you should take the opportunity to enjoy the rest. You look as if you need it."

Greg was always exhausted after the big summer push, but this year he seemed more drained than usual. His skin had a nasty sallow tinge to it and deep, dark circles hollowed out his eyes.

"We could cancel the party," I volunteered, "conserve our resources and spare you the strain."

"Oh no." Greg shook his head. "That would break the Bug's heart."

This Halloween she was particularly excited because we had decided to introduce our friends to an English festival that falls at around about the same time—Guy Fawkes Night. Traditionally, this is when the British let off their fireworks—not on the Fourth of July, as I'm often asked, when *you* are celebrating your independence from *us*.

This story goes back to November 5, 1605, when some Roman Catholics resolved to blow up the Houses of Parliament as a prelude to seizing power from the Protestant king, James I. Somebody squealed and a stack of gunpowder barrels was found in the cellars under the House of Lords. They also caught one of the conspirators, Guido, or "Guy," Fawkes, who was later burned at the stake for breaking the eleventh commandment—"Thou shalt not be found out." Every year since then, British children have stuffed pillowcases and old shirts with straw, dressed them in their fathers' hats and pants, then wheeled them around the streets through September and October, calling out, "A penny for the guy." They use their loot to buy fireworks to be set off on November 5 by a bonfire on which they will burn poor old Guido all over again.

In deference to our daughter, who loves dressing up, it would be a combination party with costumes and combustibles. Our "Guy" was already installed among the cornstalks and prize pumpkins, but would be spared the fire because our neighbors, who tolerate much in the name of international relations, would not understand.

Parties in the countryside are a culinary adventure. They are almost always a potluck, because so few could afford to lay it all on by themselves, but you never see the bits of cheese and box of crackers that someone might bring to a city affair.

Here, it's an opportunity for everybody to show off the best that their garden and kitchen have to offer, and people can spend days preparing their contribution. Along with the surprises, this year we were expecting Nancy Kappes's delicious apple-cheese torte, several different salads, and an array of chocolate-dipped fruit. We'd be providing fish ramekins, made with our own catch, a large pot of beef Stroganoff, served on a bed of noodles, and coleslaw from our fall crop of cabbages, onions, and carrots. There'd be spiced apple cider and mulled wine for the grown-ups to drink and juice or pop for the kids.

Planning the food is always fun, but the special joy of this occasion is organizing the games. I had already spent several evenings wrapping paint sets and small toys in layers and layers of paper for "Pass the Parcel"; scrubbing out an aluminum water trough, which would be filled with water and apples to be bobbed for; and selecting appropriately spooky music for the inevitable "Musical Bumps" (a variation on musical chairs where you sit on the floor instead and the last to hit the deck is out). My dream is to turn the barn into "Murphey's Haunted Madhouse," but that will have to wait until we have the time and a couple hundred dollars to waste.

"Are you sure you're feeling up to it?" I asked Greg again.

"No," my husband replied, "but I'll enjoy it anyway."

We all did—even Hotshot, who looked quite proud as he carried the little ones for short rides around the orchard. Children of all ages joined in the games and everyone ate themselves to a breathless standstill. The fireworks were the climax of the evening. Bottle rockets streaked across the lake, sparkling and shimmering in the surface of the water, and so many "Golden Showers" and "Silver Cascades" were set off that we could still smell the cordite in the air the next morning—along with a hint of the cold to come.

Over the next couple of days, the temperature began to

plummet as the jet stream dipped low over the Midwest, bringing with it frigid Canadian winds and the first threat of snow. "It could be a big one," the weatherman announced gleefully, "up to six inches, sometime tomorrow night."

In Maine or Minnesota that would be little more than a light dusting, but in central Indiana it ranked as a heavy storm. Experience had taught us that anything over four inches could block most of the county's roads and would almost always cause some kind of power cut. Even if you could get out, you did so at your own peril. Hoosiers from this part of the state have never learned to drive on ice, and a winter storm is always accompanied by its own rash of rear-endings and sliding, spinning cars that end up nose first in a ditch.

We decided to stay home for the duration and began the usual siege preparations. Greg split and stacked half a cord of wood next to the backdoor, while I went into Morgantown and stocked up on batteries, milk, kerosene, and animal feed. When I got home, we insulated the barn with extra straw and filled every vehicle to the brim with gasoline, before getting them all under cover. A snow shovel, camping stove, and a couple of flashlights were laid out neatly in the summer kitchen, where we lit the old gas stove to stop the pipes from freezing. By the evening of November 6, tendrils of frost were creeping across each window, and as I was putting Charley to bed, the first snow began to fall.

"Turn your lamp off," I suggested to the Bug, "I want to show you something." The night was thick with silent flakes—big ones—waltzing solemnly downward, coating each surface at first touch. As we watched, the spruce tree outside whitened, bathing Charley's room in pale blue light.

"It's Christmas," my daughter gasped.

"Not quite." I smiled. "But it is an early present."

The next morning, we woke up to a world muffled in white.

The first day of a winter storm always feels like a trip into the Twilight Zone. No noises penetrate from the outside—just the *thok* of melting snow and the crisp crunching of your own boots as you head out to the barn. You feel as if the farm has somehow detached itself from the surrounding Earth and is spinning silently in space.

Even Charley did not want to spoil the mood and was painting pictures quietly in the sunroom. The only sounds came from the crackle of the fire, the clink of her brush on the water jar, and a little Mozart playing softly on the stereo. "Look," said my daughter suddenly, "look—a deer!"

Greg and I crept to the big back windows and saw the doe standing under our apple trees with a front leg tentatively poised. Her head was arched back slightly as she sniffed the morning air. She knew that there were humans close by, but the scent of fallen fruit was even stronger.

We stood like statues for ten minutes as she delicately pawed at the snow, uncovering the apples one by one. The doe sensed our presence and sniffed at the air every minute or so, brown eyes scanning the horizon. By deer standards she was suicidally close to the house and guilty of almost epic folly. Finally, the tension was too much to bear and she bounded across the meadow to the safety of the trees—liquid grace in motion. Somewhere in the shadows, her buck would be waiting—like the cardinals, they send their women in first.

"Her" buck is actually a misnomer; deer only mate briefly before getting back to the serious business of survival. They, too, are superstitious in their way, following rituals learned over centuries of avoiding a list of predators that goes all the way back to the saber-toothed tiger. Our doe, for instance, is probably pregnant, and if she survives all the dangers of winter, will deliver her fawns in the spring. Her first act will be to abandon them, but not because she's an abusive mom. She knows that in their early days of life her babies have no scent, so it is safe to hide them in bushes or tall grass while she plays decoy to lure away any nearby threat.

It was a brilliant strategy in the era when wolf, bobcat, and bear were plentiful, but with the advent of modern man, it can also be a dangerous one. Every year Pat Richardson has to rescue a fawn who has been accidentally run over by a tractor or cut up by a combine harvester. The injuries can be bloody, but the does don't seem to learn. Their genetic memory tells them that the subterfuge is the only way to protect their offspring and they can't deny their instinct any more than they could switch off those supersharp senses of sight, hearing, and smell. The white-tailed deer is one of North America's oldest living mammals because no other animal is more expert at evasion, camouflage, and defense.

"Will she ever come back, Mama?" Charley asked wistfully.

"She hasn't gone away, Bug," I explained. "Her home is in those trees. She's close to us even though we can't see her."

Whenever the family walks in the forest, we know we're being watched. The air goes very still, as if a hundred creatures have paused in the midst of their busy day and are holding their breath until we've passed by. Everybody's eyes strain for the flash of a whisker or the tip of a tail, but we are too untrained to see what is happening under our very noses. Big John has promised to remedy that situation by teaching me how to track "come bow season," when he spends all his spare time in the woods.

Deer-hunting season begins in October and is split into three sections: bow hunting, rifle hunting, and musket-loaders, when the bowmen are also allowed out again. You need a different license to participate in each category, and you're allowed only one kill per weapon.

Before we moved here, I used to think that hunting in

any form was man at his barbaric worst. It does bring out the beast in some, who descend on Brown County dressed like paramilitary goons. They come with trucks full of beer and minds bent on blood. More often than not, they end up shooting themselves, or someone else, in the foot, or they make a kill and insist on skinning it by the side of the road for all the world to see.

There are others, however, who are quieter about it. They hunt only to feed their families and are often great woodsmen who pride themselves on their knowledge of nature far more than their power over life. Big John falls into this category. He learned how to track as a scout in Vietnam, where he saw things that he still finds hard to discuss. John brought the usual nightmares home with him, which haunted his sleep until he took the training he had been given to trail men and used it to follow animals. He kills only to fill the freezer and chooses to hunt with a long bow because it requires that you come very close to your prey and is the weapon that demands the greatest tracking skills. John invariably gets his buck, but his stories are usually about the animals he has seen rather than the one he has brought down.

I was given a list of specific instructions before our first lesson. "Take a long shower and don't use any perfumed soap or scent," he began. "Wear layers of clothing that you can take off when you get warm and put back on again as the day cools down. You'll need thick leather boots—not rubber, which doesn't breathe. Wear two pairs of socks and bring a spare set with you, because as you sweat—and you will sweat—the socks get wet and freeze to your feet." John advised me to carry as little as possible—just the footwear, some water, a compass, and a small pack of high-energy food like peanuts and/or raisins. "Don't bring candy," John warned. "It won't fill you up and the sugar rush will sap your strength."

I was nervous as I waited outside for him on the appointed day. Talking about hiking deep into the woods, up steep hills, and over rushing water may sound romantic in the warmth of your own living room, but actually doing it was a different matter. I'm no scaredy-cat, but certain kinds of physical discomfort—cold extremities or wet clothes—turn me into a whining child, who also suffers from fits of jelly-legged vertigo when standing on anything over five feet tall. This expedition could expose all my weaknesses, just as I was beginning to convince our neighbors that I was country through and through.

"Good morning," a voice boomed into my ear, making my breakfast leap back up my throat. The man still moves like a cat, despite his size, and he delights in sneaking up on friends unseen.

"Don't do that," I shrieked, turning to discover a John who couldn't have looked very different from the teenager in the jungle all those years ago. He was dressed in full camouflage with interesting bottles and bags hanging from his belt. An army cap was pulled down over his eyes and black streaks along his cheekbones broke up the contours of his face.

"Taking no chances, I see," John said dryly, nodding at my fluorescent orange coat—the color of choice if you don't want to get shot. "Rifle season doesn't start for a couple of weeks."

"It's the most waterproof thing I own," I replied apologetically.

"Well, doesn't look like you're going to need it," he went on, scanning the blue sky. "It's a shame that the snow's all melted, but at least we'll have the mud."

Snow on the ground makes it almost too easy for the tracker, providing a clear census of all who have passed that way. But even a heavy fall in Brown County doesn't last for more than a few days. The only evidence of our recent storm was the sponginess of the land beneath our feet as we made our way down to the lake.

"Try not to walk on any branches," John whispered. "Look carefully wherever you step."

I glued my eyes to the earth, trying to drink in every detail as we went. At first, the only tracks were from dainty birds' feet and Lady and Tramp's big paws. But then, at the back of the lake along the dam, I saw a deer print slicing into the sand: two crescent shapes, about an inch and a half long, meeting together in a sharp point.

"It's small—either a young buck or a doe," John revealed. "And it's fresh—no more than half an hour old."

"You mean it was just here?" I was excited. "How can you tell?"

John pointed with a stick. "Look at how sharp those edges are. And nothing is covering the track—no debris, no water. That makes it recent." He stood up and looked around. "There's the deer path to the lake—see it?"

All I could see was a mass of tangled undergrowth and trees.

"Crouch down," he commanded. "Now can you see it?"

More undergrowth and a mass of roots, but in the woods behind I thought I saw a worn trail where something had flattened the fallen leaves.

"Maybe," I said cautiously. "But it could be wishful thinking."

We plunged into the forest, where John seemed to spot something every few feet. "More tracks," he said, poking at the ground.

It was most frustrating—I couldn't detect a thing. He gently moved some rotting leaves aside and traced the outline of another print.

"How did you see that?" I was incredulous. "It's almost invisible."

"Just takes practice," my teacher shrugged. "In a few weeks' time, they'll leap out at you."

John followed the tracks to a grove hidden under some pines, where old needles and twigs had been scratched away to reveal a fresh patch of earth.

"A deer scrape," he grunted, and went on to explain that this is how the bucks mark their territory during their rutting season. "It's their way of saying to the doe, 'Don't go away, sweetheart, I'll be right back.'"

The males dig at the soil with their front hooves, then urinate on the area, letting the liquid run over glands in their back legs, which carries their scent down to the ground. The process is completed when they have bitten at an overhanging branch and rubbed their forehead glands along it. John reached above and showed me the broken shoot. It was still green, suggesting that the scrape, too, was recent.

The glade was so full of signs that it was almost as if the deer had put them there for my personal education. Near the scrape, the bottom of a spicebush had been pushed aside where, John said, a doe had been lying. And on the opposite edge of the clearing, a spruce sapling was missing a two-foot strip of bark about a third of the way up its trunk.

"A rub," my instructor said simply.

Bucks grow a new set of antlers every year, he went on, starting in the spring. While the antlers are sprouting, they are covered in a soft casing known as velvet, which falls off just before the mating season. As it begins to peel, the buck helps the process along by rubbing his horns up and down trees. A stag will often use the same sapling year after year, wearing the trunk smooth and leaving one of the main signs that a deer tracker is on the lookout for. The rub will help to pinpoint the deer's living area and, depending on the size of the tree, will tell you how big he is: the bigger the sapling, the bigger the rack of antlers—and usually, the bigger the rack, the bigger the buck.

John said that this fellow was of average size—"Maybe six points."

Contrary to popular legend, the number of points on a rack has nothing to do with age and everything to do with good nutrition. A young buck who's eating well could have eight or ten points. An old buck whose teeth have worn down and who is suffering from a grisly array of internal parasites would have a really scruffy set of antlers. The stag of myth, who has survived many winters and won many ruts to become lord of all he surveys, does exist, but he's a rare creature who is hunted down mercilessly.

"A twelve- or thirteen-pointer comes along once in a lifetime," John said longingly.

"Yeah." I shook my head. "And then you kill him."

"Only for the meat." The big man chuckled and turned to leave the glade.

"Well, look at this." John bent over a track to study it more closely. The print was enormous in comparison with what we had already seen. From the tip of the hoof to the dewclaw at the back, it was as long as my hand. A gleam appeared in my friend's eye, and without another word he left the path and plunged into the dense thicket, moving so fast that I fell back to avoid the whiplash of the brambles.

John was right, we did sweat. For the next couple of hours, we slashed our way through the deepest undergrowth, following the buck's trail as he visited the young bucks' bedroom, ate in a grove of oak trees, and left messages for his various does. Finally, we paused for breath at the intersection of two creeks, where John whistled through his teeth and asked me what I saw. I scanned the trees, looking for something unusual and spotted a rub on a sapling nearby. John looked impressed.

"Very good. But I didn't mean that. Take another look."

It was, of course, right in front of me. A young tree, bowed by rubbing that had stripped at least four feet of bark away, the biggest example we had seen. We crossed the creek to the bottom of a tall ridge on the other side where the buck's tracks skirted some rocks, then headed up the slope to a thick stand of pines.

"His bedroom's up there," John concluded. "He's probably watching us right now. We won't get anywhere near him today. You need to come back here before dawn, or in the early afternoon, and hide yourself in those trees at the top. If you stay still for a few hours, you'll get to see him."

We made our way home slowly, thoughts too full to talk much. I had discovered a whole new world and couldn't wait to share it all with Greg before persuading him to come on deer watch with me.

"I wish you'd been there," I called out from the kitchen door. "You would never believe how much we saw." There was no reply. "Greg, where are you?"

I found him lying on the couch in a fetal position, moaning softly. The color drained out of my face until it was almost as white as his was. "What on earth . . . ?"

"I thought it was flu," he murmured, "but now there's this burning pain in my bladder."

"Have you taken anything?"

"Some codeine; it hasn't made a dent." When my husband opened his eyes, there was an expression in them that was new to me. Greg was scared.

"You've got to see a doctor, *now*," I said firmly. "We'll worry about how to pay for it later."

The doc couldn't see him till the following morning, so I spent the night organizing my fears in order of priority. My husband is a robust man who normally could fight off the most virulent of bugs. This malady had to be something special to have hit him so hard, something that might require surgery or expensive drugs. A spectral voice whispered "cancer" in my ear, but I waved the word away, refusing to hear it unless I absolutely had to. It could be a hundred trivial things, I told myself, from a hernia to a simple urinary infection.

I clung to this optimism because life without a strong and healthy Greg was too painful to contemplate—and a major illness was too scary, because we are among America's growing group of medically uninsured.

When people gasp at the risk involved, I point out to them that we always had health insurance in Chicago until the premium topped three hundred dollars and it became a choice between that and paying the rent. Since we moved down here, where costs are lower, the economy has been so unpredictable that it has been impossible to commit to anything more than the basic monthly bills. I still had the insurance forms on my desk from a premature burst of confidence in September, when it looked as if the recession was finally in retreat. But I hadn't had the time to fill them out before business slowed again and we'd had to retrench. My last act before going to bed was to consign them to the garbage.

Greg looked a little better in the morning—well enough, in fact, to drive himself to the doctor while I took care of Charley, who was starting a cold. He was back within the hour, limping down the drive with a pained expression on his face.

"It's a prostate infection," he announced as he came in. "The doc has given me some superstrong antibiotics and says that I should be okay in ten days."

"In time for Thanksgiving—that's really good news." I sounded happier than I felt, because a little voice deep inside was warning, "Don't count on it just yet."

We hadn't planned anything special for the holiday. The only family we have are my parents in France, so it's always a quiet occasion that revolves around The Meal. The menu has become a tradition—peeled shrimp, curried Brussels sprout soup, roast turkey with all the trimmings (especially Greg's cranberry and orange sauce), and, since I'm no fan of pumpkin pie, the prizewinning French almond apple tart for dessert.

When we first arrived, we had dreamed of a time when the farm would provide all the ingredients for a feast that would be a real celebration of the harvest. This year we were getting close with our own Brussels sprouts, potatoes, green beans, onions, sage, paprika, bread, and apples. As I pointed out to Greg, we could furnish the turkey, too (and I would do the honors, happily), but he turned me down flat. So the bird will be store-bought, while Cornbread and Cranberry continue to strut around the pasture, looking even smugger than usual.

Thanksgiving is also when Charley and I begin "greening" the house, a process that builds toward the decoration of the tree, ten days before Christmas. We start by collecting acorns and pine cones in September, which are then sprayed with gold and silver paint before being attached with a glue gun to fresh boughs of cedar, juniper, and pine a couple of days before the holiday. The arrangements are set out in three large flower vases, which by Thanksgiving morning fill the downstairs with the sweet smell of resin.

The table is decorated with "Tussie Mussies" (a medieval phrase meaning "sweet posies"), which are little bunches of dried flowers and herbs. Each plant in the bouquet is supposed to convey a different meaning (Tussie Mussies were used by lovers in Victorian times to send each other quite complicated messages), and I try to choose combinations that sum up our year.

I had already dried roses (for love); apple mint (for wisdom and warmth); daisies (for hope); and lily of the valley (for peace), to which I now added sage (for good health). There are literally thousands of symbols—floriography, the language of flowers, goes back to ancient Egypt.

The house looked lovely on the day, but our celebration was a subdued affair. Greg was not improving. In fact, he seemed to be getting worse. The pain in his bladder was spreading, and that legendary appetite had almost disappeared. Seeing my husband pick at his food was as worrying as the fact that the doctor could now find nothing wrong. It was time for second opinions, specialized tests, and mounting medical bills. Like Pat and Jim Richardson, we elected not to discuss it, and I eased my stress by spending spare afternoons in the woods, returning to the ridge where the big buck slept.

Staying totally still for two or three hours is even harder than it sounds. For the first fifteen minutes or so, it's a pleasant experience, but then the prickles begin—unexplained itches that feel like bugs down the back of your neck, or a slithering across the ankles. If you resist the temptation to jump, scratch, or otherwise move, the sensations eventually fade away, to be replaced by attacks of pins and needles. I still haven't found a sitting position that avoids this and always end up with numb feet, legs or posterior parts. This stage is like hitting the athlete's wall—if you can get through it, the rest is all downhill.

It takes about forty-five minutes for the forest to forget you're there, by which time you might find yourself dozing off. During my first session, I was dreaming that I was in bed and was about to yell at Greg for opening the window in the middle of winter, when a loud cawing woke me up. I opened my eyes to the sight of two chipmunks, a few inches from my foot, fighting over some corn that I had laid down by the trail when I first arrived. The crow who had given me my alarm call was sitting in a tree nearby, preening his wings. Above his head, there was a nest perched across the top branches that must have been a couple of feet wide.

A crow's nest! I thought to myself, but I was wrong. The black big-mouth took off as a thin "peep, peep" began in the sky above and a much bigger bird came into sight, spiraling downward on the invisible breeze. It was a red-tailed hawk, probably the one who hunted above our lake. She stretched out the four-foot span of her wings to steady herself as she landed, then folded them away as she settled in for an afternoon snooze. The chipmunks had been watching her, too, frozen to the spot in midargument. As soon as they saw that the coast was clear, they dived for cover, fight forgotten, following each other into the bowels of a beech tree.

The shafts of sunlight that had pierced the foliage from above when I first arrived were now streaming in at a horizontal angle. It was getting cold. My toes, which had frozen numb some time before, now began to burn. It was time to go. The buck was either about his business or had known I was there all along and was watching the watcher in the woods. I had the feeling that if I ever saw him, it would only be with his full knowledge and consent.

I was too busy over the next few days to try again. Life up at the house was coming apart. Greg was still on the couch and Charley had contracted her first ever dose of gastric flu. She scared her mother to death by running a temperature of 102 degrees for three days and then developed an ear infection the moment the fever broke. Lady added to the general chaos by attacking one of the hens and trying to bury her alive in the garden. Amazingly, the bird survived, despite a horrendous collection of puncture wounds and having lost most of her back feathers. I cleaned her up as best I could, put Bactine on the bites, and got her settled in a cage in the summer kitchen. My day became an unbroken chain of feeding, medicating, and clearing up after all my charges, while using the few quiet moments I had to generate some work. Greg was in no condition to shoot anytime soon, and our savings account had almost dwindled away. By my calculations, we would run out of money on January 1 unless I did something about it *right now.*

There were times when I longed for my old life in Britain, with its financial security and free medical care. My former boss in London had told me the year before that there was a producer's desk with my name on it if ever I chose to return. At the time, I had scoffed at the thought, saying that the only way I'd leave here was feetfirst in a box, but now I was beginning to wish that I hadn't been so dismissive. At least, I thought grimly to myself, we'd be able to get Greg to a specialist.

We had tried to see a couple of internists in Indianapolis, but the receptionists' pleasant voices had hardened the moment they heard we weren't insured, and Greg had been put on waiting lists that were at least six months long. He made another appointment to see our GP, in the hope that some new symptoms might come to light.

The only creature who seemed to be doing well was the hen, who had a hearty appetite and drank all the water I could give her. I was really beginning to believe that she could make it until my nose caught a whiff from the summer kitchen one morning of the unmistakable stench of gangrene. I hoisted the chicken out of her cage and inspected all her wounds. They were clean and healing nicely apart from one that I had missed under her wing. The edges of that puncture were green tinged, and as I watched in horror, a maggot emerged from the hole. There was no hope for her. I took her outside and put down an extra meal of corn. While she was eating happily, I shot her from a distance. She never knew what hit her.

This had not been part of the plan. Everything was going wrong, no matter what was done to stop it. I was so crazed with frustration and anxiety that I decided to go on deer watch again before the whole family began to suffer.

We all have our own ways of communicating with our Maker and I always get closest to mine in His great outdoors. This excursion was less about seeing the buck than it was about finding some clarity amidst the confusion.

"Is all this stuff supposed to be telling me something?" I asked as I walked past the lake. "Did I really travel five thousand miles, across several lifestyles, just to be forced back to where I began?"

The air was still. Patches of ice had begun to form at the edge of the water, like globules of grease in an unwashed pan.

An unrelenting gray sky hovered over a landscape that looked as desolate as I felt. Even the beaver's lodge was beginning to decay after Tramp had sat on it, a couple of weeks back, and its disgruntled tenant had moved out. No answers here, I concluded, turning toward the woods and the long walk to "Buck's Ridge."

I had planned a new approach for this trek, circling the edge of our forest and coming at the crest from the north. It would be a much tougher hike, but it gave me a better chance of sneaking up unseen, and I would be downwind all the way. I moved as silently as possible, sometimes taking ten minutes to cover no more than a few feet. The birds kept singing and I reached the top of the ridge an hour and a half later without having snapped so much as a twig.

As I slid into place against a tree trunk, I felt bone tired. Sitting still for a couple of hours would be no problem today and within a few minutes I began to doze. I dreamed that I was in a TV control room, talking to the talent. A secretary was trying to interrupt, saying that Greg was being operated on and Charley's school had left a message that she had to be picked up. "Don't bother me," I'd snapped, "can't you see I'm busy?" I turned back to the monitors where my family's faces were on each screen, knocking at the glass and calling out my name.

I awoke with a gasp just as two raccoons waddled into view down by the creek. They stopped under a stand of oaks and began checking for fallen acorns. By this time of year, the squirrels and the deer have usually eaten or stored the best fruit and nuts. But some get trodden into the earth and the coons use their long fingers to work the acorns loose again. These two found a substantial snack and ate hearty for ten minutes or more. When the bigger one had finished, she began grooming the small one, hands petting and combing through his fur in small gestures of caretaking and affection.

"We can't leave," my heart cried out. "This is where we belong. But if it's a choice between Greg and staying here, please, God, give me my man. I'll do whatever I must do to make him well again." I discovered I'd been weeping, and the tears were now drying on my cheeks. I sniffed quietly and hoped that the saline wouldn't start to sting.

A sunbeam broke through the cloud and stroked the ridge like a consoling hand, deepening the shadows and spotlighting the rocks. As it struck the top of the crest, a bush shivered and suddenly he was there, calmly surveying his realm. His deep chest and strong neck supported a magnificent head crowned by a huge pair of antlers. I counted ten points, but they blended so well with the background of branches that there might have been more. He appeared to be looking for something, eyes searching through the trees. Rifle season had begun and gunmen sometimes stalked our woods, despite our No Hunting notices. The buck had survived a number of seasons by taking no chances.

Winters are rough on him, I thought. He avoids being killed only to face long weeks of semistarvation. In a bad season, the buck's body feeds off its own fat to such an extent that his bone marrow will turn from white to red. Yet he probably wouldn't even see it as privation—it's just a normal part of the cycle.

The buck began scanning the top of my ridge, coming to rest on the trees where I was hidden. For a long heartbeat of time, our eyes seemed to meet and he looked at me proudly, as if to say, "I endure in order to live. Life is every creature's duty." In the following second he melted away, disappearing so fast that I didn't see him go.

I started at the sunlit spot where he had stood, knowing that his home was mine as well. I would come back often in the hopes of seeing him again, and one day I would bring a healthy Greg with me—because we, too, were going to survive.

CHAPTER 11

"GOD BLESS US EVERY ONE!"

HE TEST WAS NEGATIVE, MR. MURPHEY." THE NURSE'S voice crackled over the speakerphone. "All your organs are apparently healthy. I'm sorry it wasn't more conclusive."

Greg and I looked at each other with profound expressions of relief. We still didn't know what the problem was, but now we knew what it wasn't—and it wasn't "The Big C." In fact, Greg had been feeling so much better over the past few days that we were beginning to believe our doctor, who had ascribed the pain to post-infection irritation and Greg's weakness to the strength of the antibiotic.

"So essentially, Murphey, you've been malingering," I teased. "It's time you pitched in with the Christmas preparations."

The house was beginning to look like an outpost of the North Pole, with every surface covered by some project in progress. In the dining room, large piles of greenery sat on each chair, while the table was stacked with all the necessary components for homemade decorations and wreaths.

The living room was Christmas Card Central. Charley and

I formed a production line there each evening, cutting up poster board and colored paper before attaching one to the other and decorating the images with glitter, sequins, and paint.

In the kitchen, the mess I had recently made during the creation of my Holiday Potpourri had been replaced by stacks of sterilized jars and seventy precut caps of red-and-white gingham. I still had to prepare the preserves, sauces, and vinegars to fill them with before they could join the other goodies that had been arranged in gift baskets for our friends.

It was all a far cry from Christmases past, which had basically revolved around shopping. I would begin in early November with some painstaking research around the local malls before drawing up long lists of who was to get what. Gift-giving in the city was serious politics. Who did we want to give to? Who did we have to give to? Who had bought what for whom last year? How much had we spent? How much had they spent? Who were we going to see between December 20 and January 1? And—the most important consideration—which credit card had a limit left?

My days were measured in miles of escalators and marble floors, while my nights were devoted to the nursing of sore feet and the mindless signing and sending of more than a hundred cards. Once they were mailed, I had moved on to the mass production of cookies and candies, while the family were parked in front of the nearest TV, feasting on frozen pizza. The whole thing had felt like a military campaign. Greg was always grateful on New Year's Day, when hostilities officially ceased.

My husband has enjoyed his Christmases more since we moved to the country. What little shopping I do now is spread out over the year, leaving our December weeks free for the family to have fun. These days we send out about forty cards and only give gifts to people we like.

"What do you want me to do now?" Greg came into the kitchen, purloining a couple of cookies from a batch that were cooling on the counter.

"You choose," I said as I bustled by him, "but I wouldn't eat those, unless you've developed a fondness for dog biscuits." His hand froze half an inch from his mouth and he silently put the cookies back on the rack.

"This"—he shook his head—"this is a lunatic asylum."

"Why don't you get your coat on," I suggested, "and we'll go and buy the tree."

Greg's eyes lit up and he went off without another word, wise enough to know that he should quit while he was ahead. For weeks I had been insisting that we could cut the tree from our own woods. "Don't tell me," I had pontificated at my obstinate worst, "that we can't find one good specimen in all the hundreds out there. You just don't want to look." My husband knew better than to argue with me in this mood and came along to see what we could find.

My first idea had been a white pine that was growing out of the bank of the lake. The tree would have to be cut down anyway, and it would be nice if it were used for a good cause. "What about this one?" I asked, marching over to it.

Greg folded his arms and looked at me, amazed. "Sal, it's fifteen feet tall."

"We could trim some off the bottom," I argued.

"But the branches are spaced about two feet apart. You wouldn't be able to hang more than ten ornaments on it."

Undaunted, I moved on, heading for the secret garden at the back of the big pasture where a plantation of pine had been put in many years before.

This may seem obvious, but trees are just big plants. They need to be fed, watered, and weeded, and they must be pruned to look their best. This sorry-looking bunch had been left to fend for themselves and the result was an overcrowded mess. The older pines had grown unchecked, spindly trunks and branches twisting toward the sky, competing against the young saplings that they had sprouted next to themselves. The smaller trees looked like limp ostrich feathers and my suggestion that we should try lashing four or five together was met with a well-deserved snort.

I don't know why I was being so stubborn. A visit to a tree farm last spring had shown me how much work goes into producing a good specimen, and I was aware that the odds against finding the traditional Tannenbaum growing naturally were about one million to one.

It wasn't about money, either. Things were still tight, but a marketing contract and a couple of television pieces had relieved the pressure, and we could certainly afford the twenty dollars that it costs down here to buy a decent tree.

I suppose it was about dreams. Part of my image of a country Christmas had been the trip out to the woods and the struggle to haul the spruce home. Going out and buying one seemed like such a city thing to do.

Contrary to unconventional appearances, Greg can also be a traditional man. As we bounced along in the car a little later, I realized that the family's annual tree expedition, with all its excitement and high expectations, was an important part of *his* holiday, and I cursed myself silently for having been so dense.

The process usually takes an afternoon of going around the tree farms, comparing quality and price. My husband is very serious about it, striding up and down the long rows, carefully studying each one. When he spots a contender, he crouches down, staring up the trunk to check that it's straight. In Chicago the final step in the ritual was a good shaking to see how fresh his choice was by how many needles it dropped; but here the tree continues to grow until the moment of purchase, when the farmer brings a chain saw over to liberate it from its roots. It is so fresh that we rarely have to clean up a needle between Decoration Day and Twelfth Night.

"What do you think of this one, Ladies?" Greg asked, waving at a six-foot-tall blue spruce. He always pays us the courtesy of consulting us about the decision, even though the final selection is invariably left to him.

"It's beautiful!" I nodded approvingly.

"Is that our tree?" Charley asked, dancing up and down.

"I think so," said Greg, and went off to haggle about the price.

Once we've got the Christmas tree home, our first task is to fetch the ornaments from their storage area in the rafters of the barn. This is one of the highlights of our celebrations. The boxes are put down gently in the living room by the chest, which has been covered in layers of tissue. Each item is then unwrapped reverently and laid out in its own nest of paper.

We take such care because they are cherished decorations that go back, in some cases, to our grandparents' trees. Greg and I both had pretty turbulent childhoods and found ourselves out in the world somewhat sooner than our peers. The ornaments were among the few vestiges of family life that we managed to hang on to, and it was a day of special symbolism when the two collections merged. Since then we've added new things of our own, and every Christmas there's a pause in the proceedings while we remember much-loved faces and the laughter of years past.

"What's this one from?" Charley asked, holding up a tiny white cradle.

"From the year that you were born," I replied. "As if you didn't know."

"And this?" She held up a handblown purple orb that was laced with delicate bands of gold.

"That was my mother's," Greg answered. "There's her picture on the wall."

We trooped over to study the portrait that smiled down on us year-round.

"She was your grandmother," he explained, "but she went to heaven before you were born."

Charley scrutinized the painting, before returning to the chest. "And this?" she asked, waving a banana skin colored a metallic shade of puce.

"That," I said dryly, "is your father's idea of a joke."

The last item out of the boxes is the tree stand, which is set up in a corner of the living room. Then the annual argument begins.

I hold the tree, while Greg screws it into the base.

"It's not straight . . . "

"Just wait a minute . . . "

"It's too close to the wall . . . "

"Oh, gimme a break . . . "

"Now it's dominating the whole room. Push it back a bit . . . "

"Will you make up your mind . . . "

The lines are interchangeable between us, but someone says them every year. Lips tighten and tempers flare until suddenly the tree is upright and standing in its proper place.

"I'm sorry . . . "

"No, it was my fault . . . "

"Stop fighting, you guys," my daughter shouted, handing us each a glass ball. "Let's decorate!" The dense branches of the spruce took every ornament we owned and within two hours it stood sparkling in the corner, dressed in all its yuletide best.

We celebrated with chocolate cake; then Charley was packed off to bed. I came downstairs to find Greg watching *It's a Wonderful Life* for the second time that week and Tramp sitting bolt upright in front of the tree, staring at the colored lights.

"Look at him," I said to Greg, who smiled.

"Yes, I know. You realize he's never seen anything like it before?" I thought about his last Christmas as a puppy shivering in our woods and called him over for a cuddle. He got out of the way just in time. With a creak and a rustle, the tree pitched forward, then collapsed on its side. We both gaped at it, speechless.

Greg was first up, gingerly lifting it off the floor, trying to keep the decorations intact. He set the tree back in the stand and started to screw it down. "The trunk was in crooked," he puffed. "I can tell by the scratch marks." There were a couple more energetic adjustments before he sat up. "There, now it's straight."

I cleared my throat. "I think you should come and see it from over here." The pickled pine was lurching to the left, its star leaning against the wall.

"I don't understand it," Greg muttered, disappearing beneath the branches again. "Is that better?"

"No."

"How's about that?"

"Even worse."

"Well, wait a minute. There, now what do you think?"

My husband stood up to find that the spruce was pointing like some furry finger toward the middle of the room.

"It's not so bad," he grumbled.

I shook my head. "If your daughter comes down to that tomorrow, we will never hear the end of it." The tree concurred and, with a loud groan, toppled over like the party drunk.

"It's the Christmas tree from hell," Greg hissed. "I'll deal with it in the morning."

"Only after *you've* dealt with Charley's tears."

My husband glared at me and turned back to the freaked-out fir. "What is the problem here, anyway?"

A close study of the beached balsam revealed a crescent-shaped kink in its trunk that was only obvious from the side that had been facing away from us when we bought it. It never would, and never could, stand up like a respectable tree.

"We'll have to camouflage it," Greg concluded, "after it has been realigned."

The rest of the night was a grim affair of instructions and suggestions all delivered through gritted teeth. By two in the morning, the tree was ensconced, bending toward the back wall as if it were flipping us the bird. "It's the best we can do," Greg said firmly, and staggered off to bed.

I watched my daughter carefully the next day, but Charley didn't notice anything different. She was too excited by the prospect of an Advent party that was being held at our church, where the children were going to be taught how to make Swedish tree ornaments and Advent wreaths by one of the most creative women in Brown County, Karen Anderson-Haldeman.

There are more craftspeople per square inch in this area than in any big city I know. Our local friends include accomplished potters, weavers, spinners, carpenters, lace makers, quilters, blacksmiths—even a lady who canes chairs—most of whom don't practice for money but just for the love of their craft. Karen's skills are multidisciplinary, learned over many years of giving in to an irresistible urge to create something beautiful out of simple everyday stuff.

The parish house was already buzzing with activity when we arrived. A long table at the back of the room was piled with garlands of greenery and raffia wreaths, which children were attaching to each other with large hooked pins. At another table, fathers stood around stabbing at the finished wreaths with screwdrivers, in an effort to make four holes for the traditional Advent candles, while small heads were bent over a third table, furiously coloring Advent calendars before they cut them out. The smell of baking sugar cookies floated out from the kitchen, where more children were using icing and sprinkles to decorate their wares.

Charley didn't know where to begin. "Why don't we start with your wreath?" I suggested. "We made cookies a couple of days ago, and you can color anytime." This seemed acceptable and we began pinning a garland to its base.

Karen has that twofold talent of the expert who can make the difficult appear easy and the simple look good. Her wreath design was perfect for small hands and short attention spans, and Charley had fixed the last candle into her creation before wandering off in search of the nearest pile of crayons.

I got myself a steaming mug of apple cider and watched as our instructor laid out the materials for her next project. The bare bones of craftwork have always made me nervous. Well, not always. When I was a very small child I wasn't scared of anything, but as I grew up and was scolded by a succession of teachers for untidy needlework and wobbly straight lines, I began to limit myself to the tasks I could do well. By the time my twenties rolled around, I was comfortable with my clumsy hands and had even developed a slight disdain for people who had the time for "unproductive" hobbies. In the city that was reinforced with a contempt for the amateur, an attitude that I didn't really review until we moved down here.

Pat was the first person to make me think about it, on one of my early visits to "Pickle Meadows." We had finished our usual tour of her wild guests and she invited me into the house.

"I've got something to show you," she said mysteriously, leading me past their comfortable sitting room to a door I hadn't been through before.

The room inside was like Santa's workshop. Huge lab counters dominated the center of the space, while the walls were lined, floor to ceiling, with shelves covered in thousands of dolls and tiny toys.

"This is what I make with them," Pat explained, conducting me over to a group of glass clock domes and doll's house frames, which contained the most exquisite miniature still lifes that this city snob had ever seen.

"Where do you find all the pieces?" I asked, touching a Tiffany lamp no bigger than my thumb.

"Everywhere from antique stores to garage sales," she replied, "and people bring me things. I've been collecting for a long time." The objects themselves were pretty, but it was Pat's ideas that turned the settings into art.

"They must make you a fortune," I said admiringly. She looked a little surprised. "Oh, I've never sold any," Pat laughed. "I do this purely for my own pleasure."

That thought stayed with me as I started to understand that personal fulfillment doesn't always depend on financial reward or other people's accolades. In the craft world, in fact, it doesn't even depend on traditional skills. I was delighted to discover that Pat also had been informed early in life that she would never be an artist and hadn't developed her own ways of being creative until her mid-twenties.

Her example, and my small daughter's enthusiasm, had encouraged me to try things like the Christmas wreaths and cards at home, but I had never played in public before. When I saw Karen's personal display of Swedish tree ornaments, I thought that now was not the time.

"They're so pretty," I said, picking up the delicate straw

bells, hearts, and stars, all bound in red satin ribbon. "They belong on a tree with strings of cranberries and popcorn."

"That's where I hang mine," she nodded.

"So you brought them today just to torture us with your skill."

"No." Karen grinned. "They're all real easy to make. Pick a design and I'll show you."

I chose a complicated-looking creation of interconnected circles, just to prove her wrong.

"No problem," she said airily, and instructed me to cut three strips of straw ribbon in descending order of size. I then turned them into circles with the help of a glue gun and wound the red satin around each one. Finally, I connected them at the top and covered the join with red berries and tiny sprigs of pine. Karen was right, the result was charming, despite my three thumbs. It also made me absurdly proud, like a small child producing a sticky painting or that first lopsided clay pot.

With a burst of confidence, I moved on to a heart and a star, and was about to start on a bell when I realized that Charley and I were the last ones there. Reluctantly, we helped pack up and left with a bag full of extra materials so that we could carry on at home.

"I wish we could have stayed there for ever and ever," my daughter sighed, as she carefully balanced her wreath across her knees.

"I do, too, Bug," I said, beaming at her in the rearview mirror. "I never expected to enjoy myself so much."

It would have been nice to have been able to finish the afternoon as leisurely as it had begun, but I needed to get down to some serious crafts of my own. Christmas week was just around the corner, and there were twelve gift baskets to finish before we started on the family's feast.

Giving some of our produce away is the final part of the

season. You have to share the bounty, or the process isn't complete. Hearing that my plum jam has brightened a Chicago breakfast or that Greg's peppers were eaten on a California beach is as much part of our harvest as a freezer full of food. We've made Christmas goodies for friends ever since our first garden in Chicago, but our projects have taken on a new dimension since we moved down to the farm.

"Something smells good—what are you making?" Greg asked, sniffing around the stove like a hungry dog.

"I'm baking small loaves of bread in the oven, and this," I explained, gently stirring a large pot, "will eventually be homemade cheese."

Greg peered at the coagulating mess in the pan and pulled a face. "Looks disgusting," he said with unnecessary honesty.

"Those are just the curds separating from the whey," I explained. "When it's all drained, pressed, and rolled in herbs, it should be as appealing as the store-bought stuff."

My husband paused and took a long, slow look around the kitchen. "Sal, do you realize how much time has gone into these baskets?" I followed his eyes across the rows of raspberry vinegar and jars of lemon curd to the recently filled boxes of Holiday Potpourri.

"I know," I admitted ruefully, "it has been weeks and weeks of work."

"How much would you have to charge to make these commercially worthwhile?"

"Don't ask." I winced. "It would depend on how many I produced and what size they were, but the big ones would have to cost at least a hundred dollars."

"Have you figured packaging and gardening hours into that?" Greg was unrelenting. "And wages for the extra hands that you would absolutely need?"

"No," I admitted. "But I'm beginning to realize that the baskets could only work if we were producing them in bulk—and we didn't move down here to start a factory."

"I'm relieved to hear that," he said seriously. "Now you can enjoy these for the special gifts they are and *after* the holiday turn that restless mind of yours to some practical plans for next year."

Greg had expected me to be disappointed, but I really wasn't. The past two years have been a learning process, and a new and better notion appears for each old one we scrap. The cheesemaking, for instance, was a secret experiment. April, the goat, was pregnant, and during my research into home-dairying techniques, I had discovered that chevre, in all its many forms, was the nation's hottest new cheese. If the recipes were as easy and delicious as the books made them sound, it might be worth investigating the pros and cons of producing it in bulk.

The exciting thing about the farm is that it constantly generates new ideas, which we can look into at our leisure before committing ourselves to any cost. In the end, I knew that the gardens and the greenhouse would probably be as much as we could handle, but I enjoyed playing with all the alternatives so much that I was unwilling to give it up. I had silently allowed myself one more year of looking for the agricultural can opener before pleasing Greg by concentrating on our plants. I would keep this plan to myself over Christmas so that my husband could also relax and enjoy.

I wish we could have persuaded Charley to do the same. Her expectations for Christmas had reached fever pitch and were now being inflamed by a bad case of greed. The child who had desired "nothing" when questioned by Santa last year now had a list that was growing to ridiculous lengths.

"I don't know where she's getting it from," I complained to Janet on the phone. "We're watching Christmas tapes every evening, so she's not seeing much TV, and she finished school ten days ago, which rules out pressure from friends.''

"Just look around you," Janet scoffed. "The advertising's everywhere—in newspapers, magazines, on the car radio, in the mail. The kid can't avoid it, not even down there.''

"This is more than just advertising," I said. "It's pure acquisitiveness. We were in the drugstore yesterday and she threw a tantrum over a bottle of Tylenol. 'I-Wannit' has become her middle name.''

It was the classic parental dilemma. You hope your child has a magical Christmas, but you don't want the holiday to be all about things. Janet's observation had been utterly correct. A moment's focus on the problem proved that our daughter's mind was under siege.

"She's being corrupted," I fumed. "I'm all for a consumer society, but not at our children's expense. They're setting the kids up for guaranteed disappointment. They can't have everything, and the gifts they *are* given often aren't what they seem to be in the ad. How do we convince her to care less about presents?''

Greg shrugged. "You're asking a bit much. She's only five years old. We have to set the right example and hope that time will do the rest. You've spent months putting together a great bunch of gifts for her. Don't even think of adding to it.''

I went through the list: the *Beauty and the Beast* tape; the *Beauty and the Beast* dolls; three new books; a crayon and pencil set; a doll's cradle carved by Dennis, with its own new "baby"; a Spirograph; Chutes and Ladders; animal face-paints; finger puppets; and, my one concession to her new desires, a soft-toy Rudolph whose nose lights up.

"Those," pronounced my husband, "are more than enough.''

But the pressure continued to mount. It reached its peak the day before Christmas Eve, when Charley and I took a quick trip to Target.

"Will Santa bring me that?" she asked, waving at a swing set.

"I don't think so," I hedged, trying to move her on.

"What about this?" she said, latching on to a large doll.

"Charley, stop grabbing at stuff." I finally lost it. "You don't realize how lucky you are," I bellowed, sounding like *my* parents. "You have a family and you are surrounded by people who love you. Christmas is about celebrating that love and trying to spread some of it about. It is never about being grasping or greedy. If you ask for anything else, Santa won't be stopping by this year." There was a round of light applause from a mother in the next aisle and my daughter burst into tears.

The car ride home was a quiet one. Our only conversation concerned a man who was standing by the side of the expressway, holding up a sign.

"What does his message say, Mama?"

"It says 'I will work for food.' "

"Why?"

"I suppose he's hungry, Bug. These are hard times. A lot of people can't find work, and if you don't work, you can't earn any money to pay your bills or to buy food."

Charley was silent. When we got home, she ran into the kitchen and opened the fridge. After some rummaging, she pulled out her juice boxes, two Jell-O puddings, and the chocolate brownie she'd been saving for dessert. A trip to her toy cupboard secured her schoolbag, into which she loaded the aforementioned items.

"I want to take these to the man by the road," she announced.

We walked back to the car without another word.

Christmas Eve dawned cold and clear, although we weren't up to see it. The Murphey family slept in, luxuriating in the knowledge that our preparations were complete and all Mama had left to do was some light cooking.

Our Christmas routine has evolved so comfortably over the past couple of years that its very dependability has become one of the season's pleasures. First, my husband cooks us a huge English breakfast of eggs, bacon, tomatoes, mushrooms, and fried bread to see us through to the evening. Then Greg and Charley disappear to wrap presents in the garage and I make the leek and Gorgonzola soup that always starts our holiday meal. While that's simmering away, I peel the potatoes, prepare the green beans and Brussels sprouts, and mix the batter for the Yorkshire pud. I make room in the fridge by removing our rib of beef, which is rolled in flour, cracked black pepper, and mustard before being stored in the summer kitchen to mature for the following day.

At this point, Charley usually appears for her bath and the hour-long process of washing her hair. That mane of red, which now hangs down to her hips, has to be carefully combed through and braided so she can live a normal life while it takes its four hours to dry. (We abandoned dryers, because they made her hair frizz.)

Father and daughter then settle in for the year's first viewing of A Christmas Carol (the 1938 version with Gene Lockhart), while Mom takes her turn in the tub, or, as Greg calls it, her "wallow."

This is the one day of the year when I'm left alone to get ready. That hour and a half of peace is one of my Christmas presents, when I can actually take the time to do my nails and put on some makeup without being constantly called away. The steam in the bathroom and the smell of perfume unknot the tension of muscles that have been working for weeks, and by the time I emerge I have totally unwound.

We don't dress formally on Christmas Eve—that's reserved for the day itself—but we do wear our nicest sweaters and best shoes, because the evening is a special one. At six o'clock I mix some mulled wine on the stove and set out cookies, candies, nuts, and fruit on the table for later. By 7:00 P.M. we're en route to church for the Christmas carol service. The drive takes us down one of the prettiest roads in the county, bending around wooded hills and past farmhouses that glow like jewels in the dark. This year a frost was forming and the sky was bursting with stars that painted the empty fields in soft silver light.

I reached over and touched my husband's hand. "I love you."

He smiled and squeezed my fingers. "I love you, too."

The church is always packed with people and we sat at the back, which suited Greg, who comes here twice a year just to please his wife. This man has a deep, private faith of his own, which isn't usually catered to by organized religion. It's a debate that he skirts around with our friend the Reverend Jonathan Hutchison, who began his sermon a moment before the greenery above Greg's head burst into flames.

A candle had burnt down faster than expected, catching the dry decorations of pine. Greg leapt to one side, grabbing a nearby cloth with which he started to beat at the blaze. Jonathan kept talking until he noticed two things—no one was listening and Greg was about to step on his guitar. The service came to a halt until the fire was put out and Jonathan's instrument had been moved to safety.

"Someone trying to tell you something?" the pastor asked his buddy from the pulpit. The whole congregation cracked up. It took Jonathan's wife, Deborah, and her beautiful alto voice to restore order and to fill the night with song.

We always stay at the end of the service to exchange the

season's greetings, but then it's a quick sprint home to get ready for the second part of our evening. The mulled wine is heated up, and shrimp, pâté, and a selection of cheeses join the other goodies on the table. Greg lights the fire, all our candles and oil lamps, and turns on the Christmas tree lights.

"Ready?" I call, before picking up the phone.

"Ready!"

Then I dial the number that I know as instinctively as my own.

"We're home."

"Oh yeah?" Big John grumbles. "What kept ya?"

Five minutes later, Terry, John, and Rebecca Dungan arrive at our door for one of the few social occasions that we share. The two families talk, work, hope, cry, and laugh together on an almost daily basis, but we rarely have the time to simply sit down and be. Christmas Eve has become the moment that's reserved just for us.

In a couple of hours, after they are gone, my daughter will get an important phone call. "Is Charley there?" a familiar voice will ask, and I'll reply, "Who's calling?"

"This is Santa. Put her on the line."

As she holds the phone to her ear, her blue eyes will widen and she'll whisper, "Yes, I'm off to bed right now."

Then Charley will scoot upstairs and fall asleep in seconds, with the sound of approaching sleigh bells ringing in her head.

John buys us this respite each year so that we can stuff stockings and arrange presents under the tree before going out to the barn with a big bag of corn. Legend says that you'd better take care of your animals especially well tonight, because at the stroke of twelve they are granted the gift of speech. We try to preempt any malicious gossip by giving them all a good meal.

The final assignment of the night is consuming the milk and cookies that were left out for Santa earlier in the evening. It will be the first thing that Charley checks on when she wakes up, before attacking her presents under the pickled pine.

Greg and I have decided that we bought a real Brown County tree. Not particularly fancy or expensive, but a sweet soul who makes you smile. A friendly fir, a comfortable conifer, whose Christmas spirit isn't based on appearances but on a feeling that will last us for many yuletides yet to come.

$\mathscr{S}$IMPLE GIFTS

"AT, TAT, TAT. . . . RAT, TAT, TAT."

"Greg, hear that?" I asked muzzily. "It's a bit early in the year for woodpeckers."

"Rat, tat, *tat*."

I opened my eyes. It was still dark. The alarm clock announced that it was 4:45 A.M. on a freezing Monday in late January.

"*Rat, tat, tat!*" It took a second for the horrible truth to sink in. That was no woodpecker—there was someone at the door.

"Sally, Sally!" Rebecca's voice floated up the stairs. "Sally, Hotshot's loose and we can't catch him."

"What?" I flung open the front door, hoping that I had misheard.

Rebecca looked disgusted. "Hotshot's been out all night," she explained. "He nearly caused an accident up the road and now he's over by our barn, but we can't get near him."

"I'll be right there—just let me get some clothes on."

As my hand groped for something warm to wear, it closed over the handle of the gun case. It would be so easy: One bullet straight between the eyes and then back to bed without missing a beat. "Yes, but what about the body?" asked a rational voice at the back of my mind. "You couldn't just leave it out on their front lawn. You'd have to dig a very big hole and bury it. I suppose you could trim it down with the chain saw first, but that would make a nasty mess. No, you'd have to lash it to the back of the Yugo and drag it home for the dogs."

By the time I found my boots, I was fully awake and the pleasant prospect of assassinating the horse was fading away, along with any hope of rest. If things followed their normal pattern, this was going to be a long morning.

Hotshot was in his usual spot when I arrived, standing by the Dungans' paddock, leering at Precious. Terry was waiting by the barn, her arms clutched around her in a fruitless attempt to keep warm. The facts of the story were even uglier than I had expected.

"Larry Collins called me because he didn't have your number," she began. "He would have come to help himself, but he had to fix the fence that Hotshot tore down. Apparently, one of his mules is in heat and Hotshot tried to go through the wire to get at her. When he couldn't, he ran onto the road and was nearly hit by a car." Terry always sounds phlegmatic, but this news was delivered in a total monotone. I didn't know what to wince at first.

"Was anyone hurt?" She shook her head. "Terry, I'm really sorry. You were telling me only last night how tired you were, and now I've robbed you of a night's sleep. I feel terrible."

My dear friend's mouth began to twitch. "Don't worry about it, Sally. Save your energy for the horse."

I had bought the regulation bucket of corn with me, which I now held out halfheartedly toward Hotshot. This was much too pedestrian a ploy, and it had never fooled him in the past. But to my surprise he wandered over and began to eat. He even let me touch him, at arm's length. Had he been wearing a halter, the whole incident would have come to an end right there. But he wasn't. His mane slipped through my fingers and I narrowly avoided a broken shin. If you ever need to catch a horse with no more than your bare hands, you have to get hold of his ear. Once you've established a firm grip, his heart and mind will follow. Hotshot knew this and took off for the safety of the trees, aiming a parting hoof at my legs. My heart sank. We were falling into our old pattern. From this point on, the more I tried to approach him, the more defiant and dangerous he would become. It was time to apply some new psychology.

Rebecca was sneaking up on him from the side. "No," I said quickly, "you'll only spook him." It was too late. Hotshot nickered in protest, reared slightly, and took off—in the direction of our farm. Becca and I dashed after him onto the road, the girl to warn passing traffic, while I jogged next to him to stop him from overshooting our gate. Headlights were coming over the hills, traveling fast. I tried to force the horse to the other side of the road, but his ears flattened in panic and he ran straight toward the approaching car.

Hotshot weighs about 800 pounds. Hitting him at forty or fifty miles an hour would be like driving headfirst into a brick wall. Rebecca overtook us, waving her arms wildly. The horse wheeled around and started cantering the other way. "No!" I yelled as loudly as I could, slowing him down just long enough to turn him back up the Dungans' drive. Rebecca, Hotshot, and I ended up exactly where we had begun, gasping for breath.

"Why don't we try the Precious trick?" I panted, suggesting the only thing that had worked in the past.

"Because she's pregnant," Rebecca explained, "and Mom's scared of upsetting her."

Judging by Hotshot's dejected expression, he wouldn't have been interested anyway. The animal was really frightened.

"Poor old fella," I said to him gently, "you've had a terrible night." The horse hung his head and looked very sorry for himself. I took a step closer. "Why don't you come on home, boy? There's a warm stall waiting for you and an early breakfast."

I took another step; Hotshot didn't move.

"Get my lunge line," I whispered to Becca, pointing at the rope that I had hidden by the barn.

"You're safe now," I continued, moving closer still, "I'll take care of you. I always do, don't I?"

There was a resigned expression on his face. Suddenly, I knew that Hotshot had given in. I reached up and stroked his strong neck. He nuzzled his head into my hand. I didn't even have to grab his ear. Rebecca quietly handed me the rope and I put it around his neck.

"Thank you," I said to both the girl and the horse, grateful for her help and for his first public gesture of affection.

We walked back home slowly, like good companions out for a stroll. Just before he got down to breakfast, Hotshot lifted his head and blew a warm blast down his nostrils straight into my face.

"Yes, old chum," I replied, "the feeling's mutual."

There were a couple of apologetic phone calls to make when I got in, and I was relieved to find that both Larry Collins and Terry had forgiven me. The damage to his fence had been minimal and Larry was prepared to treat the whole episode as a huge joke. My sense of humor only returned with the sensation in my feet, which had been frozen numb by the bitter cold.

The temperature continued to drop through the day and by the afternoon the weatherman was broadcasting warnings of a severe winter storm. "It could be the heaviest snow we've seen for several years," he said, looking serious for once. "We can expect at least ten inches, sometime tomorrow morning." Greg and I were actually pleased by the news, because at least it meant that the air would get a little warmer.

On the farm, snow is a temporary inconvenience, but ice can be a real problem. Icicles, for instance, had been indirectly responsible for Hotshot's escape, by shorting out the hot wire. Later in the morning, ice had frozen both doors to the barn shut, forcing us to gain access to the inside by climbing through a two-foot square hole known as the manure chute. We had already been breaking up the edge of the pond with a sledgehammer so that the animals could get to their drinking water, but now we would also have to hand deliver Hotshot's eleven gallons (through the manure chute), because he was confined to quarters until the fence could be fixed. Since the standpipe in the stable was frozen, his supply would be carried over from the house.

There is nothing more uncomfortable on a farm than hauling water in freezing weather. We've heard of people who got rid of all their stock and devoted themselves to raising corn after a winter of watering their animals. You slip and slide across the barnyard, arms twisted and stretched by two heavy buckets, while you desperately try to keep your balance. Inevitably, some of their contents will slop across your jeans, which will then bond to your skin as if they've been sprayed with superglue. By the time you reach the barn, you are wet, cold, and depressed by the prospect of repeating the entire exercise within the next few hours. If the snow was going to thaw out the plumbing and the barn doors, I welcomed it with both sprained arms.

The storm began at eleven the following morning, and by two o'clock it was snowing sideways. As the radio droned out an ever-growing list of closings and cancellations, it felt as if the world was shutting down.

"We're not going anywhere for the next few days." Greg stomped in from outside with a new stack of firewood to dry by the stove. "This is a big one."

"It doesn't matter, does it?" I looked up and smiled. "Our most important work is all at home."

Spring had already sprung in the Murphey household. The grow lights in the summer kitchen shone down over Greg's first batch of tomato seedlings, my herb and geranium cuttings were sprouting nicely in the hall, while we both sat in the living room, wielding one of the gardener's most useful tools: our pencils.

It was seed catalog time again—that delightful moment when plans and dreams promise to correct last year's mistakes. Seed catalogs are a gardener's escape route through frosted windows to sunny flower beds outside. Like an old photo album, they remind us of the early days when our love of horticulture was undamaged by bagworms, black rot, or drought. They also go a long way toward explaining why country people seem so much calmer than city folk. Wars, depressions, disease can shake society to its very core; then Burpee's or Field's drops into the mailbox to remind us that we can and must prepare for a future after all. Our urban friends are offered no such optimism. They measure their time in seconds, not seasons, and demand instant solutions to problems that have the whole nation scratching its head.

Perhaps politicians would benefit from some of nature's lessons—the ones we have to learn, if we want our gardens to grow. Simple rules like:

1. **Feed your foundation before you scatter seed.** Your stock can be the best, but without a benign environment, it will shrivel up and die.

2. **Care for your progeny plant by plant.** Not all your vegetables can conform to the same high standard. Some very useful stock might have crooked stalks or

nibbled leaves—that doesn't mean that they can't bear fruit.

3. **At harvest time, don't take it all.** You need your seed for next year and something should be ploughed back in to supplement the soil.

4. **Be generous—don't always expect to reap the best of what you've sown.** Good gardeners leave a legacy for their land and for the generations to come.

This year, Greg and I were paying even closer attention to our spring plans than usual. Several friends had asked us over the winter whether we'd have any seedlings to sell, and we had decided to produce our first commercial list. Predictably, my husband hadn't been enthused until I pointed out that we could avoid being overwhelmed by restricting its distribution to a small number of people, and by not starting the seed until the orders came in. "That seems reasonable," Greg agreed, "but is it worth doing on such a tiny scale?"

"I think so, for two reasons," I explained. "First, we only need about ten orders to cover the entire cost of our seed and fertilizers—which could save us a couple hundred dollars. And, more important, it's an interesting experiment in market research. What people want to grow is also what they're likely to buy, which will provide some ideas for the Farmer's Market in May."

"I thought you'd given up on that," Greg groaned.

"I gave up on the food baskets. The market is an altogether different matter."

Picking out our first plant list was such fun that we had finished it by dinnertime. "We have only one decision left," I announced to the family over an appropriately hot and heavy shepherd's pie. "We have to choose a name for the farm." A general moaning and grumbling broke out around the table, referring to the fact that we had tried and failed before. Greg's favorite, "The Island of Lost Souls" was obviously out, as was Charley's choice, "The Blooo Farm." My "Wild Thyme Meadows" was met with derisive stares.

"Guys, we must make up our minds," I said firmly. "We have messed around with this since we got here."

Greg looked thoughtful. "Well, I still like the one we came up with in the first place," he admitted. "It's straightforward, but a little bit different. People outside the county will think it's very pretty. Remember how we reacted to it when we first arrived?"

"That's true," I agreed. "I'm all for it. What do you think, Charley?"

My daughter nodded enthusiastically.

"What do *you* think, Oscar?" Greg asked the faithful lump at his feet, who flashed his wide bull-terrier grin. "That's it then. Oscar approves," my husband said solemnly. "From now on, we live on Bean Blossom Farm."

Doc Brester continued his battle for Oscar, but had only managed to hold his condition steady. The dog's white body was still covered in oozing sores, which looked even worse because the animal had lost so much weight. Bullterriers are supposed to be the body builders of the dog world—muscular, deep-chested, like dragging a small safe around. Oscar had been lying on the couch so long that his muscles had begun to atrophy. Now his spinal cord had curved and we could count each vertebra along his back. Greg and I didn't discuss it, but we both knew that every day with Oscar was an added bonus. City friends flinched when they saw him and dropped heavy hints about putting him down, but our country pals understood and shared our respect for the stout-hearted little dog who had never stopped fighting for his life.

"Do you think we're being cruel?" I asked Terry, knowing that she'd be honest.

"Not at all," she assured me. "Oscar enjoys himself and he's not in any real pain. I'd trust Doc Brester to tell you when it's time."

Terry had called to announce the birth of two kids, who had appeared at the height of the storm, and issue the ritual invitation to Charley to come over and give them their first pets.

The sun was out and the Bug and I had already been planning an expedition to the woods—before all those footprints in the snow melted away. It would be Charley's first tracking lesson and my chance to check up on an old friend.

We began our afternoon at John and Terry's barn, where the twin goats staggered over to us and butted at our hands. The little female was all white and had been christened Snow. The little male, as black as his sister was light, had no name yet and was the shyer of the two, running off and hiding behind his mama's legs. As Charley cuddled each of the babies in turn, I marveled at the force with which life asserts itself, even in the midst of a storm that had brought half the state to a halt.

For once my daughter was eager to move on, so we crossed back to our farm and started up the side of the big pasture. Walking across a virgin stretch of snow feels almost sinful—like leaving dirty footprints over a clean kitchen floor—but we soon found that others had been there before us.

"Look, Bug, a raccoon," I said, pointing to the handprints down the side of the hedge. "And what do you think this is?"

"A birdy," she guessed, staring at the tiny Y-shaped tracks.

"They do look like that, don't they? But what's this mark behind the prints?" I asked, pointing to a thin line that slithered through the snow.

Charley thought for a moment. "A tail?" she answered tentatively.

"Very good, Bug," I congratulated her. "Those are muskrat tracks."

The front of the field may have been relatively untouched, but the back was like Grand Central Station. We counted the hoofprints of eight deer leaving the edge of the trees to make their way to our lake. They had been supervised by a ninth, standing in a grove from where he had a sweeping view of the farm. I would have recognized his tracks anywhere. The stag had beaten the hunters for another season and was guiding his herd through the hardships of winter. I made a mental note to leave them a salt lick and some corn, to jointly celebrate our continued survival.

"Look, Mama, a kitty." Charley tugged at my sleeve, dragging me over to a set of felinelike prints along the middle of the deers' trail.

"No, Bug, they're not from a cat, but from another very clever fellow. See how he's tried to walk where the deer walk, to hide his tracks and mask his scent? And over here, where there were no deer—see how he runs zigzag from tree to tree? These are fox tracks, Charley. Let's follow them to see where they go."

Luckily, the animal had turned toward the woods and not, as I had feared, toward our chickens in the barn. We checked the perimeter of the pond pasture carefully, but there was no sign of any predator hanging around our birds.

"Mama, my feet are *freezing*," my daughter finally complained. "It's time to go home."

We walked back to the house along paths shoveled clear by my husband in our absence and found him stretched out on the couch, in front of a roaring fire. The living room was flooded with orange sunlight and the smell of roasting chicken, which Greg had already put in the oven for dinner. Charley got her finger puppets out and invented stories around the day's events, while I curled up in my chair, clutching a book and a steaming cup of tea. As the hot, sweet liquid did its restorative work, I studied the scene.

"You know," I announced, "no amount of money could buy a better life."

But Greg's snow shoveling activities cost him dearly. When he came down to breakfast the next morning, he had turned a nasty shade of green.

"What's the matter with you?" I asked as he lowered himself stiffly into his chair.

"It's the old pain again," he said grimly. "Only this time it's worse." We both looked at each other, openly scared. It was no longer a question of insurance or cost. Something had to be done to find out what was wrong.

Our doctor was as nonplussed as ever. He referred Greg to a urologist who, three weeks later, began a series of tests.

"We won't hear anything for about ten days," Greg reported, "and I don't know why, but I'm feeling better again."

"It's the psychological relief," I said. "The medical establishment has finally made a move. Let's hope that it's in the right direction."

Greg's mood had also improved because spring was threatening to burst out in a quite spectacular fashion. The daffodils were up in record numbers, the bushes all were covered in buds, and our roosters were pouncing on any bird that moved.

Chickens molt once a year, so when our flocks' tail and wing feathers started to fall out, I wasn't that perturbed. But when large bald patches began to appear on all our hens' backs, I called Doc Brester.

"I don't usually treat birds," he admitted, "but it sounds like a molt to me. Are they scratching a lot?"

"No," I replied, "I haven't seen them scratching at all."

"Well, you could try putting sassafras bough in their coop," he suggested in his characteristic mumble. "That would discourage lice."

"Is it available commercially?" There was a long pause.

"Pardon me?" asked the vet.

"Where do I get some?" I said, trying to speak clearly. Even people who know me have problems occasionally with my English accent, and Doc Brester seemed to have more difficulty than most.

"You go and cut one down in the woods," he said patiently. I felt myself turn red. This time the misunderstanding had been mine.

We followed the Doc's advice, but the hens' condition seemed to be getting worse. My poultry books, which had lurid chapters full of chicken's diseases, didn't offer a clue. There was only one person, I was sure, who could diagnose the problem. I called Pat.

"They're missing these large triangles of feathers on their backs," I explained, "and the skin underneath looks really inflamed."

"It's nothing to worry about, Sal." She sounded amused. "Your skin would be a bit irritated, too, if it was being constantly clawed. The bald patch is where the roosters hold on."

The hens were actually in more danger from the dogs, who were also suffering from a dose of spring fever. We don't clip our birds' wings, on the theory that their only defense is their limited ability to fly. The downside of this policy is that we always have a few escapees scratching around the yard. Over the winter, Lady and Tramp had generally ignored them, but now their fluffy little bottoms were like a red rag to a bull. Tramp, remembering the lessons of last year, confined himself to chasing and raising a few squawks. Lady set about her work seriously, killing three birds within the first week of March.

"What has gotten into you?" I asked the unrepentant dog.

"You're supposed to be the responsible one. I'm ashamed of you. There'll be no dinner tonight."

Her head drooped and she slunk away to sulk about her loss, but the lesson still hadn't hit home. On Saint Patrick's Day, she ran a bird down right in front of me and had to have her jaws prized apart before she'd let go. Miraculously, the hen got up and tried to run, carried along by a bad case of shock. She was trembling all over when she came to a halt and meekly submitted to being picked up. Her wounds reminded me of those of Lady's victim in the fall, and of the mistakes I'd made that had cost that bird her life. This time I was determined the patient would prevail.

Poultry are notoriously difficult to nurse, which is why most veterinarians choose not to deal with them. The country cure for an injured hen is normally a quick blow to the head and chicken stew for supper. If I wanted to doctor my birds, I'd have to teach myself how.

"What I really need is an antibiotic," I told Pat. "Is there anywhere to buy some?"

"Have you got any penicillin left over from the other animals' prescriptions?"

We had a bottle full, I remembered, from when Lady had been spayed.

"Try half a tab ground up in the chicken's water," Pat suggested. "It couldn't do her any harm."

An antibiotic of a different kind was causing an uproar in the house. Two shiny red capsules, administered twice each day, were having a dramatic effect on Oscar. He was packing on the pounds, his sores had started to dry up, and he was taking a sudden interest in the garbage. We hadn't caught him with his nose in a trash can since the last time he was well, but there had been so many disappointments in the past that initially we didn't dare to hope.

Then, one afternoon, he climbed down off the couch and, to everyone's surprise, began to play with Tramp. The Doberman regarded this new barking, wagging, bumptious bullterrier with a look of amazement before extending a gentle paw and bowling the shorter dog over. Oscar got to his feet and charged his friend, knocking him across the room with the force of a small white cannonball. There was a lot of yipping and growling, and the two of them were soon a wrestling mass of jaws, paws, and happy tails. Greg stared at the animal he had nurtured for so long with a delighted grin on his face. When the game was finished, my husband knelt on the floor and gave his proud, panting dog a big hug. Oscar, not naturally demonstrative even in the best of health, responded by treating his master to a very sloppy bath.

The world seemed to be smiling on us. Oscar continued to improve, a lucrative business contract appeared, and the chicken, now called Henrietta, was well on the mend. Greg also claimed to feel better despite the doctors, who had come up empty-handed yet again. "I'm going to do some planting," he announced one morning. "It's almost too late to put in our peas."

"You're two weeks earlier than last year," I reminded him, "and the ground has only really thawed out over the past couple of days."

"Are you coming along?" Greg asked, scraping back his chair.

"No, I've got to finish getting the incubator set up."

You might think that with three roosters strutting around the yard, we would be knee deep in baby chicks. But the only broody birds in the barn are two geese who had just gotten busy with clutches of their own. Before we began to keep hens, I had assumed that every egg layer would have her broody day, but this isn't the case. Some sit on their eggs for a morning, then move because they're bored. Others lay them and simply walk away. A few set out with good intentions but, after a meal break, forget where they left their nest. We are not talking Darwin here—it's amazing that the species has survived.

The solution to the problem occurred to me only when people started to turn up at our door wanting to buy fertilized eggs. Why not get an incubator and raise the chicks ourselves? Dennis encouraged me. "You've got a real touch for this," he said. "Not many folks have a feel for birds. You've got to be born with it."

Natural gift or not, hatching eggs is not as easy at it sounds. The incubator arrived with a list of dire warnings. Set the temperature too low, they said, and you'll end with "large, soft-bodied chicks"; set it too high and get a mysterious-sounding "sticky hatch." Forgetting to turn the eggs is likely to result in "cripples and malpositions," and bad ventilation breeds the mind-boggling "mushy chick." I put the apparatus together with extra care and had been adjusting the thermostat inside the box for two days to get it to a consistent 99 degrees.

The thermometer was right on the money and I had just finished loading in the eggs when Greg reappeared with a worried look on his face. "I don't feel so good," he confessed. "I think I should lie down."

Within a few hours, my husband's "discomfort" had turned into crippling pain. I was ready to take him straight to the emergency room, but our doctor demurred.

"They won't do anything until tomorrow," he explained. "They'll just administer pain killers, which I've already prescribed. Bring him to me first thing in the morning and we'll take it from there."

Neither of us slept much that night. As soon as one dose of codeine wore off, Greg was in agony until the next one took effect. I sat by him with my heart in my mouth, trying to reach for any possible explanation. Then, at 2:00 A.M. my husband groaned and clutched at his right side. A memory from childhood stirred at the back of my mind. A long-ago image of lying doubled over in bed, hand pressed against my lower abdomen.

"Appendix," I murmured. "Greg, what about your appendix?"

We repeated the word to the doctor the next day, whose eyebrows shot up. A blood test showed that Greg's white cell count was 17,000. "It should be 10,000," the doctor explained, "maybe 12,000 with a bad infection."

"So what would cause such an elevated count?" we asked.

"Appendicitis," he replied.

He sent us straight over to the hospital, where the surgeon agreed with the diagnosis except for the fact that it had been going on for so long. "If I hadn't heard the history," he told Greg, "you'd be on my table within the hour. But—pain since November? I think we should take a CAT scan first."

We will be eternally grateful to this man, who pulled out all the stops without even knowing whether we could pay for the treatment. Doctor David Wipperman saved Greg's life by finding an abscess the size of a large grapefruit sitting in his abdominal cavity. The appendix had rotted away long before, but my husband's strong body had cocooned the infection off in a bag that grew and grew until it had nowhere else to go. Greg's "attacks" had been small ruptures in that bag. His periods of feeling better were after his system had sealed it up again.

Doc Wipperman wisely spared us the details until after the operation, when we met in the hallway outside Greg's room. "Hauling cameras, chopping wood." The doctor shook his head. "The abscess could have burst at any time. It's a miracle, really," he concluded. "Most people would have died."

It has taken Greg about six weeks to start getting his strength back. He has spent most of that time sitting under spring blossoms that were every bit as beautiful as they had promised to be. For the first time since we moved here, the dogwood, lilac, and redbud all burst into bloom at once, filling the hedgerows with sky-sized cotton candy.

"It's going to be an incredible growing season," Greg said wistfully, "and we won't even have a vegetable garden this year."

"Now, don't you get frustrated," I warned him. "I've arranged a small surprise."

The following day, nineteen-year-old Bret Frederick turned up, employed to clear, dig, and plant under Greg's close supervision. Between them, they have started a more abundant garden than we ever will have had before.

My plans for the farmers' market have had to be postponed, but this has actually been a good moment to pause and reflect. A brush with death is the best sinus medicine I know—there's nothing quite like it for clearing the head. Greg says he has been given a second chance: "And I'm not going to waste it." He was poring over his artwork from the moment he was mobile and seems to spend more time with Charley than he used to in the past.

I've taken longer to process it all. In fact, for the first few days I was paralyzed by the unthinkable emptiness that Greg would have left behind. In the middle of the night I'd touch him to prove that he was there and move over so that I could fall asleep in the fragrance of his hair.

I was snapped out of this rather mawkish behavior by the sound of breaking shells. Twelve chicks pecked, rolled, and head-butted their way into the world with not a mushy one among them. After twelve hours in the incubator getting a slow blow-dry, they were moved to the nursery cage, where they have delighted everybody with simple tricks like eating, walking, and falling over.

"That's great," Pat enthused. "What are you going to hatch next?"

"Well, I'd thought of it more as an occasional event."

"Would you like to try some peacock eggs?" my friend went on, ignoring me.

"Would I! I've always wanted a couple of those."

I went out to share the exciting news with Greg.

"You know, I've seen those advertized in the papers for five hundred dollars a pair—which is why I never thought of getting any. If I am good at this, why not raise some of the more exotic breeds? Nothing too big to start. If the peacocks work out, we could try swans, perhaps, and some of the really ornamental ducks."

My husband's eyes twinkled. "I'm glad to see you're feeling better."

This summer we plan to build a wood fence for the garden and finish the glass in the greenhouse, but mostly we plan to relax. There is little point in being with the people you love, in such a beautiful setting, unless you take the time to enjoy it together. Our months in Brown County, culminating in Greg's illness, have taught us, above all, that time is life's most precious asset. It is not an empty vessel that needs to be filled, and at least for a while, we won't be cluttering ours up with any big projects—with the exception of one that can't wait.

Steve came down from Chicago recently to watch us start work on the stand of white pine at the back of the big pasture. Two tree surgeons had been hired to bring the lumber down, while Greg and I worked with chain saws, cutting the branches on the ground and stacking them into manageable piles. Everyone wore hard hats and safety goggles because taking out fifty-foot trees can be a dangerous operation. By the end of the day, our city friend was openmouthed.

"Why do you bother?" he asked.

I pointed to Charley, playing on her swing.

"Because one day she will inherit both the business and the farm. She probably won't need either at that point, but the moment may come when she wants to come home. If she does, she will find that we have provided for her. She will be able to live off this land and be beholden to no one—and when she's old, she will remember the time that we cut down the white pines and planted black walnuts in their place. They're an investment tree, valuable because they take seventy years to mature. We won't live to see them fully grown—but then it wasn't *our* retirement we were planning for."

* * *

The yellow swallowtail had stretched her damp wings out to dry on the warm gravel of the parking lot.

"Look! A butterfly!" Charley pointed, almost dropping her popsicle.

Jack McDonald, owner of the grocery store that his grandfather started in 1891, walked up behind us. "It has been hanging around all day," he said, before scooping the beautiful creature up and gently depositing her on Charley's outstretched hand. "Want to take it home, honey?"

My daughter nodded solemnly.

He disappeared into his store, reemerging with a cardboard box.

"What do you say to Mr. McDonald?" I asked, doing the maternal bit.

"Thank you," Charley answered breathlessly, as she settled her treasure in for the ride.

"You could put her on the honeysuckle when we get home," I suggested in the car. "They're full of nectar right now. She'd like that."

Charley nodded, pulling back the box flap for the twentieth time to outline our plan to the bemused butterfly.

My daughter stood outside for an hour that night, watching the swallowtail take delicate sips from each blossom. Getting Charley to bed was even harder than usual, and the moment she woke up in the morning, it was back to the bush in her jammies. I watched my little girl from the kitchen window, bright young face bathed in sunlight, squinting at the orange flowers.

She gasped suddenly and hopped, then turned and ran into the house. "She's still there, Mama," Charley shouted, crashing past the screen door. "She stayed, she stayed."

"Of course she did, Bug. Where else would she want to go?"

APPENDICES

THE APPENDICES: AN EXPLANATION

It probably seems a little odd to include reams of recipes and garden plans at the back of a self-contained story. I mean, what is this—a cookbook, a gardening book? Define yourself, please! Well, our reluctance to do that is where this book began, and to leave out the "Murphey's Lore" that we have picked up along the way would be to cheat the reader by telling only part of the tale. We hope you enjoy the following as much as we have.

$\mathcal{F}$OOD FROM THE FARM KITCHEN

CHAPTER 3

Golden Mushroom Soup Serves 4

Homemade soup is one of life's great luxuries, and it doesn't necessarily have to take a lot of time. This recipe is at its most delicious in the spring, when we use mushrooms that we have gathered ourselves and our own rib-of-beef broth. But we like it almost as much during the rest of the year, when the mushrooms are store-bought and the broth is canned.

1 pound fresh mushrooms,
    sliced
½ cup onions, finely diced
¼ cup butter
¼ cup flour
¼ teaspoon salt
¼ teaspoon pepper

1 pint beef stock
1 pint whole milk
1 cup heavy cream
¼ teaspoon paprika
½ teaspoon Worcestershire
    sauce
⅓ cup garlic chives, chopped

In a medium skillet sauté mushrooms and onions in butter until soft. Blend in flour, salt, and pepper. Pour mixture into a large saucepan and add remaining ingredients. Cook over medium heat, stirring constantly, for about 25 minutes until the broth and all the flavors have blended into a creamy soup. Do not boil. Serve garnished with chopped chives and a little floating pat of butter.

Betty Cooper's Roast Capon   Serves 6

Although I would never admit it to his face, my husband is the finest cook I know. He never forgets a meal that he liked, and he can re-create almost any dish at will. This recipe was first made for him by his much-loved nurse, Betty Cooper, when he was a very small child. It was one of his favorite Sunday dinners and one of the first things that the teenage Greg taught himself to cook.

1 roasting capon (6–7 lbs., preferably free-range)	1 tablespoon parsley, finely chopped
Salt	1 tablespoon basil, finely chopped
Six slices bacon	
2 sticks of butter	2 capfuls Kitchen Bouquet
1 medium/large onion, finely chopped	1 14-ounce can chicken broth
4 celery stalks, finely chopped	2 slices white bread, toasted
1 small green pepper, finely chopped	2 slices brown bread, toasted
3 teaspoons paprika	1 cup cornbread stuffing
Seasoned salt	¼ pound of mushrooms, washed and diced
Seasoned pepper	¼ pint heavy cream
	4 teaspoons unbleached flour

Remove giblets from capon, wash and set aside in a pan of water. Rinse bird inside and out with cold water, pat dry with paper towel, and rub inside and out with salt.

Stuffing

Fry bacon slices in a large skillet and set aside.
Melt 1 stick of butter in bacon grease and fry onions until soft.
Add similar amount of celery and green pepper.
Season with some of the paprika, seasoned salt and pepper, some of the parsley, a little basil, and a capful of Kitchen Bouquet. Add ⅓ of a can of chicken broth. Crumble bread into stuffing mixture, add cornbread, mushrooms, and crumble in bacon.

The Bird

Preheat oven to 450°F. Stuff bird, add a little chicken broth to bottom of roasting pan. Cover with foil, put into oven, and turn temperature down to 350°F. Baste every 30 minutes. Cook for 2 to 2½ hours, taking tent off at 1 hour, 45 minutes, so bird can brown. When done, let stand for 20 minutes before carving.

Gravy

After the bird has been put in the oven, boil all giblets (apart from liver) with paprika, seasoned salt and pepper, parsley, and basil for 30 minutes. Allow to cool in pan. When the bird is ready, mix strained giblet water with juices from the roasting pan. Stir in cream, the other capful of Kitchen Bouquet, seasoned pepper, and a little more paprika. In a small dish, beat 2 teaspoons of flour with a little cold water, and whisk into gravy, using an egg whisk. (The gravy should be very thick, the consistency of heavy cream. Whisk in more flour and water mixture if necessary.) Cook over very low heat, stirring constantly, for 10 minutes.

Russian Raspberry Pudding   Serves 4

This is the ideal pudding for those who don't like their desserts
to be too sweet. If fresh berries aren't available, you can substitute canned or frozen, but drain off some of the liquid after
they have been warmed in the oven, otherwise the batter will
end up floating in its own juice.

1½ pounds raspberries   3 eggs
   (or blackberries)   ¾ pint sour cream
4 tablespoons sugar   1½ tablespoons flour
½ lemon

Preheat oven to 300°F. Wash berries, drain, and turn into an
ovenproof dish. Sprinkle with 1 tablespoon of the sugar and a
little lemon juice. Warm the dish in the oven for 10 minutes.
Meanwhile, beat the eggs first, then add the sour cream and
flour until the ingredients form a smooth, pourable batter. Pour
the batter over the warm berries and cook for about 50
minutes, until firm and golden. Serve with heavy cream on the
side.

Butterscotch Cookies   Makes 20–24 cookies

I'm not usually the one caught with my hand in the cookie jar, but these are so delicious that they disappear almost as soon as they're made. The cookies only take about 15 minutes from start to finish, so I sometimes bake them on the spur of the moment when somebody drops by for tea. They are at their most scrumptious when they're warm and soft, straight from the oven.

1 stick butter	1 capful vanilla essence
4 tablespoons dark brown sugar	1 cup all-purpose unbleached flour
4 tablespoons white sugar	½ teaspoon baking soda
1 egg	1 cup butterscotch chips

Preheat oven to 375°F. Beat butter and sugars together until fluffy. Beat in egg and vanilla, followed by flour and baking soda. Stir in butterscotch chips. Using a teaspoon, drop mixture onto greased cookie sheets, allowing an inch and a half between each heap, so the cookie has room to expand. Bake until golden (about 12 minutes). Cool on wire rack.

Charley's Famous Brownies   Makes 15 brownies

There's nothing children enjoy more than something they have made themselves. Charley began "helping" in the kitchen, arranging salad vegetables in the bowl or "rounding" (stirring) things when she was three. By the time she was three and a half, she had graduated to decorating sugar cookies and making her own peanut butter on bread, and we started baking together when she was four. This is the first recipe she cooked herself. All I do is handle the oven and help her with the measuring. I have to pack an extra portion of these in her school lunch because her teachers love them so much. (They *say* they just want to encourage her cooking because it helps her practice her fractions!)

1 cup cocoa	1 teaspoon vanilla
2 cups sugar	1 cup flour
1 cup melted butter	½ teaspoon baking powder
4 eggs (at room temperature)	½ teaspoon salt

Preheat oven to 350°F. Stir cocoa and sugar into the melted butter. Gently beat the eggs and vanilla together and add to the butter mix. Sift in flour, baking powder, and salt. Mix together well and pour into a buttered, floured, square brownie baking dish. Bake for 35 to 40 minutes, testing center with a round-bladed knife to see if it is done. (When the knife comes away clean, the brownies are cooked.) Allow to cool for 20 minutes before cutting into squares.

CHAPTER 4

Cheezy Scalloped Potatoes   Serves 4

We all have at least one family recipe whose very name conjures up feelings of security and warmth and being cared for by a big person. Greg and I recently discovered that scalloped potatoes were a shared childhood favorite, which, we're delighted to say, has now been passed on to Charley.

5 or 6 large potatoes	Nutmeg
½ stick of butter	1 cup Parmesan cheese,
1 cup of milk	grated
Seasoned salt	Paprika
Black pepper	

Preheat oven to 375°F. Peel and finely slice potatoes. Put the butter and milk in a saucepan and warm gently until the butter is melted. Grease an 8-inch by 8-inch baking dish (or equivalent) and line with one well-overlapped layer of potatoes. Sprinkle generously with seasoned salt, pepper, nutmeg, and Parmesan, then cover with the next layer of potatoes and season as before. Add the third and final layer and sprinkle with paprika and Parmesan. Pour milk and melted butter over potatoes. Bake in the center of the oven for about 45 minutes, or until the crust is golden brown.

CHAPTER 5

Greg's Tacos Serves 4

As the weather heats up each year, we go through a period of adjustment, switching from the "stick-to-the-ribs" meals of winter to the lighter foods of spring. Greg's tacos, which are substantial without being heavy, bridge the gap perfectly. He also makes them in the summer, using fresh herbs and produce from our garden.

1 large onion, finely chopped
1 clove garlic, chopped
1 tablespoon peanut oil
1 pound ground sirloin or 1 pound shredded steak meat
1 jar medium-hot salsa
1 14-ounce can beef broth
1 tablespoon Kitchen Bouquet

2 tablespoons tomato ketchup
2 sprigs fresh cilantro, chopped
Pinch of cumin
Pinch of chili powder
Pinch of cayenne pepper
Pinch of black pepper
Pinch of turmeric
12 to 15 large taco shells

Toppings

1½ cups shredded lettuce
1½ cups chopped tomatoes
1½ cups chopped scallions
1½ cups grated cheddar

1½ cups diced avocado
1 cup sliced black olives
1 cup chopped fresh cilantro
1 cup taco sauce

Sauté onion and garlic in one tablespoon of oil until brown. Add meat and sauté until brown. Stir in the rest of the ingredients, mixing well, and turn heat down to low. Simmer for 30 minutes. Preheat oven to 300°F. Spoon meat into shells and place on cookie sheet or in a baking dish. Cook for 15 to 20 minutes, until shells soften to the touch and are thoroughly warm. Serve with toppings (set out in separate dishes), refried beans, and rice.

CHAPTER 7

Terry's Baked Bean Casserole Serves 8

When you ask Terry Dungan for a recipe, she just grunts and says, "I dunno—I just throw stuff together." I wheedled this out of her because it is one of the highlights of her family's fall barbecue party every year.

¼ pound bacon, chopped
1 medium onion, chopped
1 2-pound can of pork and
 beans or 2 pounds of
 homemade baked beans.

⅓ cup brown sugar
½ cup ketchup
½ teaspoon mustard
¼ cup barbecue sauce

Preheat oven to 375°F. Gently brown bacon and chopped onion in a frying pan. Mix all other ingredients together in a casserole. Add browned bacon and onion. Stir well and bake in oven for 1 hour. Serve with coleslaw and pit-barbecued pork.

Blue Ribbon French Almond Apple Tart
Serves 6 to 8

I always thought that this was a prizewinner. I'm so happy that Brown County has made it official. The secret, as with all good pastry, is to work it (touch it) as little as possible. Keep your hands and tools cool (I soak my hands in cold water and put my rolling pin in the fridge for 15 minutes), and you'll cook up a crust light enough to please the angels.

The Crust
1¼ cups unbleached all-purpose flour
Pinch of salt
5 tablespoons butter
¾ tablespoon white sugar
¾ tablespoon demerara sugar
2 teaspoons ground almonds
1 egg yolk
2 to 4 tablespoons cold water

The Filling
1½ pounds Granny Smith apples
½ teaspoon lemon juice
¼ cup demerara sugar
½ teaspoon nutmeg
½ teaspoon cinnamon
½ teaspoon ground cloves
3 large cooking apples, peeled, cored, finely sliced

The Glaze
1 small jar apricot jam
1 teaspoon lemon juice

Preheat oven to 400°F.

The Crust
Sift flour and salt together, then rub in butter until the mixture looks like bread crumbs. Stir in sugars and almonds. Add egg

yolk and enough water to make a dough. Wrap dough in plastic wrap and chill in refrigerator.

The Filling

Peel, core, and chop Granny Smith apples. Put in heavy-based saucepan with lemon juice and sugar. Slowly bring to boil, reduce heat, and simmer. Mash with a potato masher, then add nutmeg, cinnamon, and cloves to taste, a little at a time. Roll out dough and line an 8-inch flan dish. Fill with apple puree. Cover top with overlapped apple slices, starting at the edge and working inward until the tart is covered with a wheel of apples. Bake in oven for 25 to 30 minutes, until the edges of the apple slices are golden brown.

The Glaze

Melt apricot jam in a small pan, over a gentle heat, until liquid. Mix in lemon juice. (You could strain the glaze at this point, but I think the little bits of apricot make the glaze.) Pour over the top of the dish, using a pastry brush to spread it to the edges. Allow to cool and set. This is particularly delicious when served warm with a dollop of whipped cream.

CHAPTER 8

About Preserving

Canning, preserving, and pickling are crafts that go back in history to the first caveman who salted his kill. It can take a lifetime to learn all the subtleties of food preservation, but the basic how-tos are relatively easy. The rules below come from several publications that I would recommend highly to anyone who would like to go beyond the simple recipes in this book: the *Ball Blue Book* (published by the Ball Corporation, Muncie, Indiana); *Stocking Up: How to Preserve the Foods You Grow, Naturally,* (Rodale Press, 1977); and my favorite, *Fancy Pantry* by Helen Witty (Workman Publishing, 1986).

Preserving Rules

1. Use only self-sealing Mason jars for foods that have to be processed. Old jelly jars or pickle jars may have scratches or dents inside them that harbor germs, and they do not have lids that will seal properly. The number of jars used in a recipe may vary each time you make it. Density, evaporation, even the weather can affect the bulk of food you have to preserve, so don't be surprised if the recipe that yielded ten jars last time now only produces eight. It's a natural mystery, like lost socks at the Laundromat.

2. Make sure that all your equipment is scrupulously clean. You don't want to process any bacteria along with your food. Sterilize all jars, bottles, lids, and seals by washing them in the dishwasher or by washing them in hot soapy water (do not use any abrasive scourers

or brushes, as they will scratch the glass surfaces), and then boiling them in a water bath for at least 10 minutes. (This is done by boiling water in your canner—which is simply a large enamel pot—and soaking your equipment in it for 10 minutes. Just make sure that all the jars are covered with at least 2 inches of water, which is kept at a rolling boil throughout.) Allow your jars, lids etc., to air dry on a wooden board or on paper towels. Never put the hot jars on a cold counter because they will crack or shatter.

3. Fill the warm jars with the food to be processed, leaving at least ½-inch of headspace at the top. Run a wooden or plastic spoon around the inside to squash any air bubbles before screwing the lid down tightly.

4. If the food is to be processed, lower the jars into the canner using a jar holder, leaving an inch of space between each. Make sure that they are covered by at least 2 inches of boiling water. If the water has cooled, bring it back to a rolling boil and time your processing from there.

5. Cool jars on towels or a wooden board. Listen for a loud *ping* as each lid seals itself. Children love to be given the job of counting the *pings* to make sure that there's one for every jar.

6. Allow to cool for about 24 hours, then test lids. If the center feels solid, with no give to it, the jar is sealed. If the lid is still flexible, the jar hasn't sealed and you should refrigerate and eat the food immediately.

7. Label the cool jars (what it is, when made, etc.) and store in a cool, dark cupboard.

Tomato Paste   Makes about four 8-ounce jars

This is the homemade version of those little cans of paste that we throw into everything from spaghetti sauce to stews. I bottle it in small jelly jars, which yield enough for two to three meals. Refrigerate once open.

5 pounds ripe tomatoes   Seasoned salt
1 stick butter   Celery salt
1 cup dark brown sugar

Dip tomatoes in boiling water and peel. Melt butter and stir in sugar. Chop tomato flesh and add to butter. Season to taste with salts and cook over very gentle heat, stirring regularly, until the mixture has reduced to a thick paste. Bottle in sterilized jelly jars and process in a boiling water bath for 1 hour. (See "About Preserving," page 236.)

Tomato Ketchup   Makes about 1 gallon

I don't encourage the use of ketchup with everything, but I do feel better about my family using it when it's homemade. Charley still insists on eating the store-bought stuff!

10 pounds ripe tomatoes	½ tablespoon coarse ground
4 yellow onions, finely	black pepper
chopped or grated	1 tablespoon cinnamon
2 teaspoons horseradish	½ teaspoon cloves
mustard	½ teaspoon ginger
2 cups demerara sugar	½ teaspoon nutmeg
1 cup red wine vinegar	¼ teaspoon paprika
1 tablespoon salt	Dash of Worcestershire
2 tablespoons seasoned salt	Sauce

Dip tomatoes in boiling water and peel. Chop flesh and mix with chopped or grated onion. Cook in a preserving pan or heavy saucepan until stewy (about 25 minutes). Sieve sauce and return to pan. Add other ingredients and mix well. Cook over a very gentle heat for about 7 to 8 hours, until it is smooth and thick. Bottle and process in a boiling water bath for 20 minutes. (See "About Preserving," page 236.)

Tomato Soup
Serves 4

A steaming bowl of this is our standard central heating on cold winter days. For dinner parties, I serve it with a teaspoon of sour cream floating in each bowl, which has been sprinkled with chopped garlic chives or the tender green part of a scallion.

4 tablespoons butter plus 1 pat	4 tablespoons flour
1 tablespoon onion, grated	2½ quarts hot milk
1 tablespoon green pepper, minced	½ pint heavy cream
1 tablespoon celery, minced	1 egg yolk, beaten
4 cups cooked or canned tomatoes, strained	1 teaspoon basil, fresh or dried
1 teaspoon salt	1 teaspoon parsley
3 teaspoons demerara sugar	Pinch of nutmeg
½ teaspoon coarse ground black pepper	Pinch of paprika
	Dash of lemon juice

Melt a large pat of butter in a skillet, and soften onion, peppers, and celery. Add tomatoes, salt, sugar, pepper. Cook over gentle heat for 35 minutes, then put through blender. In a large saucepan, melt the 4 tablespoons of butter over a moderate heat, and mix in the flour with a wooden spoon until all the lumps have gone. Cook this roux for 3 minutes. Slowly add hot milk to roux, a little at a time, stirring constantly. When well blended, add cream and beaten egg yolk. Beat in blended tomato mixture and bring to boiling point. Reduce heat and simmer, adding spices, lemon juice, and herbs to taste. Cook for 10 minutes. If you can fight the family off from eating this immediately, allow it to cool, then store in doubled-up freezer bags and freeze. Will keep for 6 months.

Cacciatore Sauce   Serves 8

Directly translated, this is huntsman's sauce—designed to go over any kind of grilled meat. We like it best over steaks or chicken breasts, with baked potatoes and a green salad.

1 tablespoon peanut oil
2 heaped teaspoons garlic, minced (either fresh or in oil)
1 large onion, finely chopped
1 small can tomato paste

2 pounds of cooked or canned tomatoes, drained
1 glass red wine
Seasoned salt to taste
Coarse black pepper to taste
½ pound mushrooms, cleaned and chopped
½ teaspoon basil (fresh or dried)

Warm oil in skillet. Gently sauté garlic and onions, until soft. Add tomato paste and mix in well. Add tomatoes and mash up in pan, then pour in the red wine. Season to taste with salt and pepper, then add mushrooms, and a pinch of basil. Cook on low heat for at least 30 minutes, stirring occasionally. If you are going to use it right away, put it into an ovenproof dish and keep warm in the oven while you are grilling your meat. When the meat is done, spoon sauce over it before serving. If you want to store it, just allow it to cool in the skillet. Double-wrap in freezer bags before freezing. It will keep for 6 months.

Gazpacho Andaluz

Serves 6

This is my favorite summer soup. It will freeze, but it is best eaten fresh. Add crusty garlic bread and side plates of hams, salamis, and cheeses, and it makes a meal in itself.

4 thick slices white bread
2 tablespoons red wine
    vinegar
3 large cloves garlic, crushed
3–4 tablespoons olive oil
1½ pounds cooked or
    canned tomatoes, drained

1 cup tomato juice
2 pimientos from a small
    can, finely chopped
1 large onion, grated
1 small cucumber, grated
1 teaspoon salt
Pepper to taste

Garnishes (all chopped)

1 cup cucumber
2 cups green and red peppers
4–6 scallions
1 cup celery

1 cup tomatoes
1 cup croutons (we like the
    cheese ones with this)

Cut the crusts off the bread and blend them to make fine bread crumbs. Turn into a large bowl and mix in the vinegar and the crushed garlic. Gradually add as much of the olive oil as the crumbs will absorb. Stir in the tomato pulp, the tomato juice, and the very finely chopped pimientos. Grate in the onion and cucumber, and add salt and pepper to taste. Mix together well and blend until smooth. Color, if necessary, with a little tomato paste. Season again and add more tomato juice or water (keep tasting to decide), if you need to thin out the soup—it should be very thin. Chill. Finely chop the garnishes and serve on separate dishes. Load up your bowls with these—think of this as less of a soup and more of a floating salad.

Salsa

Makes about 2 pints

There are dozens of different recipes for salsa. I like this one because it's quick! Having said that, it tastes best when it has been left for a few hours to absorb all the flavors of the various ingredients. I usually make it the night before I plan to use it and store it in the fridge. This will also freeze.

2 pounds tomatoes, peeled
   and chopped
3 tablespoons lemon juice
1 tablespoon lime juice
6 ounces green chili peppers,
   diced
3 tablespoons cilantro
1 tablespoon parsley
1 cup scallions, chopped
2 heaped teaspoons minced
   garlic in oil

½ cup green pepper,
   chopped
½ cup sweet red pepper,
   chopped
½ teaspoon black pepper
¼ teaspoon cayenne pepper
½ cup tomato sauce
Splash of Tabasco sauce

Mix everything together in a large bowl. Take one cup of mixture and blend thoroughly. Then mix it back into the other ingredients. Chill overnight, then serve or freeze.

Sal's White Bread

Makes 3 loaves

Freshly cut grass and baking bread are two of the world's best smells. City friends claim that they're too busy to bake their own, but I make this on a Saturday morning, once every two or three weeks, as I'm doing my chores. I prepare three loaves at one time, freezing two of them. Thirty minutes in the oven at 300°F will defrost the loaf, and it will taste as good as it did when it was just baked.

Since there are no preservatives in the bread, feel free to eat it in large chunks. Once left out, it will probably mold within four days.

1 level tablespoon dried yeast	3 pounds unbleached or bread flour
2 level teaspoons sugar plus 1 level tablespoon sugar	4–6 level teaspoons salt
1½ pints warm water	4 tablespoons peanut oil

Grease and flour 3 large loaf tins. In a small bowl, mix yeast with 2 teaspoons sugar and add half of the warm water (¾ pint). Leave in a warm place for 15 minutes, or until mix has foamed up. In a separate bowl, sift together the flour and salt. Stir in 1 tablespoon sugar. Make a well in the center and pour in the oil. Add yeast liquid and remaining water *at the same time,* then draw ingredients together with a fork or your fingertips. Turn out onto floured surface and knead for at least 10 minutes, until dough is smooth. Bread-making machines— *bah!* Kneading is great therapy—and it's free. Go on, take out all your frustrations: punch it, pull it, pound it—just stop when it's not sticky anymore, or the dough will get tough. Shape dough into a ball and put into a large greased bowl. Cover with greased plate and leave to rise in a warm place until it has doubled in size. Punch down and turn out again onto floured surface and knead until smooth. Divide equally into 3 pieces, shaped to fit tins. Place in tins, dust lightly with flour and cover with greased waxed paper. Leave to rise in a warm place for about an hour, until light, puffy, and at least double in size. Bake for about 45 minutes, just above oven center, at 450°F. The loaves are ready when the bottoms sound hollow if tapped. Turn out onto wire cooling racks.

To Freeze
Double-wrap in freezer wrap and label with date of baking. Take out of the freezer two hours before you want to eat it, or heat in a moderate oven for 30 minutes.

Mustard Vinaigrette

Makes enough for 1 salad

We use this dressing in the summer on our *insalata tricolore,* or sometimes simply over a split, ripe avocado. (If you want to make the avocado a bit more elaborate, add a spoonful of crabmeat to its center, or some baby shrimp, then dribble the dressing over it.) For the salad, use beefsteak tomatoes, preferably homegrown, fresh buffalo mozzarella cheese, and fresh lettuce leaf basil. Arrange in alternate strips of green, white, and red on a serving dish. Pour the dressing over the salad just before you eat.

2 teaspoons horseradish mustard	1 teaspoon salt
2 teaspoons red wine vinegar	1½ teaspoons sugar
	1 cup peanut oil

Using an eggbeater, mix mustard and vinegar together in a bowl. Add salt and sugar, then dribble in oil, a little at a time, beating hard all the way. This should be light and frothy, and shiny, almost like mayonnaise. Don't be afraid to use extra oil if you need it.

Greg's Belt-Buster Steak   Serves 6

You will probably have to ask your supermarket butcher to cut this especially for you. Don't be put off by the large quantity of meat. Six people at a dinner party will eat it all, and when we cook it just for ourselves, we use the leftovers to make tacos (Chapter 5) or beef Stroganoff (Chapter 10).

1 5 to 7-pound sirloin steak,
   2–3 inches thick (the
   thickness is essential)

Marinade

¼ cup dark soy sauce
2 tablespoons maple syrup
¼ cup teriyaki sauce
4 tablespoons Worcestershire
   sauce
4 tablespoons Chinese oyster
   sauce
4 tablespoons ketchup
1 teaspoon ground ginger (or
   2 teaspoons grated fresh
   ginger)

1 teaspoon seasoned salt
1 tablespoon coarse ground
   pepper
1 teaspoon paprika
1 clove crushed garlic (or 1
   teaspoon garlic in oil)
2 tablespoons steak sauce
½ teaspoon cayenne pepper

Combine all marinade ingredients and soak the steak in them for at least 2 hours, preferably 4–5 hours. Turn steak occasionally to cover in marinade. On a very hot grill or barbecue sear one side of the steak for 1 minute before flipping the meat over and cooking it for 8–10 minutes for medium-rare, 15 minutes for medium-well. *Never* pierce the steak with a fork—use tongs or a spatula *only*. Flip the steak and grill the seared side for five minutes. Serve, sliced across the width, not across the length, using the juices as gravy.

CHAPTER 9

Egg Recipes

As you can imagine, I have become an avid collector and inventor of recipes that use large quantities of eggs—the more the merrier. I thought I would include some of our favorites here. But first I thought I should include some tips on how to keep eggs fresh.

Storing Eggs

Stored properly, eggs will stay fresh for three months. If you have farm-fresh eggs, don't wash them. The shells have their own natural seal, which you will wash off, and the eggs will spoil much more quickly. At most, wipe them with a moist kitchen towel and store in the refrigerator *point down*. Eggs will absorb the smells or tastes of food around them, so it is best to keep them in cartons.

Frozen eggs will keep for six months. The best freezing method I have found is to break the eggs into the individual compartments of an ice tray. Once frozen, turn them out and store in double-wrapped freezer bags.

Quiche Lorraine   Serves 6

The leathery, dried-up offerings that are usually served to us in restaurants have given this dish a bad name. It should be a deep, fluffy golden mixture, dripping in all the richest dairy products. The basic batter remains the same, whether you are using bacon, mushrooms, broccoli, crab meat, or all of the above. When quiche is made properly, "real men" will fight for seconds!

The Crust
3 cups unbleached all-
purpose flour
Pinch of salt
1 stick of butter

½ cup Crisco
1 egg
Splash of white vinegar
Iced water

The Filling
1 tablespoon butter
8–10 slices strongly smoked
bacon, finely chopped
5 eggs and 1 yolk
¾ pint heavy whipping
cream
½ cup cheddar cheese,
grated

½ cup Swiss cheese, grated
Seasoned salt
Ground white pepper
1 bunch scallions, finely
chopped

The Garnish
Tomato slices

Parsley

Preheat oven to 400°F. Pour flour and pinch of salt into a large
bowl. Rub in butter and Crisco until flour has the texture of
fine bread crumbs. Make a well in the center and break in the
egg. Add the splash of vinegar and mix dough together with a
fork. If the pastry is still too hard, add a little iced water until
it is the right consistency. Wrap in plastic wrap and chill for
30 minutes. Melt butter in a skillet. Sauté bacon gently. Beat
the eggs and yolk in a bowl until frothy. Add cream, cheeses,
and seasonings. Mix scallions with the bacon and fry until softened, then turn the entire contents of the skillet into the egg
mixture. Roll out pastry on a floured board and line a 10-inch
flan dish. Pour in filling and bake until golden—about 45
minutes. Garnish with thin slices of tomato and a small bunch
of parsley in the center.

Baked Egg Custard

My Nana Moyce used to make *the* best egg custard in my small child's world. I have experimented with all sorts of different recipes to come up with the closest to hers. This is it. The orange is my addition. It can be left out for a more traditional taste.

1 pint milk	2 egg yolks
1 tablespoon butter	1 capful vanilla extract
Zest of a small orange	1½ tablespoons white sugar
2 eggs	Whole nutmeg, grated

Preheat oven to 350°F. Heat milk, butter, and orange zest in a pan until it is just simmering. Beat the eggs, yolks, vanilla, and sugar together in a bowl until just frothy. Stir in the hot milk. Strain into a greased pie dish and finely grate nutmeg over the top. Set in a roasting pan, in ½-inch of hot water, and bake in the oven for about 30 minutes, until light gold on top. Serve immediately. Some people will also eat this cold, but not in this house!

Norwegian Cream   Serves 6–8

Put aside your diet, shelve your morals. This is the killer dinner party dessert of all time. People have been known to groan when they see it approach, but only because they know that they are going to eat it all.

¾ pint milk
5 eggs
2 tablespoons sugar
½ teaspoon vanilla
1 pint heavy whipping cream
1 12-ounce jar apricot jam
1 egg white (freeze the yolk
    for another time)

Approximately 1 cup
    coarsely grated dark
    chocolate (not baker's
    chocolate)

Preheat oven to 325°F. Warm milk over a low heat. In a mixing bowl, beat 4 eggs and 1 egg yolk together with sugar and a little cold milk (saving the fifth egg white for the topping). Add warmed milk and vanilla, and strain into a lightly buttered 2-pint oval pie dish. Bake in a warm bath (just put ½-inch hot water in a roasting pan and stand dish in it), for about 1 hour, until firm and a little brown on top. Whip cream until thick and chill in the fridge for at least an hour. Remove custard from oven and leave to cool. Warm apricot jam in a small pan until fairly liquid and spread on top of custard. Chill in the refrigerator for at least 90 minutes. Whip the 2 remaining egg whites until very stiff and gently fold into the whipped cream. Heap on top of the pudding, in soft peaks (the pudding should be set firm and cold before you try this, or the cream will melt), and decorate *lavishly* with the grated dark chocolate!

Victoria Jam Sponge Cake   Serves 6–8

We each have our own talents and our own incapacities. As I
have confessed before, I am totally incompetent when it comes
to fine work. I can't draw a straight line, sew a neat stitch, or
ice cakes with that delicate lacework we all admire so much.
So when it comes to my family's birthday cakes, I have had to
improvise. My solution has been to create pleasing shapes instead of pretty designs. Charley gets a ladybug, sniffing at the
flowers; Greg, a camera or a basket of tomatoes. Every part of
the cakes is edible. I begin with the sponge recipe below—
baking it in an appropriately shaped bowl, dish, or tin before
covering it with colored almond paste or marzipan and decorating accordingly.

For less formal occasions, I make the cake as specified and just
sift confectioners' sugar over a lace doily that has been laid on
top of the cooled sponge. When the doily is removed, the beautiful sugar pattern remains.

1½ sticks butter
¾ cup white sugar
3 large eggs
1 capful vanilla extract
1½ heaping cups self-rising
   flour

1 12-ounce jar black
   raspberry (my favorite),
   plum (good substitute), or
   strawberry (if you insist)
   jam

Preheat oven to 350°F. Grease and lightly flour two 9-inch cake
tins. In a bowl, beat the butter and sugar together until creamy
white and very fluffy. Add the eggs, one at a time, beating each
time. Mix in the vanilla and beat in the flour. Divide the sponge
mixture between the two cake tins and bake in the middle of

the oven for about 30 minutes. When a round-bladed knife slipped into the cake's center comes out clean, the sponge is done. Turn out onto wire cooling racks and allow to cool for at least 30 minutes. Place the bottom half on your display dish (browned side down), then spoon the jam onto the middle of the cake. Press the other half down on top, *gently,* and dust with confectioners' sugar.

Hotel Scrambled Eggs
Serves 4

Most master chefs say that it is the simplest dishes that are the hardest to cook well. Scrambled eggs are no exception. This recipe is a compilation of hints collected from hotels like the Dorchester in London, the Crillon in Paris, and the Hotel Taprobane in Sri Lanka. You can add cheese, ham, or diced smoked salmon, but this recipe is so deliciously rich that it really needs no amendments.

8–10 large eggs
½ cup milk or half-and-half

½ teaspoon salt
¼ stick butter

Break the eggs into a large bowl. Using a shell, remove the thin white membrane from around the yolks. Mix in milk and salt. Don't whip the eggs: beat gently until the whites and yolks have combined and the mix is smooth and consistent. Melt the butter in a large skillet over low heat. Pour in egg mixture, gradually increasing heat to no more than medium. Let eggs begin to form up (as in an omelet), then keep from sticking to the pan by gently scraping away from the sides and bottom of the skillet. Turn heat down as eggs begin to harden and keep breaking them up and turning them with a spatula. Serve with buttered toast and bacon.

Greg's Pan-fried Fish   Serves 4

This will work with just about any fish—but obviously the fresher, the better. Try and find out what is caught in your area rather than use what's shipped in frozen.

1 cup peanut oil
1 stick of butter
3 large eggs
3 cups unbleached flour
2 tablespoons seasoned
    pepper
2 tablespoons seasoned salt

2 tablespoons paprika
1 tablespoon garlic powder
1 tablespoon chopped
    parsley
1 tablespoon chopped basil
2 pounds skinned and filleted
    fish—your choice

Heat oil with butter in skillet. Do not let butter burn. Beat eggs in one bowl until frothy. Mix flour with seasonings in separate bowl. Dip fish pieces in egg batter, then roll in flour mixture. Drop into hot fat and cook, turning regularly until golden brown. Serve with wedges of fresh lemon and/or tartar sauce.

Green Salad
Serves 4

Green salads can be *so* boring. This is our attempt at trying to avoid the same old, same old.

1 head romaine lettuce
1 cup cucumber
¾ cup scallions
¾ cup green pepper
½ cup garlic chives
2 teaspoons minced garlic
1 teaspoon salt
½ teaspoons white sugar

Freshly ground black pepper
½ cup balsamic vinegar
Dash lemon juice
⅔ cup olive oil
½ cup Parmesan cheese, grated
Caesar salad croutons

Wash, drain, and shred lettuce. Finely chop rest of vegetables and chives. Put 2 teaspoons of garlic in bottom of salad bowl, mix with 1 teaspoon of salt, 1½ teaspoons of sugar, and freshly grated black pepper. Add about ½ cup of balsamic vinegar and a small dash of lemon juice. Mix together thoroughly. Beat in about ⅔ cup of olive oil. Put salad on top of dressing and sprinkle generously with Parmesan and croutons. Toss just before serving.

Brown County Apple Butter   About 22 12-ounce jars

I hadn't tasted this sweet, cinnamony spread until we moved here and I was quite suspicious of it at first. Now I am an addict. The butter is a local specialty, served with warm, fluffy biscuits. Everyone has his or her own version, but no one makes it better than the Nashville House restaurant. My thanks to them for this recipe.

2½ gallons of applesauce
   (preferably homemade)
1 gallon hot water

⅓ cup ground cinnamon
8 cups of sugar

Preheat oven to 350°F. Mix all the ingredients together in a large Dutch oven and bake for 6 to 8 hours, stirring at least once an hour. Geraldine, from the Nashville House, says that the butter is done when it is medium thick and a deep burgundy color. There should be no liquid on top of it. Pour into warm sterilized jars and screw lids down tight immediately. Store in a cool, dark cupboard. Will keep for up to a year unopened. Once open, refrigerate.

Mustard Piccalilli
Makes about 15 12-ounce jars

The British do love their relishes so. I have tried to introduce Greg to the whole range, but this is one of the few that he likes. I serve it on cheese sandwiches, as a relish with cold cuts and baked potatoes, and on the side with chicken pot pie. If the quantities seem a little much, just halve them.

12 pounds vegetables (cauliflower, onions, marrow or zucchini, cucumber)
Salt
1½ quarts cider vinegar
1 pound white sugar
5 tablespoons mustard powder
2 tablespoons ginger root, grated
⅔ cup unbleached flour
3½ tablespoons turmeric
2 teaspoons garlic powder
½ teaspoon allspice

Peel and chop vegetables into small florets or 1-inch cubes. Soak overnight in salted cold water. Warm the vinegar in a heavy-based saucepan until gently simmering. Add the sugar and stir until dissolved. Add the mustard and ginger. Mix the flour, turmeric, garlic powder, and allspice with a little of the hot vinegar, then add to the pan. Stir until thickened, then add the vegetables. Simmer over a very low heat for about 45 minutes, until vegetables are soft but not mushy. Pour into warm, sterilized jars and process in a boiling water bath for 25 minutes. (See "About Preserving," page 236.) Store in a cool, dark cupboard. Refrigerate once open.

Sweet and Sour Red Cabbage

Makes about 5
12-ounce jars

Generally, we eat this with roast pork loin or maple-baked ham. But I have also learned to use it as an ingredient in beef stew and in the meat filling for shepherd's pie (chapter 12). It adds a subtle, tangy kick.

¼ cup peanut oil	1 cup cider vinegar
3 large cooking apples, peeled and chopped	1 cup dark brown sugar
1 large onion, chopped	1 teaspoon ground cloves
10 cups red cabbage (about 4 pounds), shredded	1 teaspoon ground allspice
	1 tablespoon orange juice
	Salt and pepper

Heat oil in a Dutch oven, then add apples and onion. Cook, uncovered, over moderate heat until softened. Add cabbage and cook for about ten minutes, until cabbage has also softened. Add vinegar, then stir in sugar, spices, and orange juice. Salt and pepper to taste. Reduce heat, cover, then cook for 20–25 minutes, or until the liquid has been absorbed. Transfer pan to oven and bake at 250°F. for a further 30 minutes. Ladle cabbage into warm, sterilized jars, and put in canner at a rolling boil for 20 minutes. (See "About Preserving," page 236.) Store in cool, dark cupboard. Refrigerate once open. Keeps for about 6 months.

Greg's Roman Peppers

Makes about 4
1-quart jars

The Romans knew a thing or two. These are a delicious addition to winter bean, pasta, and potato salads, or eaten as a relish with simple grilled meats. Use the leftover oil in salad dressings.

15–20 fresh green and/or red sweet peppers	1 gallon olive oil
	4 large sprigs purple basil
1 cup pickling salt	8 whole cloves fresh garlic

Preheat oven to 350°F. Wash and slice peppers into four pieces. Spread on a lightly greased cookie sheet. Bake for 20–30 minutes, until you can peel them easily. Cool them on counter, then sprinkle with pickling salt. Cover with paper towels and leave for 1–2 hours, to allow salt to leach peppers' moisture. Towel-dry peppers. Warm the olive oil over medium–low heat. Put a sprig of the basil and two peeled cloves of garlic in the bottom of each warmed, sterile quart-size jar, then cover with a layer of the peppers. Pour in enough of the oil to cover the layer. Add another layer of peppers and cover again with oil. Continue until the jar is full. Put lid on immediately and screw down tight. Store in a dark, cool cupboard. Refrigerate once open.

Steak and Kidney Pie   Serves 6

The use of oysters in this recipe may seem very extravagant today, but a century ago, when this dish became popular in Britain, the shellfish were poor man's eating. They are worth including because they make the gravy so rich—but you can leave them out if the idea doesn't appeal to you. Do try and use a good cut of beef, like sirloin tip or round steak—it makes all the difference to the taste. Serve the pie with buttered boiled potatoes and cabbage or greens that have just been shown the boiling water!

The Crust

3 cups unbleached all-purpose flour	1 stick of butter
Pinch of salt	½ cup Crisco
½ teaspoon sage	1 egg
½ teaspoon thyme	Splash of white vinegar
	Iced water

The Filling

1 cup flour	1 stick of butter
2 teaspoons (approx.) salt	1 large onion, finely chopped
2 teaspoons coarse ground black pepper	1 heaping teaspoon minced garlic in oil
2 teaspoons paprika	1 12-ounce can beef broth
2 teaspoons fresh parsley	2 cups red wine
2 pounds beef, cut into 1-inch cubes	Splash Worcestershire sauce
1 pound kidneys, washed and sliced	1 capful Kitchen Bouquet
	1 dozen canned oysters
	1 egg yolk, beaten

The Crust

Mix flour, salt, and herbs together. Rub in the butter and Crisco with your fingertips until the mix looks like fine bread crumbs.

Make a well in the center and add the egg and the vinegar. Draw together with a fork, adding water, if necessary, to form a smooth, firm dough. Wrap in plastic wrap and chill for at least 30 minutes.

The Filling

In a large bowl, mix flour, with 1 teaspoon each of salt, pepper, paprika, and parsley. Turn beef cubes and kidneys into flour mixture and toss until thoroughly coated. Melt butter in the bottom of a Dutch oven. Add onion and garlic and cook gently until softened. Add beef and kidneys and brown on a higher flame. Add beef broth and stir until thickened. If the filling seems too liquid at this point (it should be creamy), pour off some of the broth. Add the red wine and season with a good splash of the Worcestershire sauce, the Kitchen Bouquet, and salt, pepper, paprika, and parsley to taste. Cook on a very gentle heat for about 20 minutes, until the meat is tender. Drain off any excess liquid and add the oysters. Cook for a further 5 minutes. Preheat the oven to 425°F. Pour filling into a large pot pie dish and cover top with rolled-out crust. Make sure that the crust isn't touching the filling. You can trim this to look neat, but I leave the edges hanging over for a more rustic look. Using a fork, prick a cross of holes in the center of the crust, and brush it with a beaten egg yolk. Bake in the oven for 15 minutes, then lower the temperature to 350°F. and continue cooking for another 50 minutes.

Bread and Butter Pudding   Serves 4

Don't confuse this with the rich, fat-filled bread pudding. This is a light, golden custard, which used to be served in nurseries all over Britain by stern nannies of the nineteenth century. Today it is one of my most popular desserts among American adults.

8 slices white bread, lightly buttered	2 eggs
2 ounces golden raisins	3 level tablespoons sugar
Rind of 1 lemon, grated	1 pint vanilla-flavored milk

Remove crusts and cut the lightly buttered bread into 1-inch squares. Put them in a greased ovenproof dish, with alternate layers of golden raisins mixed with the grated lemon rind. Beat the eggs with 2 tablespoons of the sugar and all the milk. Pour this custard over the bread. Sprinkle the remaining sugar over the top, and bake the pudding in a preheated oven, at 350°F. for about 30 minutes, until fluffy and golden.

Roast Beef and Yorkshire Pudding   Serves 6

One of the best international combinations in our household is the American standing rib roast, cooked using this British recipe, which was originally published by the London Sunday *Times*. We now serve it for Christmas dinner every year, and at other times, when I'm feeling homesick.

The Yorkshire Pudding

1 cup flour

¼ teaspoon salt

1 egg

1 egg yolk

8 ounces milk

The Beef

Rib of beef (allow ½ pound
   per person)

1 teaspoon mustard powder

1 tablespoon flour

1 tablespoon black pepper

2 glasses red wine

The Yorkshire Pudding

In a bowl, sift together the flour and the salt. Make a well in center and break in the egg and the egg yolk. Beat by hand, then pour in milk while still beating. Let batter stand in the refrigerator for at least an hour.

The Beef

Preheat oven to 425°F. Rub mustard, flour, and black pepper over beef. Place in roasting pan and sear uncovered in oven (without turning) for 20 minutes. Turn temperature down to 375°F. and roast meat according to weight. (Allow 20 minutes per pound + 20 minutes searing time for medium-rare. Subtract 20 minutes for rare, add 20 minutes for well-done.) Baste surfaces of meat with pan juices every 30 minutes. Halfway through, pour off fat and set aside. Pour 1 glass of red wine over beef and keep basting. Five minutes before beef is done, heat the beef drippings that were set aside in an 8-inch cake tin in oven. Take beef out and allow to stand for 30 minutes. Turn oven up to 450°F. and pour Yorkshire pudding batter into drippings when they are smoking hot. Cook for 20–25 minutes until the pudding is puffy and golden brown. Just before carving beef, make gravy by pouring 1 glass of wine into pan and simmering with juices. Serve with horseradish sauce, roast potatoes, and a green vegetable.

Murphey's Meat Loaf   Serves 6

Equating this recipe with those of most other meat loaves is like comparing chuck steak with the finest filet mignon. It is my husband's concoction, and he'll spend a whole winter's afternoon carefully preparing it. Greg serves it with buttered Dutch noodles and green beans. We eat the leftovers in toasted sandwiches with lettuce, tomato, and mayonnaise.

1 pound ground sirloin
1 pound ground veal
1 pound ground pork
2 eggs, lightly beaten
¼ cup bread crumbs
 (homemade—grind a slice
 of white bread in the
 blender)
½ cup ketchup plus 3
 tablespoons
2¼ cups red wine
1 onion, finely chopped
1 small green pepper, finely
 chopped
1 small carrot, finely
 chopped

½ stick butter
1 tablespoon seasoned
 pepper
1 tablespoon paprika
1 teaspoon seasoned salt
½ pound mushrooms,
 cleaned and sliced
1 12-ounce can beef broth
2 tablespoons Worcestershire
 sauce
¼ cup heavy whipping
 cream
1 teaspoon Kitchen Bouquet
¼ cup flour

Preheat oven to 350°F. Combine the meats in a bowl and mix in lightly beaten eggs, bread crumbs, ½ cup ketchup, and ¼ cup red wine. In a skillet, sauté onion, green pepper, carrot in butter until soft. Add to meat mixture and mix in pepper, paprika, and salt. With your fingers, kneed together and form into a rectangular loaf. Bake uncovered in a greased ovenproof dish for 15 minutes. In a skillet, sauté mushrooms in a little butter.

Add beef broth, 3 tablespoons ketchup, the remaining ¼ cup red wine, and 2 tablespoons Worcestershire sauce. Bring to boil and simmer until mushrooms are cooked, about 10 minutes. Remove gravy from heat. Remove meat loaf from oven and pour ½ inch of mushroom gravy into the bottom of the meat loaf pan. Do not pour over the top of the loaf. Set remainder of the gravy aside and return pan to oven. Continue cooking for another 75 minutes. When meat loaf is cooked, remove from oven and put on a plate to cool. Add remainder of mushroom gravy to the drippings in the pan and bring to simmer over a low heat. Add ¼ cup of cream and a teaspoon of Kitchen Bouquet. Mix in well and bring back to a simmer. In a small bowl, mix ¼ cup of flour with very hot water from the tap, until it has a creamy consistency. Pour slowly into the simmering gravy and stir until thick, adding more flour and water mix if necessary. Slice meat loaf and pour gravy over top.

Garam Masala Chicken Curry   Serves 4

In Britain, Indian restaurants abound in the way that Chinese restaurants do over here. I was raised on curry—the hot stuff, guaranteed to bring a blush to the cheek and a tear to the eye. As an adult, I discovered that all this suffering was unnecessary. These five-alarm curries come from the southern parts of the subcontinent. The northern areas, like Kashmir, have a much milder and more subtle cuisine. Even Charley loves this dish, served on a bed of saffron or tumeric rice, with mango chutney on the side.

1 tablespoon peanut oil
1 large onion, finely chopped
1 teaspoon minced garlic
1 heaping tablespoon Madras curry paste
1 heaping tablespoon garam masala curry powder
1 small can tomato paste

1 cup canned or homemade chicken broth
Splash lemon juice
2 pounds boneless, skinned chicken breasts, chopped into bite-sized pieces
½ cup sour cream
¼ cup slivered blanched almonds

Warm the peanut oil in a large skillet and fry the onion and garlic until just brown. Add the curry paste and the garam masala curry powder. Mix in well and cook for 5 minutes, stirring continually. Add tomato paste and thin down to a runny consistency with chicken broth and a splash of lemon juice. Put in chicken pieces and simmer for at least 45 minutes, stirring occasionally, until the chicken is cooked. Allow the sauce to thicken; it must be the consistency of thick gravy when ready. Add about ½ cup of sour cream. The curry should be golden orange in color. Before serving, mix in almonds and cook for another 5 minutes.

CHAPTER 10

Nancy Kappes's Apple Cheese Torte   Serves 6

This is one of those recipes that makes the most rank amateur look like a pastry chef—which is not to underrate Nancy, who is one of the best dessert makers I know.

The Crust

1 cup butter
⅔ cup granulated white sugar

½ teaspoon vanilla
2 cups flour

The Filling

1 8-ounce package cream cheese, softened
¼ cup sugar plus ⅓ cup sugar
1 egg, beaten
1 teaspoon vanilla
6 Granny Smith apples, peeled, cored, and sliced

½ teaspoon cinnamon
½ teaspoon ground cloves
Lemon juice
¼ cup blanched and sliced almonds
Dark brown sugar

Preheat oven to 450°F. To make crust, cream butter and sugar together, then add vanilla and flour. Mix well and press into the bottom of an 8- or 9-inch springform pan. Chill for 20 minutes. Beat the cream cheese, ¼ cup granulated white sugar, egg, and vanilla together and set aside. Combine the apples with ⅓ cup granulated white sugar, spices, and a couple of drops of lemon juice. Pour cheese mixture over the chilled crust, followed by the apple mixture. Do not combine. Sprinkle the top with almonds and a little dark brown sugar. Bake at 450°F. for 10 minutes, then reduce heat to 400°F. and bake for another 25 minutes. The torte can be eaten hot or cold, but we think it's at its best when warm.

Fish Ramekins   Serves 6

My favorite way of preparing this is with crab, but any richer-
fleshed fish will do. When we're relying on what we can find in
the lake, we make this with catfish.

½ cup onion, finely chopped
2 tablespoons butter
½ pound heavy-fleshed fish
  (like catfish or bass), or
  canned white crabmeat
¾ cup fresh bread crumbs
2 level teaspoons horseradish
  mustard

1 cup plain yogurt
3 tablespoons heavy cream
Cayenne pepper
Salt
Grated Cheddar cheese

Fry onion in the butter until golden brown. Bone and flake the
fish, then mix with the onion and bread crumbs. Stir in the
mustard with the yogurt and cream. Sprinkle generously with
cayenne and add salt to taste. Spoon the mixture into 6 individual ramekin dishes. (At this point, you could wrap the
dishes and freeze them. They will keep for about two months.
When defrosted, proceed as outlined below.) Sprinkle with
grated Cheddar cheese and bake at 325°F. for 25–30 minutes,
until bubbling and golden brown. Serve on its own as an appetizer, or with creamed potatoes and salad as a main course.

Brussels Sprout Soup Serves 4

When we serve this soup to guests for the first time, we never identify it by name. We only tell them what it is once they have emptied their bowls and are coming back for seconds. Children enjoy it, too, and we have found that this recipe is one way of getting even the most hardened hot dog consumers to eat at least some of their greens.

1 pound Brussels sprouts	1 pint chicken stock
1 small onion, finely chopped	1 egg yolk
1 small potato, peeled and diced	4 tablespoons heavy cream
2 tablespoons butter	Sour cream
½ teaspoon curry paste	Paprika

Trim and chop Brussels sprouts into quarters. Wash thoroughly and drain. Sauté onion and potato in butter for 5 minutes, until softened. Add sprouts and stir in curry paste. Cook gently for 2 minutes. Stir in stock and bring to a boil. Cover and simmer for 15 minutes, until vegetables are tender. Cool slightly, then puree a little at a time in a blender. Return soup to rinsed-out pan. In a small bowl, mix egg yolk and cream together, then beat in a little of the soup. Pour mixture into soup and reheat gently without boiling, stirring continuously. Season to taste, and serve with a swirl of sour cream and a little paprika in each dish.

Beef Stroganoff   Serves 4

Another of Greg's personal assaults on the Healthy Eating Movement. When we first met, he used to make this once every couple of weeks. In the interests of a long and happy life together, I have managed to restrict him to three or four times a year.

1 pound sirloin tip or strip steak
1½ sticks of butter
2 small onions, finely chopped
Paprika, to taste
Seasoned pepper, to taste
Seasoned salt, to taste

1 teaspoon basil, fresh or dried
1 tablespoon parsley
2 tablespoons Kitchen Bouquet
2 cups mushrooms, washed and sliced
1 15-ounce can whole tomatoes, drained
⅔ tablespoon sour cream

Beat beef flat with a rolling pin and slice into very thin, long strips. Melt 1 stick of butter in a skillet and soften half the chopped onion in it. Add the beef and season with paprika, seasoned pepper, seasoned salt, basil, parsley, and 1 tablespoon of Kitchen Bouquet. Sauté until brown. Remove beef, butter, and onion from pan and set to one side. Melt half stick of butter and soften other half of onion. Add mushrooms, season with paprika, seasoned salt, and pepper, and sauté until brown. Add beef, onions, and butter to mushrooms, and combine with 1 tablespoon of Kitchen Bouquet. Add can of chopped whole tomatoes and ⅔ tablespoon of sour cream. Bring to slow boil, reduce to simmer, and cook uncovered for at least 1 hour until very thick. Serve on buttered and "parsleyed" noodles with a green salad.

Mulled Wine   Serves 8–10 approx.

This always sounds so Dickensian, conjuring up pictures of men in top hats shoving red-hot pokers into pewter tankards. But my recipe is an adaptation of one I got from Denmark, where they warm up their freezing winter nights with what the Danish call *Glüvine.*

Your guests should be warned in advance that this has a slow kick. Any more than a couple of glasses is likely to affect the motor coordination of their knees!

One 2-liter jug of red wine or two 1-liter bottles	15 cloves
	½ teaspoon ground nutmeg
1 firmly packed cup dark brown sugar	½ teaspoon ground cinnamon
2 cups brandy	½ teaspoon ground ginger
1 cup raisins	½ cup orange juice
1 cup golden raisins	1 tablespoon slivered
3 cinnamon sticks	blanched almonds

In a large kettle, slowly warm the wine, then dissolve the brown sugar in it. Add brandy, raisins, golden raisins, cinnamon sticks, and cloves, cover, and bring to a simmer. Cook for 15 minutes, before tasting and adding any extra sugar you might like. Season with at least half a teaspoon of nutmeg, cinnamon, and ginger, replace cover, and cook again, over a low heat, for another 25 minutes. Taste and adjust seasonings before adding ½ cup of orange juice and 1 tablespoon blanched almonds. Replace cover and cook for a final 15 minutes. Before serving, remove cinnamon sticks and cloves. Serve in Irish coffee glasses or mugs, with a generous helping of the fruit and nuts.

During the party, keep the wine on top of the stove, always covered, over a very low heat.

Cranberry and Orange Sauce   Makes about six 8-ounce jars

We don't make foods just for the sake of it. Unless it's a special occasion, for instance, I always buy mayonnaise, and the same goes for horseradish or tartar sauce. But when it comes to cranberries, nothing beats homemade. I haven't found a commercial brand yet that doesn't leave that dry "sucking lemons" feeling in the roof of your mouth.

2–3 bags fresh cranberries	1 cup white sugar
1 cup fresh orange juice	1 cup grated orange rind

Wash berries and discard any old or rotten ones. Put orange juice, berries, sugar, and orange rind in a large kettle and bring slowly to the boil. Reduce heat and simmer gently for 30 minutes on low. Allow to cool. Pour into sterilized jars and screw down caps immediately. Store in a cool, dark cupboard. Refrigerate when open. Will keep for about 6 months. Serve chilled.

CHAPTER 11

Christmas Gift Baskets

The best part about making gift baskets is choosing what to put in them. In the past, I have used gift baskets for everything from giving a girlfriend a night off (the contents included bubble bath, a new book, chocolates, and a split of champagne), to providing new homeowners with an instant picnic to be eaten while they unpacked (breads, a salami, cheeses, fruit, the Greek dips—tsaziki and taramasalata—a flask of coffee, and brownies for dessert). The secret to making these successful presents is attention to detail—the contents should fit the recipients' needs or tastes—i.e., the right book for my girlfriend, or not making the movers scramble for knives, plates, sugar, and cream.

This Christmas is the first time I have made baskets for Brown County friends, so I kept the contents pretty general. As the years go by and we get to know each other well, the baskets will be more and more tailored to each individual. The offerings for this year were

Raspberry vinegar
Lemon curd
Plum jam
Cranberry and orange sauce
(see recipe page 273)
Greg's Roman peppers (see recipe page 259)
Garlic and herb cheese

Homemade bread (see recipe page 244, dividing recipe into miniature loaf tins)
Holiday potpourri (see page 304)
Herbal bubble bath and bath oil (see page 305)

Raspberry Vinegar Makes about 3 pints

People always love this vinegar's deep ruby color and sweet/ tart smell, but they often don't know what to do with it once they have taken it home. So now I tie a list of suggested uses (included below) on a little scroll around the bottle's neck, because wasting a drop of this would almost be a sin.

3 pounds raspberries White sugar
2 pints white vinegar

Put vinegar and raspberries in a bowl. Mash the fruit up with a potato masher and cover bowl with plastic wrap. Leave in a warm place for 3 days. Mash the fruit up again and strain the mixture over another bowl. Repeat the process until the liquid is clear. Measure the juice and add 1 pound of sugar for every pint of liquid. Bring mixture slowly to a boil in a thick-bottomed pan, stirring until the sugar has dissolved, then boil for 15 minutes, or until the vinegar clings to the back of a teaspoon. Pour into sterilized bottles and screw tops down tight. Label when cool.

Some Uses For Raspberry Vinegar

- As a replacement for lemon juice in salad dressings, sauces, and in the frying pan with pork chops or chicken breasts.
- Over fruit salads, mixed with orange or pineapple juice.
- A spoonful over fresh berries in the summer.

- Warm gently and use as a sauce over winter sponge puddings or cakes.
- As a glaze for roast ham.
- Dribbled over buttermilk pancakes instead of maple syrup.

Lemon Curd   Makes about four 8-ounce jars

The simplest of all preserves, a wonderful present, and even better hoarded at home, where it's used as a filling for tarts, an ingredient in cakes, or simply on toast with a cup of tea in front of the fire!

3 lemons	1¼ cups superfine sugar
1 stick of butter	3 eggs, beaten

Rub whole lemons against small-toothed grater to remove the yellow part of the peel. (Try to avoid digging into the white pith, as this tastes bitter.) Set grated peel aside and cut lemons in half. Squeeze juice into a small bowl and remove any stray lemon pips. Place the butter and sugar in the top of a double boiler with simmering water in the lower part. (If you don't have a double boiler, use a basin over a pan of water.) Stir well until the butter has melted. Stir the finely grated rind and juice from the lemons into the pan, together with the eggs. Continue to stir over the simmering water until the curd thickens, about 20–25 minutes. Remove from heat and pour into warm, sterilized jars. Put lids on immediately and screw down tight. Label when cold. Store in the fridge, where it will keep for about nine weeks.

Microwave Plum Jam

Makes about six
8-ounce jars

The ingredients for this recipe are the same whether making the jam the old-fashioned way or doing it in the microwave. We also like our plum jam on the tart side, so you may want to add more sugar.

4 pounds dark plums	3 tablespoons lemon juice
½ cup water	5 cups sugar

Sterilize 6 8-ounce screw-top preserve jars by half filling them with water and putting in the microwave on high until the water boils (about 10 minutes). Remove from microwave, pour out water, and set aside. Pit plums and finely chop. Do not peel. Mix fruit with ½ cup of water and add lemon juice. Place mixture in a microwave-safe bowl, cover, and cook on HIGH for about 5 minutes, until soft and bubbling. Stir thoroughly, then add sugar. Return mixture to microwave and cook on HIGH for 15–20 minutes, until setting point has been reached. (This can be determined by dropping a teaspoon of the hot mixture onto a cold saucer, where it should form a crinkly skin as it cools. If it does not, return to microwave and cook again for a few more minutes.) Skim jam to remove scum. Fill jars to the brim and screw tops on *immediately.* Do not screw tops down tight. Place jars in microwave, about 2 inches apart, and cook on MEDIUM HIGH for 2–3 minutes. Place on towel, newspaper, or a chopping board to prevent cracking. Screw lids down tightly, using a towel or oven mitt, and leave to cool. Refrigerate once open. Will keep for about 6 months.

(Preserving instructions from *Preserving with a Microwave* by Isabel Webb [New York: Sterling Publishing Company, Inc., 1991]).

Garlic and Herb Cream Cheese

Makes about eight portions

Making cheese yourself may be fun because of all the boasting you can do afterward, but unless you have your own source of milk, it isn't very economical. I watched in astonishment while the gallon and a half I used turned into a small 6-inch square of pressed cream cheese. Since I had twelve gift baskets to provide for, I developed the recipe below—which may have been cheating, but was delicious nonetheless.

4 8-ounce packages cream cheese	¼ cup fresh tarragon
2 tablespoons sour cream	Seasoned salt
Chopped garlic in oil	Cracked black pepper
½ cup fresh parsley	2 teaspoons *white*
½ cup fresh chives	Worcestershire sauce
	Paprika

Cream cheese by hand or in a processor. Fold in sour cream and 2 heaping teaspoons of chopped garlic. Add ½ cup each of chopped parsley and chives, then add ¼ cup chopped tarragon. Season with seasoned salt, black pepper, and a teaspoon of the white Worcestershire sauce. Taste and adjust, adding more garlic if necessary. Pot in small glass dishes, cover in plastic wrap, and chill in the refrigerator overnight. In the morning, sprinkle the tops of the cheeses with paprika. Store, covered, in the refrigerator until the gift is to be exchanged, when you can garnish the top of the dishes with fresh sprigs of parsley. The dishes, of course, become part of the present. This can be made up to 5 days before and should be kept in the fridge by the recipient for no more than 10 days. A nice final touch is to include a small pack of gourmet crackers.

Leek and Gorgonzola Soup

This is one of the family's all-time favorites. It freezes beauti-fully, so I always make large batches. The frozen soup will keep for six months.

1½ pounds leeks	¾ cup Gorgonzola cheese,
½ stick butter	softened
1 tablespoon flour	Black pepper
1½ pints chicken stock	Nutmeg

Clean leeks thoroughly under running water and pat dry with paper towels, then chop finely. Melt butter in a saucepan and sweat the leeks (let them sauté gently in the butter without turning them) over a low heat for 7 minutes. Stir in the flour, let it cook for 1 minute, then mix in the stock. Bring to a boil and simmer for 15 minutes. Crumble the cheese into a bowl and cream with a little of the soup. Gradually work into the soup, keeping the mixture smooth. Reheat soup and season with the black pepper and nutmeg to taste. Serve with hot crusty bread.

CHAPTER 12

Shepherd's Pie   Serves 4

This recipe was traditionally served on Mondays in Britain, because it made use of the leftovers from the Sunday roast. Originally the dish was made with ground lamb (hence the "shepherd"), but in modern times beef is generally preferred. As with Murphey's Meat Loaf, this version is the Rolls-Royce of shepherd's pies.

The Filling

1 large onion, chopped	Salt
1 heaped teaspoon minced garlic	Pepper
	Nutmeg
1 tablespoon olive oil	Basil
1½ pounds ground sirloin	Dry red wine
½ cup carrots, chopped	¼ pound mushrooms, washed and chopped
½ cup celery, chopped	
1 15-ounce can whole peeled tomatoes	1 heaped tablespoon pickled red cabbage
1 small can tomato puree	

The Mashed Potatoes

6 large potatoes	Pepper
1 egg	1–2 tablespoons mayonnaise
1 tablespoon butter	Grated Cheddar cheese
Salt	

The Filling

In a large skillet or Dutch oven, soften onion and a generous amount of garlic in olive oil. Add beef and brown. Add carrots and celery, and mix with meat. Drain tomatoes and mix in, along with the tomato puree. Season with salt, pepper, a little nutmeg, and a little basil. Reduce over a gentle heat for about 10 minutes, then add a generous glass of dry red wine. Cook for 45 minutes, stirring occasionally. Add chopped mushrooms and red cabbage. Cook gently for another 30 minutes. Set half of the mixture aside for freezer (it can be turned into another pie or used as Bolognese sauce on top of spaghetti). Spoon other half into an ovenproof dish (a 3-pint gratin dish is ideal), leaving 1½ inches of space on top to spare.

The Mashed Potatoes

Peel potatoes, boil until soft, and drain. Mash with a potato masher, then, using a fork, beat in the egg, 1 tablespoon of butter, salt, and pepper. Add a tablespoon or two of mayonnaise and cream potatoes until very fluffy. Spread potatoes over meat mixture, sprinkle with grated Cheddar cheese, and bake at 375°F for 25–30 minutes. Serve with peas or green beans.

$\mathcal{H}$ERBAL RECIPES
AND GARDEN
PLANS

CHAPTER 2

Spiced Rose Potpourri

People always seem to be terribly impressed by homemade potpourri. Yet given the right ingredients, nothing could be simpler—and you don't need to have a garden to collect the materials you need. When I lived in the big city, I used to dry the flowers from bouquets I had been given, or had bought, and clip the blossoms off my potted geraniums, chrysanthemums, or roses. By the fall of each year, I had enough petals to fill several large storage jars, and a potpourri that would be a mix of happy memories rekindled.

The essential oils and the fixatives used in making potpourri are available from many good craft stores and mail-order catalogs. I get mine from Nichols Garden Nursery, 1190 North Pacific Highway, Albany, OR 97321-4598—which is also where I buy most of my seed.

It is worth making potpourri yourself, because so many of the commercial varieties are full of dyed wood shavings, which lose their scent very quickly. If a homemade variety seems to be fading, just turn it into a plastic bag, add a few drops of brandy, and shake. It will smell as good as new.

The two important things to remember when concocting your first recipes are

1. The presentation is as important as the perfume. Combine interesting colors and a variety of textures—and try not to crush your ingredients.

2. This should be alchemy at its most fun. There are no rules other than what is pleasing to your nose and eye, so feel free to experiment. My potpourri recipes are intended only as guides. Go ahead and substitute any ingredients or oils that take your fancy.

4 tablespoons chopped orris root
½ teaspoon rose oil
½ teaspoon clove bud oil
¼ teaspoon cassia bark (cinnamon) oil
A few drops of vanilla oil
1 cup dried rose petals
1 cup dried rose buds
1 cup dried pom-pom chrysanthemums

1 cup dried P. G. hydrangea blooms (cream and light green)
1 cup whole bay leaves
½ cup dried red celosia
1½ cups whole cloves
12 nutmegs
2 teaspoons powdered nutmeg

(There are almost as many different methods of drying flowers as there are species themselves. I usually dry whole blooms in a box between layers of sand or silica gel. Our rose petals are collected in a shallow basket and put somewhere airy, dark, and dry, while the hydrangeas are water-dried, which means they are arranged in a vase of water, which is then allowed to evaporate. A good source of reference for the various techniques is *Flowers That Last Forever: Growing, Harvesting, & Preserving* by Betty E. Jacobs (Pownal, Vt.: Storey Communications, Inc., 1988.)

Using a wooden or plastic spoon, combine the orris root and the essential oils in a glass or china bowl and mix thoroughly. Pour into a quart-size preserving jar and store in a dark cupboard for a week, taking the jar out to shake once a day. By the end of the week, the perfumes should have combined to produce the potpourri's basic scent. Turn the mixture back out into a large bowl and add the remaining ingredients, gently mixing with a wooden spoon, so that all the petals and spices are coated with the little bits of orris root. Return the potpourri to the preserving jar and put it back in the dark for another couple of weeks, shaking it once every few days. At this point, you will have your finished scent. If you're not happy with it, turn the mix out into a bowl, adjust the scent with a few drops of the appropriate essential oil, and store in the dark again for a few days. This is also a good opportunity to add more petals or leaves should you need to. Sometimes the ingredients settle in the jar and have to be beefed up. When you are satisfied with the scent, turn the potpourri into pretty glass or china bowls and display.

Rose Petal Beads

If you could fight your way through the plants in our sunroom, you would find a wall lined with gardening and herb books. Many of them are in immaculate condition—looked at and set aside, to be referred to once or twice in the decades to come.

A few are so dog-eared and broken-backed that they fall apart in your hands when you pull them off the shelves. These are the much-loved ones that have been consulted a thousand times. They are full of old Post-its and muddy fingermarks from where we have grabbed them, straight from the garden. John Jeavons's *How to Grow More Vegetables Than You Ever Thought Possible on Less Land Than You Can Imagine* (Berkeley, Calif.: Ten Speed Press, 1991) and Nancy Bubel's *Seed-Starters Handbook* (Emmaus, Pa.: Rodale Press, 1988) fall into this category, along with anything Phyllis V. Shaudys cares to write on the subject of herbs. Her book *Herbal Treasures: Inspiring Month-By-Month Projects for Gardening, Cooking, and Crafts* (Pownal, Vt.: Storey Communications, Inc., 1990), which is a collection of herbal secrets from around the country, spends most of its time by my bed, where I often dip into it before drifting off at night. My thanks to her for many happy dreams and for the use of this recipe, which was originally included in her work.

Gather about a shopping bag full of fresh wild rose petals. Put them through a hand food grinder—they should end up looking like modeling clay.

Store this in a cast-iron skillet or pot (make sure there's no rust in it), and regrind daily for two weeks. The paste will get thicker every day until it reaches a consistency where it can be formed into hard beads. To do this, roll little lumps between the palms of your hands until smooth. Put a large pin through the center of each bead and pin to a soft board. Continue rolling, piercing, and attaching to the soft board (at least ½ inch apart) until you have as many beads as you need. (It takes about 60 to make an adult-sized necklace. Keep in mind that the finished bead will be about half the size of the freshly made one.)

Let the beads dry for two weeks—longer if the weather is humid. Then remove each one, take it off the pin and polish with a soft flannel or cloth. String them on button bead or jeweler's thread, in a color that will blend with the dark mahogany of the beads. Polish the entire string again when it is finished.

(Original recipe by Barbara Radcliffe Rogers, Herbitage Farm, Richmond, NH 03470.)

Culinary Herb Garden Plan

Choosing what plants to put in a culinary garden is about as personal as picking out the bedroom wallpaper. Your selection will depend on individual taste, the amount and direction of sunlight, and the space you have to work with. There are literally thousands of culinary plants to choose from. Over the years, these few are the ones that have proved most useful in the Murphey kitchen.

The Basils

Lettuce leaf basil   One of the essential ingredients for *insalata tricolore* and any number of summer salads. We grow and eat at least six full-size bushes each season.

Purple ruffles basil   Makes the best dried basil we have found. It has to be started early and doesn't seem to like more than six hours of full sun. But it is very easy to harvest—just uproot and dry the bush whole. Makes very pretty herbal vinegar and oil, turning olive oil or white vinegar a deep shade of rose pink.

Lemon basil   My favorite of the three, because it adds a subtle zest of citrus, mixed with the peppery taste of basil, to soups, salads, sauces, and summer marinades. One of the most versatile herbs in my kitchen garden.

Bay Leaf

Oh, how I've nurtured my little bay tree! At the beginning, these plants are painfully slow growing. They usually have to be housed in a pot, as they don't take kindly to any winter freeze. Mine grew by millimeters last season, before being brought inside in the fall. Despite its size, it provided enough leaves for all our winter stews and for two dozen bags of bouquet garni at Christmas. This spring the little bush has suddenly taken off, and we now have to move its pot around, perched on a skateboard!

Cilantro/Chinese Parsley/Coriander

Again, one of those workhorse herbs that we use in Mexican, Chinese, and Thai cooking, as well as freshly chopped in soups, salads, avocado dip, and salsa. The flowers are pretty and milder than the leaves. We use them as a garnish for dozens of different cold summer dishes. In September I allow the whole plant to go to seed, saving some to plant and some to grind up for the spice jar. I haven't bought new cilantro seed for about five years.

Dill

This is the first of two herbs that are a "must grow" now that we eat so much fish. Its feathery leaves impart a subtle aniseed flavor to oven-baked bluegill or bass, and the seeds are an essential ingredient in many of the pickles we make.

Edible Flowers

Many people might question whether these belong in an herb garden, but the definition of the word "herb" is actually much wider than is usually imagined. My dictionary describes it thus: "A plant with no woody stem above ground, as distinguished from a tree or a shrub." Edible flowers certainly fall into this category, but they also earn their place in my garden because of their many uses in the kitchen.

Bachelor's button/cornflower   One of the bees' favorite plants throughout the summer, I use its bright blue blossoms to garnish egg dishes, fish, and mashed potatoes. The taste of the blossoms is so mild that I have also used it, finely chopped, sprinkled over the top of raspberry syllabub or lemon sorbet.

Nasturtium   This is our favorite edible flower for two reasons: It is a member of the watercress family and has the same spicy taste that we enjoy so much, and every part of this plant is usable. We use the leaves as a direct substitute for watercress in sandwiches with egg salad or cheese; as the main ingredient in a delicate soup; and as part of a mixed salad, or with orange slices as a salad on its own. The blossoms, which grow in every color of the sunset, are a little milder than the leaves and we use them in salads and as a garnish. They can also be stuffed like dolmades for a breathtakingly pretty appetizer. If you can bear to pick the buds before they flower, you can pickle them in vinegar to make "poor man's capers." We use these as flavoring in winter stews and sprinkled over prosciutto and shaved Parmesan for a summer lunch.

Fennel

I plant two types: **Florence fennel,** for its thick bulb, which tastes like aniseed-flavored celery, at its most delicious when braised in a little butter and black pepper; and **Bronze fennel,** which I use both as a seasoning and to make a soothing wash for Greg's eyes, which often get red and sore after a long photo shoot.

Garlic Chives

We used to grow the common chive until we discovered a stand of this flourishing by our backdoor. Its subtle mix of onion and garlic flavors make it our favorite herb. Leaving some to go to seed for the following season demands self-control, particularly since its attractive flowers are as delicious as its leaves.

Sweet Marjoram

Greg finds oregano a little pungent for his taste, so marjoram has proved to be the ideal substitute. Mild and peppery, it goes well with any Greek or Italian dish.

The Mints: Spearmint, Peppermint, Apple Mint, and Chocolate Mint

I use apple mint to make the jelly that we serve with lamb and spearmint for the mint sauce. Peppermint is used as a flavoring in some of my cookie and candy recipes, and chocolate mint is the garnish on most of our chocolate desserts.

Parsley

Again, we grow two kinds: **moss-curled,** with its classic tightly curled leaves, which we use in every type of cooking; and plain parsley, which I planted by mistake a couple of years ago, and which has been coming back ever since. We found that this dries better than the moss-curled, although the other type is best for freezing.

Rosemary

Last year I gave up trying to overwinter this in the ground. I now raise my rosemary bush in a gigantic pot, which we bring into the sunroom when the weather gets cold. I water it very sparingly over the winter and harden it off gently again in the spring. The strategy has been a success. I now have a bush that is more than a year old, whose leaves are used for lamb and pork dishes, and in some recipes for potpourri.

Sage

I overlooked this herb for years, but have recently found an increasing number of uses for it. I rediscovered it when cooking a saltimbocca (veal scallopini beaten thin, then curled with bacon and sage into little rolls, which are braised in butter and Marsala wine), and now use it with pork, in sage and lemon sauce; in classic sage and onion stuffing, and in a spicy tomato pizza sauce. I will be looking for more recipes this season.

Tarragon

The other essential herb for fish dishes, I grew this originally to make herbal vinegar. Now we use it in a number of recipes, including Eggs Florentine, Egg Mayonnaise, Salmon Soufflé and Fisherman's Pie.

Thyme

We don't cook with this herb much on its own, but it is an essential ingredient in a bouquet garni—which we use to season many of our winter stews, soups and sauces.

Fragrance Garden Plan

There are essentially two types of fragrance garden: the garden planted for its scents during the growing season and the garden planted for its preservable perfumes. Luckily, we don't have to worry about the former, because there are aromatic bushes and flowers all over the farm. The air smells fragrant here from the time that the lilacs blossom in the spring, through the honeysuckle sweetness of summer, to the rich perfume of the P. G. hydrangea, just before the fall. Mock orange and wild roses add to the medley and provide hips and dried petals for many potpourris.

The plants in our fragrance garden are chosen specifically with this craft in mind, and as ingredients for sachets, bath products, and wreaths. Their blooms are harvested continually through the summer, just before they open fully, and are dried immediately to seal in their perfume. Most of the plants listed below must be grown in pots, so they can be brought in for the winter.

Gardenia

To a Brit, the heady scent of gardenias is nothing short of exotic—this is what summer evenings at Tara must have smelled like before the Civil War, when Southern belles wore gardenia blossoms braided in their hair. These aren't the easiest plants to grow. In Indiana they must be raised in pots, with *exactly* the right amount of moisture or the little trees will wilt. But their creamy blooms are worth all the trouble—either preserved whole in fine sand or silica gel, or dried in baskets, petal by petal.

Geraniums, Scented

I started to collect these unusual cousins of the familiar patio flower two years ago. So far, we have the **mint, lemon-scented, apple, attar of roses, chocolate,** and **citronella** varieties, and I'm always on the lookout for more. The qualities of these modest-looking plants can't be really appreciated until you have picked a leaf and rubbed it between your palms. Their perfume is overwhelming and it doesn't diminish when the plant is dried. They have become a required ingredient for sachets and potpourri.

Jasmine

My first introduction to this tropical-smelling flower was in North Africa, at the age of thirteen. Every evening, the local boys would pick fresh jasmine blossoms and string them together into necklaces, which they would sell for a few cents. My father never failed to buy me one, and I kept them all in a little clay jar that we had bought at the hotel *souk.* Their fragrance lingered on for months after we had returned to a cold and rainy London—a little piece of the desert trapped inside the vase. My Hoosier jasmine holds its bouquet just as well and will infuse a bath oil or Chinese tea for up to a year after it has been picked.

Lavender

Predictably, I prefer the English varieties to the French, finding them to be more pungent. After dozens of casualties to the Midwest winter, our lavender is now grown in pots, which are brought into the back hall before the first frost. They are lined up next to the bay tree and the scented geraniums, where they are all allowed to go dormant until the first signs of spring. I harvest the lavender throughout the summer, air-drying it in bunches, which are crumbled into lace sachets and pillows to store among our clothes.

Lemon Balm

The clean scent of citrus is my favorite smell of all, and no plant produces it more prolifically than lemon balm. This unstoppable herb will grow anyplace where there's sun, and will march around the garden like its cousin, mint. It maintains its tangy essence of lemons throughout the drying process and is my chosen base plant for a citrus potpourri.

Mignonette

Paris made this plain yellow flower famous in the nineteenth century by planting it all over the city's balconies, because of its glorious scent. Mignonette is another temperamental plant that needs just the right amount of water and sun. I grow mine in a very big pot, because it hates to have its roots disturbed and it is better not to transplant.

Orange/Bergamot/Eau de Cologne Mint

This most highly scented of all the mints richly deserves each of its three names. Like lemon balm, its aromatic oil seems to survive almost any treatment. One of my favorite ways of using it is steeped in chilled water, as a finger bowl for a very special meal.

Sweetgrass/Southernwood

When people in the Middle Ages strewed rushes on their floors, they included sweetgrass to cancel out some of their nastier smells. Its bouquet is a fresh mixture of mint and flowers, but history is my main reason for raising it—we're sharing a fragrance with Shakespeare or Henry VIII.

CHAPTER 4

A Child's Garden Plan

There's no such thing as a green thumb among kids. Little ones are all natural gardeners who love to grow things—even if it's just mustard and cress on a paper towel. When the seed sprouts and throws out leaves, they think they have made magic, and when they proudly present you with the first fruits of their labors, you'll be inclined to agree with them.

Plans for a child's garden can be as varied as the weather and the places where we plant them. Here are a few general rules for success.

Make It Fun

It's up to us parents to present children with all the information they need to make as many of the creative decisions as possible (what to plant, where to plant, and in what pattern).

Maximize Their Chances of Success

Select the right site or window for the plants that you think your child will want to grow. (This usually means south- or west-facing, because kids love the bright flowers, fruits, and veggies that need full sun.)

If the garden is going to be outside, you also must watch the shape of the bed. Last summer we forgot how short Charley's arms and legs are and made her garden too wide. As a result, she had to step into it to harvest or weed and a lot of stems were crushed under small feet—which also compacted the earth into a hard crust. This year we have moved her to a more permanent location, which we have equipped with a network of stepping-stones so that Charley can move around her garden without squashing anything!

Once you have selected a spot, collect pictures of plants that would do well there from catalogs, magazines, seed packets, and so on. Since variety is the key to capturing young minds, try to give them a good mix of flowers, herbs, and vegetables that will keep doing interesting things throughout the growing season and provide them with a range of products in the fall.

Do prepare the beds or planters for them. Children aren't equipped to do the heavy work yet, and they can get discouraged by their own lack of coordination or strength. Charley is happy playing the role of assistant during this part of the process: holding the tools, filling the wheelbarrow with disgarded weeds, and bringing her exhausted parents large glasses of ice water!

When the children are putting in their seed, encourage them to plant a little more closely than we would do in a grown-up garden. The more densely planted the plot, the fewer the weeds. When the seeds are in, show them how to mulch the bed, preferably using straw. (Commercial wood chips can be very acidic, which many plants hate. If you want the chips for a more decorative look, try to avoid pine or cedar, which are the most acid of all.) Mulch will also keep the weeds to a minimum and it will hold the moisture in, which is an advantage when short attention spans forget to do the watering.

Let Them Make Mistakes

This is the one I'm bad at, but if you intervene to do the weeding or watering for them, it becomes your garden, not theirs. Charley soon learned that plants will wither if you don't water them and weeds will run rampant when left unchecked. If your children insist on growing violets in full sun or pineapples in

Zone 2, stand aside. They will soon see why you advised them against it and they will have learned something about climates and botany along the way.

Charley's new garden will be planted with a selection of perennials and bulbs to give her flowers from the early spring through to the end of fall. It is also large enough for the miniature apple tree and the new roses that she wants so much.

I will be able to watch the Bug at work from my office, where I keep a small box of dried petals from the sticky bouquets I was given last year. They will remind me of the pride and love that went into each flower long after their fragrance has faded and their gardener has gone.

Charley's Garden Selections

(P = Perennial; A = Annual; B = Biennial)

Spring Flowers

Winter aconite (P)   The first flowers of coming spring, these bloom unfailingly in February, reminding the young and the restless of the warmer days to come. When they have finished flowering, their star-shaped leaves provide a pretty ground cover around their taller summer cousins.

Narcissus, mixed colors (P)   Surprise is another key to holding a small person's interest. These grow in such a variety of colors and textures that Charley never gets tired of watching them flower. They also divide and multiply prolifically without any effort on the gardener's part.

Dwarf crocus, mixed (P)   Charley has planted these around her stones so they will peek up at the same time as the narcissi blossom.

Hyacinth, mixed colors (P)   These flowers always remind me of Nana Moyce, who used to keep a bowl of them on her dining table each spring. They were a granny plant, made to be displayed on lace doilies. My daughter suffers from no such perception. She's in love with their fragrance and insists on having bunches of them in her bedroom whenever they are in bloom.

King Alfred daffodil (P)   I think that the only reason Charley wants these is so she can put them in "blooo water" and watch them turn green! (We color the water with blue food dye, which the flowers then absorb up their stems into the petals.)

Peonies (P)   When we first arrived at the farm, we found a row of about twenty unidentifiable bushes just planted in the middle of a field. We couldn't imagine what they were until the spring came and they burst into beautiful flower. They were peonies and Charley fell in love with their big cabbage blooms and their honey-sweet scent. We have finally begun to move them into the garden this year and Charley has chosen a deep red one and a pink one for her plot.

Dutch irises (P)   Before we moved here, I thought that irises were just a flower with dark blue petals and yellow stripes. Then we discovered light blue and pink varieties that have a delicacy similar to orchids. Charley likes them for their unusual shapes, which, she says, makes them look like birds.

Summer Flowers

Painted and Shasta daisies (P)   These are flowers as a child would draw them. Charley says she chose them for their bright, sunny faces.

Giant hollyhocks (P)   Talk about drama! They grow taller than Charley, with huge double blooms in a bright range of colors.

Lupines (P)   As dramatic as hollyhocks in their way. Charley claims that lupines make her laugh.

Snapdragons (A)   Charley was first drawn to these last year when I grew them in my cottage garden. I think she was attracted by their constantly changing variety of colors that go from the hues of a sunset to a citrus yellow.

Klondyke cosmos and giant zinnias (A)   Charley first spotted these in a garden that we pass on the way to school. Their colors vibrated in the September sun, making the whole bed sparkle with orange, pink, purple, yellow, and red. Both species are also very hardy and will stand up to most of the mistakes a young gardener will make.

Giant Russian sunflowers (A)   Everything is big about this variety. The seeds are the ideal size for small fingers, they sprout at an incredible rate, and the final plant is between eight and ten feet tall! Charley's garden wouldn't be the same without them and she loves giving her crop of sunflower seeds to the birds in the fall.

Creeping phlox (P)   The catalog picture of this shows a sea of dense pink and white blossoms cascading over a rock garden. "It looks like cotton candy," Charley observed. She wants to use it to edge her bed.

Roses (P)   I wasn't sure that Charley would enjoy growing roses—all those thorns and scratched hands. But the Tropicana, with its bright orange flowers and strong scent, was a great success last summer. This year, she wants to add two more to her collection: Mr. Lincoln, a large and very fragrant red rose, and the Blue Girl Rose, which, as its name suggests, is an unusual shade of pale blue. In the interest of my daughter's fingers, I still do the pruning.

Vegetables

We grow such a huge amount of vegetables in the family garden that Charley has confined her interest this year to the foods she's particularly fond of. Gardening organically is especially important when it comes to children's vegetables, and not just for philosophical reasons. In their enthusiasm, young gardeners tend to eat their produce right off the plant. Any pesticide or chemical fertilizer residue can give them a nasty burning sensation in their mouths, which is off-putting for the child and worrying for parents, who might then wonder about other, more dangerous side effects.

Pink Bo Peep and Baby Blue popping corn   Both these sweet corns produce an abundance of mini-ears, about 3 to 4 inches long. They are, as we say, "Charley-sized." The few that might escape my daughter's culinary efforts will end up in the dried-flower arrangements that we make together in the fall.

Kleckley Sweets watermelon   Squashes and melons thrive under corn, where their vines can be supported by the stalks. An added advantage to companion planting this way is that raccoons and rabbits are deterred from feasting on the cobs. Kleckley Sweets is the family's favorite watermelon, for its succulent taste and compact size.

Baby Nantes Carrots   As far as Charley is concerned, any kind of carrot would do, but we persuaded her to grow these because they are bite-sized and perfect for her lunch box or a snack.

The Early Girl Tomato   As with the carrot, Charley doesn't care about the type of tomato, just so long as it produces "lots"! So it was left to my husband, the tomato king, to settle on the variety. Greg chose this one, he says, because it produces prolific numbers of small to medium-sized fruit from early in the season and throughout the summer.

Rouge d'Estampes Cinderella Pumpkin   When we told Charley that this was the original model for the Cinderella coach, that was all she needed to know. We liked her choice because the flesh of this type is delicious, so at Halloween there will be no waste.

Herbs

I used to think that herbs had little to offer the small child, until I saw my daughter's growing interest in my herb garden. She loves to pick the leaves and rub them in her hands to release their fragrance, and she enjoys the different shapes and textures of the leaves.

Chocolate mint   Her favorite because it smells like an After Eight. In the summer we use it to garnish our homemade chocolate mousse and I use a sprig to decorate Charley's chilled glass of chocolate malt.

Twickle purple lavender   Again, fragrance is the attraction. Charley has learned to dry the flowers and the leaves, which she stores in her treasure box or ties in her hankies to keep in her clothes.

Woolly betony, or lamb's ears   Charley chose this one for its furry silver leaves, which keep their soft texture even when they are dried.

Creeping lemon thyme   Texture and smell combine in the decision here. The tiny leaves produce a carpet of deep green, which, when stepped on or picked, gives off a pungent citrus scent.

Monarda, or bee balm   When Charley discovered that bees, butterflies, and hummingbirds were wonderful for her garden and would increase her yield, she asked me whether there was a plant that they all particularly liked. She had already chosen a number of flowers that would have fitted the bill, but I felt that she wanted something specific, and this is one of the best bee plants that I know.

One final note: Your young gardener's pleasure is only really complete if his produce is displayed, dried, eaten, cooked, or preserved properly. Some of the happiest times Charley and I have ever spent together have been in the kitchen, or in front of the fire in late fall, carefully putting the fruits of her garden to some final good use. They were worth any amount of time and effort.

CHAPTER 10

A Lexicon of Flowers

"Floriography," or the symbolism of flowers, goes back at least as far as ancient Egypt. It creeps into Greek and Roman mythology and floral symbols are scattered throughout the Bible. But it was the publication of *Le Langage des fleurs* by Charlotte de La Tour in 1818 that led to floriography's widespread popularity, particularly among Victorian lovers, who would send each other quite complicated messages in fresh or dried bouquets.

I do not have enough room here to include even a tiny percentage of the known floral symbols, but I have listed the twenty-five meanings that crop up most frequently in my Tussie Mussies and potpourri.

Allysum	= Worth beyond beauty
Bluebell	= Constancy
Borage	= Bluntness
Carnation	= Bonds of affection
Chamomile	= Energy in adversity
Daisy	= Hope
Yellow daylily	= Flirtatiousness
Fennel	= Strength

Hyacinth	= Playfulness
Iris	= A message
Ivy	= Matrimony
Lavender	= Devotion
Lemon balm	= Sympathy
Lily of the valley	= Peace/happiness regained
Marigold	= Sadness
Marjoram	= Joy
Nasturtium	= Patriotism
Pansy	= Devotion
Parsley	= Festivity
Red rose	= Love
White rose	= Innocence/innocent love
Rosemary	= Remembrance
Sage	= Good health
Sweet peas	= Departure
Violets	= Faith

CHAPTER 11

Holiday Potpourri

Charley and I start collecting for this in September, when we gather acorns and pine cones in our woods, and harvest wild rose hips from the hedgerows around the big pasture. In October we pick and dry teasel and bittersweet. Then, in the middle of November, we cut the first large bunch of evergreen, which is hung in the hayloft to dry.

After Thanksgiving is over, the acorns and teasel are spray-painted gold, the pine cones silver, and the basic potpourri (below) is mixed. The recipe has obviously become more complicated since we moved here and have access to such a large range of plants, but I used to make something similar in Chicago, growing some materials in our garden and collecting others on winter walks.

½ teaspoon clove bud
    essential oil
½ teaspoon cassia bark
    essential oil
4 tablespoons chopped orris
    root
¾ cup dried silver artemisia
¾ cup white pine and blue
    spruce needles
¾ cup dried cedar leaves
½ cup dried rosemary
½ cup bittersweet berries

½ cup rose hips
½ cup dried red celosia (or
    any other dried red flower)
½ cup woolly betony leaves
12 bay leaves
3 tablespoons whole allspice
6 smashed cinnamon sticks
2 tablespoons ground allspice
12 whole nutmegs
1 tablespoon ground nutmeg
A few drops of vanilla
    essential oil (*not* extract!)

Mix the clove bud and cassia bark oils with the chopped orris root in a glass or china bowl, using a wooden chopstick. Turn into a quart-size glass storage jar and keep in a dark cupboard for 3 days, shaking the jar once daily. By this time, the orris root will have fully absorbed the oils, and you will be ready to mix the potpourri. Pour mixture into a glass or china bowl and add the rest of the ingredients, with the exception of the nutmegs and vanilla. Mix thoroughly, but very gently, trying not to break up the leaves or flowers. Fold in the nutmegs and put contents back into the clean, dry glass storage jar. Keep in the dark cupboard for two weeks, gently shaking the jar daily to keep the orris root distributed throughout. At the end of two weeks, pour into a bowl and add a few drops of vanilla essential oil (*not* vanilla extract, which will ruin the whole mixture). Store in the dark for one more week, shaking gently once a day before turning out into decorative containers or boxing it up for gifts. In either case, decorate the top of the potpourri with the painted acorns and pine cones and small heads of teasel. If these aren't available, you can use miniature gold, silver, and red glass balls—the ornaments you would normally buy for a tiny tree.

Herbal Bubble Bath and Bath Oil

I have always been wary of giving friends products that might affect their skin, until I hit on the idea of using baby soaps and oils for my base. They are as gentle as they are cheap, but you must buy the *unscented* varieties. The following recipes can be used as models with any fragrance; just substitute the essential oil of your choice.

Southern Belle Bath Bubbles

4 cups unscented liquid baby   1 teaspoon gardenia essential
    soap   oil

Mix soap and oil together well and decant into one or two decorative bottles. Keep in a dark cupboard for ten days, shaking
gently once a day. Label and decorate the bottles with ribbons
around the neck and, if you're feeling creative, a white satin
gardenia blossom!

Lavender Bath Oil

2 cups unscented baby oil   2 small bunches dried
⅓ cup lavender essential oil   lavender stalks
1 cup (approx.) dried
    lavender blossoms

Mix oils together in a glass or china bowl before floating the
blossoms in the mixture. Place lavender stalks into a decorative
glass bottle and gently pour the oil over them. Decorate the top
of the bottle with a little lace or cloth cap tied down with ribbons. I always try to color code my ribbons to go with the
fragrance I'm using—i.e., purple and pink for lavender or green
and yellow for a citrus scent.

CHAPTER 12

(Some of the entries below already have been mentioned else-
where in the Appendix, but we wanted to record our list as it
was sent out to potential customers.)

Bean Blossom Farm
Seedlings on Offer for Spring 1994

Our seedlings are organically raised and will be delivered at the
correct time for planting. Most of our plants are annuals that
need full sun—unless otherwise indicated.

Herbs

Lettuce leaf basil   Large, bright green leaves, which we eat
fresh in salads all summer long and which freeze nicely for
cooking in the winter.

Purple ruffles basil   Deep purple leaves with very crinkly
edges. This is the ideal basil for drying. Will also impart a pretty
rose color when steeped in white vinegar. Very strong flavor.

Lemon basil   Tangy lemon taste mixed with the usual basil
spice. My favorite of the basils. We use it in soups, salads, sandwiches, and all types of cooking throughout the summer. In the
fall, I let the plant flower and use the buds in sachets and in
citrus potpourris.

Anise basil   Strong flavor and smell of aniseed. This is delicious in salads with nuts and/or white cheeses like mozzarella.

Also a pretty garnish for summer drinks, particularly any with a liquorice base. The bright pink flowers dry very well and hold their scent for a spicier potpourri.

Cinnamon basil   Smells just like the spice and can be used in its place for a milder, fresher flavor in most summer dishes. A really delicious addition to iced tea.

Greek mini window-box basil   If you are tired of edging your annuals with candytuft, you might try this as a decorative and edible alternative. When the season is over, just pull out the whole plant and hang it somewhere warm and dark to dry.

Bergamot (Perennial)   Also known as bee balm. Showy scarlet flowers that attract bees, butterflies, and hummingbirds—who, in turn, will pollinate the rest of your garden.

Borage   Cucumber-flavored plant with pretty sky blue flowers. I use it to garnish iced drinks.

Garlic chives (Perennial)   Just like the common chive, but with a distinct taste of garlic. I use this almost every day over the summer: in soups, salads, chopped finely over new potatoes, or as a garnish to a stew. Plant lots!

Roman chamomile (Perennial)   A pretty and fragrant ground cover. Chamomile is said to be good for the stomach. The little white flowers are used to make chamomile tea, which is very soothing at the end of the day. You can also use the flowers to make a hair rinse that is famous for bringing out the blond in blond hair and giving any color a deep shine.

Coriander/cilantro   A must for anyone who makes salsa and/ or cooks Mexican food. This variety is the most bolt-resistant that we have grown. Also use the delicate white flowers, which are as flavorful as the leaf and very decorative. In the fall, let the plant go to seed and grind some for the winter, while saving some seeds to start next year's crop.

Dill   We use the feathery leaves in fish dishes and with potatoes. The flower heads and seeds are an essential ingredient in almost every kind of pickle.

Fleabane (Perennial)   As its name suggests, the main purpose of this plant is to repel insects. Make a strong tea and spray on plants. Will flourish in sun or semishade.

Parsley   Extra-curled. Used in almost all cooking as an ingredient or a garnish. We grow lots and freeze what is left over in the fall.

Pennyroyal (Perennial)   The *best* insect repellent I know. A member of the mint family, this pungent little plant will fight off everything from fleas to the clothes moth. Can be used both dried and as a spray.

Rue (Perennial)   This is an answer for those whose garden plants suffer from the Japanese beetle. The beetles hate this herb, but it is loved by roses—one of the beetles' favorite targets. Companion plant it around your rosebushes for munch-free blooms.

Sweet marjoram (Perennial)   Tastes like a mild form of oregano. Perfect for more subtle Italian cooking—especially good with lamb.

Sage (Perennial)   I only rediscovered this diligent little herb last summer. It adds a wonderful peppery twist to chicken Marsala, roast pork loin with lemon and sage, or duck with sage and onion stuffing.

Tarragon, French (Perennial)   A very fragrant variety. We use some of our crop in egg and fish dishes, but most goes into my tarragon and herb garden vinegars.

Creeping thyme (Perennial)   A wonderful ground cover, producing a thick mat of dark green leaves and rose pink flowers after its first year. Has a spicy fragrance that attracts bees, and can be used in cooking just like ordinary thyme.

Edible Flowers

Our favorite edible flower, the nasturtium, is not included here because it does best when seeded directly into the garden. If you are going to grow edible flowers, please include this member of the watercress family. You can use the leaves as a milder substitute for watercress in salads and sandwiches; the blossoms, which taste milder yet, make a beautiful garnish—or can be served stuffed like dolmades; and the buds can be pickled in vinegar to make "poor man's capers." I plant them in our herb garden with bright blue bachelor's buttons and Lemon Drop marigolds for a bright display of color throughout the summer.

Lemon Drop marigolds   A bright citrus yellow flower that blooms all season long. Especially pretty when used to garnish tomato soups and salads.

Bachelor's button Also known as the blue cornflower. Bright blue blossoms used whole or snipped up to decorate egg, fish, and potato dishes.

Jewels in the Kitchen Crown A package offering nasturtium, bachelor's button, coriander, and sunflower seeds—with a farm letter on the how-tos and what-withs of edible flowers.

Everlastings
Like the edibles, most strains of everlasting flowers do better when seeded directly. But the ones on offer below appreciate an earlier start than they can get outside. Plant them with straw-flowers, globe amaranth, and baby asters for blooms that will last you all year round.

Cockscomb Bright scarlet, pink, and gold blossoms that look as if they belong on another planet. With sun and a little fertilizer, these blooms can grow up to 4 or 5 inches across. In the fall, dry them and use whole in everlasting arrangements or clip into small pieces as an ingredient for potpourri.

Celosia, mixed Bright red and yellow feathery flower heads, which will keep their color if you dry them in the dark. Also makes a colorful border plant and an unusual addition to fresh flower arrangements.

Annual Flowers
Every year, most nurseries and garden centers have the same old stock on offer. We got so bored with little pink vincas and bronze marigolds that we decided to comb the catalogs for something more unusual. Below is a selection of what we found,

which can be combined with shop stock for a more exciting look.

Impatiens   A hardy little annual that will grow in shady spots, but which has become devalued with overuse around train stations and corporate headquarters. A change in color scheme helps to alleviate the boredom. We are offering two this year: *tango hybrid,* a flaming orange variety, grows to 24 inches and mixes well with *dwarf white baby,* with true white blossoms with pale yellow centers, which grows to 12 inches—a wonderful window-box plant.

Watercolor pansies   Imagine the brightest colors on the Impressionists' paint palettes and translate them into floral terms. These little flowers will give a dazzling display of yellow, orange, purple, blue, pink, red, and white, all summer long. Will do equally well in containers or in the ground.

Moss rose—portulaca   More beautiful color, set in attractive feathery green foliage. The little moss roses will bloom in a mix of scarlet, tangerine, yellow, and white, throughout the season, changing their color combinations all the time. They grow about 6 inches tall and are happy everywhere from sunny garden borders to plain clay pots.

When our big greenhouse is up and going next year, we will offer a much wider selection of flowers to choose from. In the meantime, each order will be grown specifically for the customer and delivered, ready-to-plant, by the middle of May. Orders cannot be accepted after March 21st.

Vegetables

Cabbages

Offenham 2—Flower of Spring. English variety producing early tender greens, like collards, but not so tough. Lightly boil for a couple of minutes and toss in butter and black pepper.

Mammoth Rock Red Cabbage. An excellent performer for us last season—growing through the summer without bolting once. Produced large 5- to 6-pound crisp heads, all a deep blue-red.

Cauliflower

Snow Crown Hybrid. A midseason variety. Tie outer leaves around heads when still small to ensure a creamy white floret.

Cucumbers

French Cornichon. Sweet, cocktail-size gherkins, direct from France. Pickle whole in dill and vinegar in the fall.

Rollinson's Telegraph. The long European-style cucumber that can be eaten with the skin on. Very sweet, the stuff of cucumber sandwiches.

Peppers

Purple Beauty. Inside it is a sweet green pepper. Outside it has the shining purple skin of an eggplant. Very

decorative in summer salads or served stuffed from the
oven.

Pimiento Perfection. Sweet red pepper. Preserve in oil for
use year-round in stews, chilis, and as a garnish to
winter dishes.

Peto Wonder Hybrid. Very large green bell pepper. Keep
the seeds and grow some next year.

Small Red Chili Pepper. The name says it all. These fiery-
hot little peppers are ideal for stringing in *ristras,* to
decorate the kitchen and preserve the harvest for many
months to come.

Super Cayenne. Very hot and ornamental pepper, which
we grate and store in spice jars, come the fall. The
plant, with its bright red little peppers, is particularly
pretty when grown in a container.

Paprika Pepper. Again, we grow this to dry and grate, for
use as a kitchen seasoning. Much richer flavor than the
store-bought variety.

Tomatoes "Why do you grow so many varieties?" asked a
neighbor, the other day.

"Because," I explained, "each one is uniquely different from
the other—in looks, taste, and time of harvest."

We'll be planting twenty-two different kinds this year. Some
will be old favorites, while others will be experiments that, if
delicious, will be added to our list for 1994. The seven types
listed below are the best of all the varieties we grow. Choose a
selection that will give you a harvest through the summer of
both eating tomatoes and fruit to be preserved.

The Early Girl. Our earliest slicing tomato. Small to
medium size fruit with a very sweet taste. This strain is
known for its resistance to disease.

The 1884. My personal favorite, because of its rich tomato taste. A *huge* midseason pink from the Ohio flood of 1884. It was discovered growing on a pile of debris on the river at Friendly, West Virginia.

The Nepal. Mid-size to large fruit, ready midseason. Old-fashioned tart flavor.

San Marzano. Italian plant, with pear-shaped fruit. We grow it exclusively for tomato paste and sauce. Ready to harvest, mid to late in the season.

Brandywine. I think this is Greg's favorite. Again, *huge* dark pink fruit—we have had them at 2–3 pounds each, where one slice makes a side salad—but its size doesn't spoil its flavor. Also excellent cooked, canned, or frozen. This is an Amish variety that dates back to 1885. Mid to late in the season.

Abraham Lincoln. Late-season dark red, with really big round fruit. Very meaty and sweet, delicious in salads and makes great juice.

Patio Hybrid. Grow this as a container plant. It gives medium-size fruit on a compact bush that will be about 20 to 30 inches tall. Also ideal for the apartment dweller, where it can be grown in a window. I give them as presents to friends without a garden of their own.

Miscellaneous

Greg's Good Green Earth   You won't get the best results from your plants unless you feed them. We give ours a flying start by putting about half a cupful of this fertilizer blend in each hole, and mixing it with a little soil, before planting the seedling on top. There are no chemicals in this, just a combination of nature's best foods: bat guano, worm castings, bone meal, etc. A 5-pound bag should last the home gardener one full season.

Sal's Potpourri Kit   People would love to make their own, but they get nonplussed by unusual-sounding ingredients and strange instructions. This is a basic kit to get you going. It contains 4 essential oils, 2 fixatives, a selection of dried flowers and leaves, an instruction booklet with easy-to-follow guidelines, and a selection of recipes. Unfortunately, the oils are not cheap, but a little goes a long way and these should last through a couple of seasons. (For delivery in midsummer.)

FTERWORD

I would like to offer my sincerest thanks to the following people who made this book possible:

Mike & Gela J.: Or, as they are known in this house, my parents, Pa & G. My father's spidery scrawl has been all over my writing since I was fifteen. This book was no exception and, as usual, he set the highest standards of personal and professional truth. Gela (officially my stepmother, but more like my sister), also brought her razor-sharp mind to bear, making suggestions that were always the cherry on the ice cream. Thank you both for laughing and crying in all the right places and giving this project so much of your time.

Toni Sciarra: My editor at William Morrow. The relationship between writer and editor can be like an arranged marriage, cordial if you're lucky. Our case was the delightful exception where we became the best of friends. Thank you, Toni, for all those good ideas. You are a source of energy down the phone line.

Regula Noetzli: My agent in New York, who had the nerve to take me on in the midst of a recession. Thank you for your faith.

My thanks also go to Shelley Powers for suggesting this book; to Mike Lewis, editor of the *Brown County Democrat*, for publishing the column that began the whole process; to Steve Kowalski and Janet Ginsburg, who listened tolerantly to every word; to State Naturalist Jim Eagleman for answering all my silly questions; to Extension Agent Jon Cain for putting me in touch with the right people; to Mike Nickels for his wholehearted support; to Joyce Probst, Genie Garrett, and Jean Suttles for the love and learning they have lavished on Charley, which allowed me to write with a clear conscience; and to all the people of Brown County for the warmth and openness that makes this such a special place to live.

Finally, I have to thank Greg and Charley for their endless patience. Not quite "zip, zip, zip," Greg, but now it's done, and, Charley Bug, this summer is all yours.